Medieval English

Political Writings

Middle English Texts

General Editor

Russell A. Peck
University of Rochester

Associate Editor

Alan Lupack
University of Rochester

Advisory Board

Rita Copeland
University of Minnesota

Thomas G. Hahn
University of Rochester

Lisa Kiser
Ohio State University

Thomas Seiler
Western Michigan University

R. A. Shoaf
University of Florida

Bonnie Wheeler
Southern Methodist University

The Middle English Texts Series is designed for classroom use. Its goal is to make available to teachers and students texts which occupy an important place in the literary and cultural canon but which have not been readily available in student editions. The series does not include those authors such as Chaucer, Langland, the Pearl-poet, or Malory, whose English works are normally in print in good student editions. The focus is, instead, upon Middle English literature adjacent to those authors that teachers need in compiling the syllabuses they wish to teach. The editions maintain the linguistic integrity of the original work but within the parameters of modern reading conventions. The texts are printed in the modern alphabet and follow the practices of modern capitalization and punctuation. Manuscript abbreviations are expanded, and u/v and j/i spellings are regularized according to modern orthography. Hard words, difficult phrases, and unusual idioms are glossed on the page, either in the right margin or at the foot of the page. Textual and explanatory notes appear at the end of each section, along with a glossary at the back. The sections include short introductions on the history of the works, their merits and points of topical interest, and also include briefly annotated bibliographies.

Medieval English Political Writings

Edited by
James M. Dean

Published for TEAMS
(The Consortium for the Teaching of the Middle Ages)
in Association with the University of Rochester

by

Medieval Institute Publications

WESTERN MICHIGAN UNIVERSITY

Kalamazoo, Michigan – 1996

Library of Congress Cataloging-in-Publication Data

Medieval English political writings / edited by James M. Dean.
     p.   cm. -- (Middle English texts)
    Includes bibliographical references.
    ISBN 1-879288-64-8 (paperbound)
    1. Political poetry, English (Middle)   2. English prose
literature--Middle English, 1100-1500.   3. Great Britain--Politics
and government--1066-1485--Sources.   4. Great Britain--Politics and
government--1066-1485--Poetry.   5. Political science--Early works to
1800.   I. Dean, James M. (James McMurrin)   II. Series: Middle
English texts (Kalamazoo, Mich.)
PR1120.M3735   1966
821'.108--dc20

                                     96-5082
                                       CIP

Printed in the United States of America

P   6   5   4   3

Cover design by Elizabeth King

Contents

Preface

This edition contains selected poems and documents — some not printed since the nineteenth century, others often reprinted — which help illuminate political issues in fourteenth- and fifteenth-century England. It makes available to teachers and students representative political poems and documents ranging from a Latin poem on the venality of judges (reign of Edward I) to an antifraternal, macaronic lyric of about 1490. Here one hears, represented, voices of the overtaxed farmer, the outraged or fearful cleric, and the somber prophet, voices which reveal the persistent concerns of educated classes, especially the clergy. None of these is optimistic about England's future. The authors of the poems and documents, mostly anonymous or pseudonymous, speak in the traditional language of complaint and satire; but the outlines of their anxiety are fairly clear. They worry about misuses of power (especially in the Church), about their wealth and taxes, and about declines in moral standards. Sometimes they attack the king — particularly Richard II, who governed a troubled realm from 1388 (when he reached majority) to 1399 (when Henry of Lancaster deposed him) — but more often they censure the king's ministers or powerful barons of the realm.

The volume contains five sections representing subcategories of medieval English political writings: Poems of Political Prophecy (which forecast the imminent demise of England based on ominous foreshadowings); Anticlerical Poems and Documents (which record the passions swirling around clerical abuses, mendicancy and the uses of poverty, and Lollardy); Literature of Richard II's Reign and the Peasants' Revolt (which chronicle the schemes of rebel leaders and the woes of Richard's kingdom); Poems against Simony and the Abuse of Money (which reveal the depths of avarice in the Church and in courts of law); and Plowman Writings (which register the ostensible complaints of tenant farmers and peasants against their oppression by overlords). This selection of poems and documents reflects a variety of English political concerns. I include writings especially that tell a story, such as the poems and documents centered in Richard II's turbulent career (which witnessed the Peasants' Rising of 1381), or the poems about ideal plowmen or writings about corrupt clerics; and I regard this material as companion pieces to my previously-published *Six Ecclesiastical Satires*. For want of space I have excluded panegyrics to rulers and elegies (such as the well-known verses on the death of Edward III from the Vernon manuscript or the Agincourt carol beginning "Owre kynge went forth to

Normandy") as well as documents and poems satirizing women (misogynistic writings), or contemning sumptuous clothing.

The largest section concerns anticlerical poems and documents because the chief political issues of the later Middle Ages involved abuses within the ecclesiastical hierarchy. The late medieval Church, in England as well as on the continent, was a highly politicized institution, from the Avignon papacy and the Great Schism (beginning in 1378) to the English statute of 1401 permitting the civil authorities to burn heretics (*De haeretico comburendo*) and Arundel's *Constitutions* (drafted 1407, promulgated 1409), which prohibited unlicensed preaching and the unauthorized production of Holy Scripture in English. Most of the authors of medieval political literature were clerics — regular, secular, or heterodox — and their writings naturally reflect their interests. But even so, much of what passed for political controversy in the later Middle Ages concerned ecclesiastical issues: what it means to be poor (and whether friars or Lollards adequately represented poverty in their life); who should have access to the Bible and under what circumstances; what measures authorities should take against Lollardy; how rural officials (many of them clerical) should treat vulnerable churls. Even problems of lordship and dominion (governance and property rights) were debated chiefly by clerks; and the question of *gentilesse* — does true nobility reside in inherited wealth or in the soul? — had theological as well as political ramifications in fourteenth-century England.

Scholars have increasingly challenged the genuineness of these writings as witnesses to political events, claiming that they are conventional satires or complaints expressed in commonplace language. Literary works that seem to contain political material may shade into formulaic language, owing more to Latin and vernacular complaint genres than to contemporary material conditions.[1] A poem on statecraft such as *Treuthe, reste, and pes* may include contemporary references (the statute *De haeretico comburendo*) together with proverbial sayings and commonplace sentiments ("The world is like a fals lemman"; "The world is like a chery fayre"). Similarly, *Song of the Husbandman* contains valuable portraits of regional oppression but also

---

[1] For an airing of the issues, see Thomas J. Elliott, "Middle English Complaints Against the Times: To Contemn the World or to Reform It?," *Annuale Mediaevalia* 14 (1973), 22–34; Rossell Hope Robbins, "Dissent in Middle English Literature: The Spirit of (Thirteen) Seventy-Six," *Medievalia et Humanistica*, New Series 9 (1979), 25–51; Siegfried Wenzel, *Preachers, Poets, and the Early English Lyric* (Princeton: Princeton University Press, 1986), chapter 6; and George Kane, "Some Fourteenth-Century 'Political' Poems," in *Medieval English Religious and Ethical Literature: Essays in Honour of G. H. Russell*, ed. Gregory Kratzmann and James Simpson (Cambridge: D. S. Brewer, 1986), pp. 82–91. Kane particularly objects to Robbins's alleged romanticizing of politics and dissent in "Middle English Poems of Protest," *Anglia* 78 (1960), 193–203.

abstract moralizations: "Thus wil walketh in lond." Perhaps medieval writers felt that they could make sense of political events only by framing them in conventional moral statements; perhaps they regarded moral pronouncements, proverbs, gnomic utterances, and apocalyptic warnings as essential features of their poetic style. Richard W. Kaeuper argues that medieval writers were unsophisticated as regards statecraft and that they knew only *local* conditions:

> Not only are the sources painfully inadequate, the very abstraction, state, was scarcely conceived by men who saw, experienced, and wrote about only particular rulers, officials, and courts, and whose critical acumen ran more along the lines of moral denunciations of particular orders in society, rather than analyses of institutions which were often thought to be immutable, even while they were changing rapidly and with powerful effect.[1]

A plausible explanation for the forms of medieval political complaint is that writers analyzed and understood their political situations through general statements and that they provided specific instances to illustrate universal formulations. They recognized and represented local injustice, if at all, with the help of timeless commonplaces.

A good example of the intertwining of politics and morality occurs in the beginning of the Wycliffite tract *The Lanterne of Light.* The anonymous author first mentions "thise daies of greet tribulacioun," which sounds conventional and formulaic, since Christ alludes to the "greet tribulacioun" in Matthew 24. But then the author claims that "manye" apparently virtuous people — Lollards — have "fallen from her holi purpose, dredyng losse of worldli goodis and bodili peyne," probably an allusion to the persecutions of Lollards after *De haeretico comburendo* (1401) and Arundel's *Constitutions* (1409). According to the *Constitutions* of 1409 a heretic's "worldli goodis" were confiscate; and the 1401 statute allowed ecclesiastical authorities to hand over heretics and schismatics to the state for burning ("bodili peyne"). Finally, the Lollard author cites Christ's words in Matthew 24:12: "*Quoniam habundabit iniquitas, refrigescet caritas multorum.* That is to seie: 'The greet plenté and habundaunce of wickidnesse schal kele or make coolde the charité of many.'" Medieval exegetes regularly understood this scriptural statement as an instance of *senium mundi*, the commonplace notion that the world has grown old, sick, and morally corrupt in preparation for Christ's second coming. The Wycliffite author of *The Lanterne of Light* regards the persecution of Lollards as an instance of the world's

---

[1] *War, Justice, and Public Order: England and France in the Later Middle Ages* (Oxford: Clarendon, 1988), pp. 269–70.

moral cooling prior to Christ's return as Judge in the days of great Tribulation. In other words, politics are interpreted against a backdrop of cataclysmic moral decline.

The larger question in many of these issues — though one seldom treated straightforwardly in medieval writings — was the uneven distribution of wealth and unequal applications of the law. Fourteenth- and fifteenth-century England had an agrarian economy, with a system of bondsmen, husbandmen, and tenant farmers attached to manors; and most medieval English people spent their lives within the vill and the parish, relying on ties of mutual obligation and customary services.[1] For the most part the villein class and their struggles went undepicted in the literature. But in moments of historical crisis versions of their stories could emerge, especially as poets and chroniclers represented — and misrepresented — their plights. The prophetic writers attacked lords and priests and present times generally, under the guise of predicting the future, while anticlerical, Lollard, and antisimoniac authors assailed wealthy friars, the established church (with its pomp, arrogance, and ruthless disregard of material deprivation), and the unethical use of money. Political writers could offer critiques of statutory laws or systems of governance, as do poems on the articles of trailbaston (1304–05 to the reign of Richard II), which permitted, among other things and contrary to common law, indictments without oaths of twelve jurors as well as powers to assess heavy financial damages.[2] Thirteenth- and fourteenth-century poets frequently complained that ordinary citizens were overtaxed but that the monies never reached the king. In political prophecies as well as in venality satires, they decried the elevation of churls or bastards into positions of social prominence to the detriment of state and church; and they deplored the collusion, extortion, and oppression of rural officials — the greedy, unaccountable deans, beadles, constables, summoners, bailiffs, woodwards, reeves, and friars who preyed upon the poor. The topic of money became especially important in fifteenth-century England. The poets who wrote about the abuse of money and the importance of meed in contemporary affairs seemed by turns dumbfounded and outraged at these new circumstances.

---

[1] Barbara A. Hanawalt, *The Ties That Bound: Peasant Families in Medieval England* (New York: Oxford University Press, 1986).

[2] See Isabel S. T. Aspin, ed., *Anglo-Norman Political Songs*, Anglo-Norman Texts 11 (Oxford: Blackwell, 1953), pp. 67–68, and the poem *Trailbaston*. The *OED* s.v. *Trailbaston*, in its full linguistic account, first defines the term as "a class of evil-doers in the reign of Edward I," and adds: "also applied to their system of violence, for the suppression of which special justices were instituted in 1304–05; thence contextually applied also to the ordinances issued against them (*ordinatio de trailbastons*), and to the inquisitions, trials, courts, and justices (*justices sur les traylbastouns*), appointed for their suppression. In living use from 1304 to c 1390; afterwards only a historical term, often misunderstood." Reasons for the confusion may be found in Aspin's note to line 5 of *Trailbaston*, pp. 76–77.

Preface

The science of politics did not exist in the Middle Ages, at least in our disciplinary sense of the term. Universities did not recognize politics as a separate category or discipline; and the analysis of political theory arose chiefly in theological discussions, especially as regards kingship versus the papacy. The origins of medieval politics may be sought in St. Augustine's *The City of God*, in which he posited two especially significant institutions: the earthly city (for Augustine embodied in Rome) and the city of God (the Christian Church, more specifically the "saints"). For Augustine, as for many later medieval thinkers, the city of man must be subordinate to the city of God; earthly institutions should be used (not enjoyed) for the greater glory of God. The prevailing theory was the doctrine of the two swords, an allegorical interpretation of Luke 22:38, whereby God is said to have authorized two institutions to govern humans: kingship (*imperium*) and the papacy (*sacerdotium*). Even John of Salisbury (1110–80), distinguishing between the just and the unjust ruler, who may be resisted (*Policraticus* 10.8), believed that the king derives his earthly sword from the priest. Thomas Aquinas harmonized Aristotle's focus on man as a political animal with descending theocratic formulations of kingship characteristic of the earlier Middle Ages. He developed the concept of the "political government (*regimen politicum*)" and reconciled it with the "regal government (*regimen regale*)"; and his definition of the state — "the State is nothing but the congregation of men" — had its counterpart in his concept of the Church as "a mystical body."[1] Giles of Rome, in his influential *De ecclesiastica potestate* (1301), argued that the ruler must be a loyal servant of the Church in order to be considered a just king; these ideas found expression in the papal bull of Boniface VIII, *Unam sanctam* (1302). Dante Alighieri, in *De monarchia* (perhaps written 1312–13), challenged the papal interpretation of the "two swords" passage, maintaining that a universal emperor should have sole authority in the earthly sphere while the priesthood should govern in spiritual matters, while John of Paris argued that the king governed by the will of the people. In *Defensor pacis* (1324), Marsiglio of Padua contended that the king (the *pars principans* or "ruling part" of the community) derives his authority from the people — that is, people of prominence and substance — while the priesthood governs by virtue of secular authority. Politics also emerged in medieval theories about the polity: the so-called

---

[1] Walter Ullmann, *A History of Political Thought: The Middle Ages* (Baltimore: Penguin, 1965), pp. 178–80. Ullmann argues that Thomas created the science of politics through his idea of the state as a social, political system of human organization (pp. 178–79). Throughout his book Ullmann distinguishes between the "descending" (or feudal/theocratic) and "ascending" (or popular) theories of government and law. For further introductory remarks concerning medieval political science, see Ullmann's *Principles of Government and Politics in the Middle Ages* (London: Methuen, 1961).

three estates. Estates theory emphasized an ordered hierarchy of knights, or those who fight (*bellatores*), clerics, or those who pray (*oratores*), and peasants, or those who work (*laboratores*). By the fourteenth century, this crude scheme, though often invoked in complaint and satire, had become obsolete, wholly inadequate as a description of the English commonwealth and its citizenry. The third estate was by the mid to late fourteenth century a congeries of *arriviste* gentry, prosperous (and not so prosperous) merchants, craftsmen, burgesses, yeomen, villeins, and serfs. Simply put, the peasant class consisted of all those who were not noble and not clerics; and many of the middle strata of the third estate — those who did not take an active role in governance — participated in the misnamed "Peasants' Revolt" of 1381. By at least 1376 and the Good Parliament, the Commons were an integral part of Parliament and of government. They promulgated statutory law, suggested tax policy, and impeached ministers. They could no longer be ignored or taken for granted, as they once were. Richard II's kingship was a constitutional and limited rather than a feudal monarchy.

The fourteenth century in England was a time of political and economic crisis. From the disappointing reign, mortifying deposition, and probable murder of Edward II toward the beginning of the century through the dethronement and murder of his great grandson, Richard II, in 1399–1400, the period experienced turbulence and misery. Edward III (reigned 1327–77) enjoyed some military success in campaigns against the French — at Sluys (1340), at Crécy (1346), and at Poitiers (1356) — but at home there was lawlessness and chaos. As May McKisack has said of this period:

> The evidence at our disposal makes it abundantly plain that fourteenth-century England, for all its multiplicity of courts, statutes, and justices, was not a law-abiding country and that those responsible for the maintenance of order were faced with obstacles beyond their power to surmount.[1]

The problems have been explained in terms of economic contraction and of decline;[2] and one historian has argued that the fourteenth century generally provides a "mirror" of our own times.[3]

Some of the events that help define the century as calamitous include anxieties concerning the papacy; wrangling between barons and parliament, on one hand, and

---

[1] *The Fourteenth Century 1307–1399* (Oxford: Clarendon, 1959), p. 203.

[2] Respectively: Robert E. Lerner, *The Age of Adversity: The Fourteenth Century* (Ithaca: Cornell University Press, 1968); and Charles Muscatine, *Poetry and Crisis in the Age of Chaucer* (Notre Dame: University of Notre Dame Press, 1972).

[3] Barbara W. Tuchman, *A Distant Mirror: The Calamitous Fourteenth Century* (New York: Ballantine, 1978).

the crown, on the other; crop failures and famines; devastating plagues which created labor shortages, price gouging, and crime waves; urban riots and a general Rising that included many elements of the commonalty; criminal gangs which operated with impunity; a corrupt judicial system; wars against Scotland, Ireland, and France, which provided a constant drain on the treasury; a bloody "crusade" against Flanders on behalf of the Roman pope Urban VI; and a growing threat of heresy along with measures to suppress it. In 1309 the papacy removed to Avignon, France, in order to escape civil unrest in Rome. Meanwhile, England was at war with France — though not continuously — from 1337–1453 (the Hundred Years' War); and when the papacy divided into two popes, with dual bureaucracies — at Avignon and Rome, beginning in 1378 (the Great Schism) — England supported Rome. At home the monarchy waged frequent, often bitter power struggles with magnates intent on strengthening their positions.

Disputes between barons or commons and the crown occurred with alarming frequency, including prior to and during 1311, when the Lords Ordainers challenged Edward II; in 1340–41, when the populace refused to pay Edward III's ninth (a tax) for his French wars and when parliament forced concessions regarding Edward's Walton Ordinances of 1338; in 1351 and 1352, when Edward issued militant statutes on laborers and on treason; in 1376, when the Good Parliament, led by the speaker, Peter de la Mare, challenged the duke of Lancaster and the lords concerning new taxes, impeached Lord William Latimer and Richard Lyons over the wool Staple, confronted the aged Edward III, and condemned his influential mistress, Alice Perrers; in the Gloucester parliament, 1378, when the restless Commons again defied Lancaster (representing the crown), and protested the need for further taxes; in the Wonderful Parliament of 1386, when the duke of Gloucester, Thomas of Woodstock, Thomas Arundel, and others forced Richard (not yet in his majority) to dismiss his Chancellor and Treasurer and hinted at deposition; in December, 1387, when Gloucester and the Appellant Lords confronted and apparently threatened Richard in the Tower; in the Merciless Parliament of 1388, when the Appellants managed to execute as traitors a number of Richard's faction, including Robert Tresilian, Chief Justice of the King's Bench; Nicholas Brembre, formerly mayor of London who had quarreled often and violently with the present mayor; Simon Burley, Richard's tutor; John Beauchamp, Steward of the Household; and John Salisbury, Knight of the Chamber. The 1390s were filled with political ferment and crisis, leading to Richard's deposition and death. On these years, see the Introduction to Richard's Reign, below pp. 119–27.

Fifteenth-century England was also troubled, at least in part because of Richard's government and his downfall. Serious challenges to and revolts against Henry's reign began almost immediately after he assumed the kingship — so many that the early fifteenth century might be characterized as a period of crisis management. The

Preface

Appellants of 1397 mounted an unsuccessful rebellion in 1400; and Richard, in confinement at Pontefract, died (probably murdered) shortly afterwards. The Northumberland Percies crushed a Scottish invasion at Homildon Hill, 1402, but in the following year these same Percies, who now supported the earl of March as Richard's true heir, defied Henry and were defeated at the battle of Shrewsbury. Meanwhile, in 1402 and again in 1404, the Commons demanded oversight of taxation for the war efforts. Henry repelled other challenges from anti-Lancastrian forces in 1405; and he and his son, the future Henry V, contained the Welsh nationalism inspired and led by Owen Glendower during the period 1400–16. Henry IV died in 1413. Next year the new king, Henry V, was forced to suppress a feeble but troubling rebellion by a Lollard knight, Sir John Oldcastle. (See the Introduction to Anticlerical Poems and Documents, p. 37.) In August, 1415 — the year of Henry's great victory over the French at Agincourt — Henry put down another magnate plot on behalf of the earl of March, executing Richard, earl of Cambridge, Henry, Lord Scrope, and Sir Thomas Grey. When Henry died in 1422 of complications from dysentery after the protracted siege of Meaux, he left as heir his infant son, Henry VI. Because Henry V had been recognized as king of France in the treaty of Troyes, 1420, the succession of the very young Henry VI precipitated a crisis of command, when the rule of France and England was divided between the surviving brothers of Henry V — John, Duke of Bedford, serving as regent of France, and Humphrey, Duke of Gloucester, serving as protector of Henry and regent of England. Gloucester was opposed at home by magnates jealous of his power in the realm. His special adversary was the wealthy and politically capable cardinal Henry Beaufort, chancellor of England in 1403–1405, 1413–17, and 1424–26, who jockeyed with him for power from the 1420s into the 1440s. In 1425 Bedford returned from France to mediate between the disputing protector and the cardinal with the result that Gloucester's power was limited.

Opposed to the abuses of the age was the humble plowman or husbandman, a figure representing the right use of poverty, who rebuked the grasping friars or wealthy prelates by his form of living. If "Bishop Golias" of the Latin satirical poets was a negative norm — drinking, jangling, gambling, scheming — the plowman offered a positive standard of virtue and right conduct. But the husbandman was also a political figure, as John Ball and rebellious peasants recognized, since his virtue was in part a function of his lack of power and wealth. The plowman became a modern-day surrogate for Christ in Langland's poem: *Petrus id est Christus*. Chaucer characterizes his pilgrim Plowman as "A trewe swynkere and a good," who labors "For Cristes sake, for every povre wight" (I.531, 537). He tacitly repudiates the worldly Monk, whose chief passion is hunting, and the devil-may-care Friar, who refuses contact with the poor and sick — the "poraille" or riff-raff — on the grounds that distressed folk will not serve his cause. The anonymous author of *Piers the Plowman's Crede* emphasizes

Preface

Piers's indigence, for this plowman, who teaches the narrator his Apostles' Creed when four orders of friars cannot, plows in the muck with tattered clothing, barefoot on the bare ice, so that "the blode folwede" (line 436). When Piers denounces the sumptuous hypocrisy of fraternal orders and reminds the narrator of St. Francis's humility, he speaks with authority as one who knows Christian poverty through experience.

Biblical translations unless otherwise noted are from the Douay version. The following abbreviations appear throughout the volume: Alford, *Glossary* = John A. Alford, *Piers Plowman: A Glossary of Legal Diction* (Cambridge: D. S. Brewer, 1988); *EETS* = *Early English Text Society*; *Index* = *The Index of Middle English Verse*, ed. Carleton Brown and Rossell Hope Robbins (New York: Columbia University Press, 1943), cited by entry numbers; *Supplement* = *Supplement to the Index of Middle English Verse*, ed. R. H. Robbins and John L. Cutler (Lexington: University of Kentucky Press, 1965); RHR = Rossell Hope Robbins, ed., *Historical Poems of the XIVth and XVth Centuries* (New York: Columbia University Press, 1959); Robbins, "Poems" = Rossell Hope Robbins, "XIII. Poems Dealing with Contemporary Conditions," *A Manual of the Writings in Middle English 1050–1500*, gen. ed. Albert E. Hartung, vol. 5 (New Haven: The Connecticut Academy of Arts and Sciences, 1975), pp. 1385–1536, 1631–1725; Scattergood, *Politics* = V. J. Scattergood, *Politics and Poetry in the Fifteenth Century* (London: Blandford; New York: Barnes and Noble, 1971); *STC* = *Short Title Catalogue*; UMI = University Microfilms International (with reel numbers); Whiting, *Proverbs* = B. J. Whiting, *Proverbs, Sentences, and Proverbial Phrases* (Cambridge: Harvard University Press, 1968); Wr *PPS* = Thomas Wright, ed., *Political Poems and Songs*, Rolls Series 41.1 (1859); Wr *PSE* = Thomas Wright, ed., *Political Songs of England* (Camden Society, 1839). Citations from *Piers the Plowman's Crede (PPC)*, *The Plowman's Tale (PlT)*, *Jack Upland (JU)*, *Friar Daw's Reply (FDR)*, and *Upland's Rejoinder (UR)* are from my edition of *Six Ecclesiastical Satires* (Kalamazoo: Medieval Institute Publications, 1991).

It remains to thank David Wallace, who conceived the original idea for this volume and who generously advised me on it; Mary P. Richards, who read the entire edition in manuscript and offered important suggestions; Lawrence Duggan, who read the introductory sections; Paul F. Schaffner, Ruth Karras, Siegfried Wenzel, Thomas O. Calhoun, George H. Brown, and Philip Flynn, who furnished valuable, timely help on various matters; Leo Lemay, who forwarded material to me from the British Library; Richard Kaeuper, who provided suggestions for works included in this volume; and especially Russell A. Peck, general editor of the Middle English Texts Series, who corrected errors and offered suggestions at every stage; and Alan Lupack, associate editor, who checked the volume in its final draft. For the preparation of this

Preface

volume and of *Six Ecclesiastical Satires* I am fortunate to have had his broad experience and deep learning. Richard Firth Green and Elizabeth Revell, along with Thomas Hahn and Harry Butler, have puzzled over the Latin passages in *On the Times*; I am indebted to them all, but especially to Richard Firth Green for his numerous suggestions regarding that difficult poem. Thomas Seiler carefully copyedited both volumes, Karen Saupe and Jennifer Church helped shape them into camera-ready copy, and Richard Duggan provided valuable technical assistance on matters of style and format. The preparation of both volumes has been aided by a University of Delaware General Research grant and by summer research-assistant grants from the Department of English. I have profited from the research skills of Hugh P. Campbell, William Frost, Stephen Palley, and Lisa Kochanek.

I wish to acknowledge the following institutions and people for furnishing manuscript reproductions: Stuart O. Seanóir, Assistant Librarian, Manuscripts Department, Trinity College Library, Dublin, for supplying a paper copy from microfilm of MS 516 fol. 115*r* and a microfilm copy of Trinity College Dublin 516 fols. 108–10; Michael Boggan, Executive Officer in Chief, Photography, The Manuscript Collections, and The British Library for supplying electrostatic prints of MSS Harley 913 fols. 59*r–v*; Harley 2253 fols. 64*r* and 127*r–v*; Harley 2324 fols. 1*r–4r*, 5*v–13r*; Lansdowne 762 fols. 5*r–6v*; Arundel 57 fol. 8*v*; Cotton Cleopatra B. ii fols. 63*v–65v*; and Cotton Vespasian B. xvi fols. 2*v–3r*; Miss J. A. Ringrose, Under-Librarian of the Department of Manuscript and Archives, Cambridge University Library, for supplying photostatic copies of MSS Kk. 1. 5 (4) fols. 33*r–34r*; Dd. 14. 2 fol. 312*r*; and Peterhouse 104 fols. 210*r–212r*; Mrs. E. M. Coleman, Assistant Librarian of the Pepys Library, and the Master and Fellows, Magdalene College, Cambridge, for supplying a glossy black and white photograph of MS Pepys 1236 fol. 91*r*; the Sub-Librarian of Trinity College, Cambridge, for supplying an electrostatic copy of Trinity College Cambridge MS 1144 fol. 58*v*; Mrs. G. Cannell, Assistant Librarian of The Parker Library, Corpus Christi College, Cambridge, for supplying electrostatic prints of Corpus Christi College Cambridge MS 369 fol. 46*v*; Miss E. A. Quarmby, Assistant Library, Special Collections, of St. John's College, Cambridge, for supplying electrostatic enlargements of MS 195 (G. 28) fols. 1*v–2r*; and the Keeper of Western Manuscripts, Bodleian College, Oxford, for supplying electrostatic prints of MSS Bodley 48 fols. 325*v–331r*; Ashmole 59 fol. 78*r*; Archbishop Selden B. 26 fol. 19*r*; and Digby 102 fols. 100*r–101r*. Finally, I wish to thank the National Endowment for the Humanities for its support in the completing of the volume.

General Bibliography

Coleman, Janet. *Medieval Readers and Writers 1350–1400*. New York: Columbia University Press, 1981.

Dean, James. *Six Ecclesiastical Satires*. Kalamazoo: Medieval Institute Publications, 1991.

Dobson, R. B. *The Peasants' Revolt of 1381*. 2nd ed. London: Macmillan, 1983.

Hudson, Anne. *The Premature Reformation: Wycliffite Texts and Lollard History*. Oxford: Clarendon, 1988.

Jacob, E. F. *The Fifteenth Century 1399–1485*. The Oxford History of England, 6. Oxford: Clarendon, 1961.

Kaeuper, Richard W. *War, Justice, and Public Order: England and France in the Later Middle Ages*. Oxford: Clarendon, 1988.

Mann, Jill. *Chaucer and Medieval Estates Satire: The Literature of Social Classes and the General Prologue to the Canterbury Tales*. Cambridge: Cambridge University Press, 1973.

McKisack, May. *The Fourteenth Century 1307–1399*. The Oxford History of England, 5. Oxford: Clarendon, 1959.

Pearsall, Derek. *Old English and Middle English Poetry*. The Routledge History of English Poetry, Vol. 1. London: Routledge, 1977.

Peter, John. *Complaint and Satire in Early English Literature*. Oxford: Clarendon, 1956.

Robbins, Rossell Hope. "XIII. Poems Dealing with Contemporary Conditions." *A Manual of the Writings in Middle English 1050–1500*. Vol. 5. Gen. ed. Albert E. Hartung. New Haven: The Connecticut Academy of Arts and Sciences, 1975. Pages 1385–1536, 1631–1725.

Scattergood, V. J. *Politics and Poetry in the Fifteenth Century*. London: Blandford, 1971.

General Bibliography

Taylor, John. *English Historical Literature in the Fourteenth Century*. Oxford: Clarendon, 1987.

Thomson, John A. F. *The Transformation of Medieval England 1370–1529*. Foundations of Modern Britain. London and New York: Longman, 1983.

Ullmann, Walter. *Principles of Government and Politics in the Middle Ages*. London: Methuen, 1961.

Yunck, John A. *The Lineage of Lady Meed: The Development of Mediaeval Venality Satire*. Notre Dame: University of Notre Dame Press, 1963.

Chronology of Political and Literary Events

1301	Giles of Rome's *De ecclesiastica potestate* (On Ecclesiastical Power)
1302	Boniface VIII's bull *Unam sanctam* (temporal power subject to ecclesiastical)
1304–05	Articles of Trailbaston
1305-78	Babylonian captivity (Papacy moves to Avignon)
1307	Accession of Edward II
	Battle of Loudon Hill (Robert Bruce of Scotland defeats the English)
1309	Beginning of Avignon papacy
1311	Lords Ordainers challenge Edward II
1312	Execution of Piers Gaveston
c1312–13	Dante's *De monarchia* (On Monarchy)
1314	Scots defeat the English at Bannockburn
1315–17	Famines in Europe
1322	Statute of York (Commons recognized as essential part of government)
	Thomas of Lancaster and Contrariants defeated at battle of Boroughbridge
	Rise of the Despensers
1324	Marsilius of Padua's *Defensor pacis* (Defender of Peace)
1326	Queen Isabella invades England against Edward II
1327	Accession of Edward III
	Urban unrest at St. Albans, Dunstable, and elsewhere
c1330	Birth of John Gower
	Auchinleck MS (*The Simonie*)
	Harley MS 2253 (*Erceldoune's Prophecy; Song of the Husbandman*)
1333	Battle of Halidon Hill (Edward III defeats the Scots)
c1333	Laurence Minot's *Halidon Hill*
1337	Beginning of Hundred Years' War
1338	Walton Ordinances (call for annual record of state of treasury)
1340	English defeat the French at Sluys in naval battle

Chronology

	Birth of John of Gaunt, Earl of Richmond (later Duke of Lancaster)
c1340–50	*Ercyldoun's Prophecy*
c1343	Birth of Chaucer
1346	English defeat the French at Crécy
1347	English defeat the Scots at Neville's Cross; take David II of Scotland prisoner
1348–49	Black Plague in Europe, including England
1349	English Ordinance of Laborers
1351	First Statute of Laborers
	First Statute of Provisors (allowing English crown patronage in ecclesiastical preferment)
1352	Second Statute of Laborers
	Peter Ceffons of Clairvaux's *Epistola Luciferi ad cleros*
c1352–53	*Wynnere and Wastoure*
1353	First Statute of Praemunire (antipapal statute)
1355	Riots at Oxford (St. Scholastica's Day)
1356	Black Prince and English defeat French at Poitiers, capture French king John
1356–57	FitzRalph's antifraternal sermons at St. Paul's Cross
1358	Jacquerie revolt in France
1360	Treaty of Brétigny (Truce between England and France: Edward abandons claim on French crown)
1361-62	Severe outbreak of plague in England (Mortalité des Enfants)
1363	Sumptuary laws (restricts clothing according to class)
1365	Second Statute of Praemunire
1366	Birth of Henry Bolingbroke, Earl of Derby
1368–74	*Piers Plowman* A text
1369-70	Severe plague years. Death of Blanche, Duchess of Lancaster
1372	English naval defeat off La Rochelle
1373	John of Gaunt leads unsuccessful *chevauchée* (raid) from Calais to Bordeaux
1375	John Barbour's *The Bruce*

Chronology

Chronology

Chronology

Chronology

1408	Death of John Gower
1409	Arundel's *Constitutions*
1409–15	*The Lanterne of Light*
1410	John Badby executed for heresy
	John Huss defends Wyclif; excommunicated
c1410	Presentation of Lollard Disendowment Bill
	Ellesmere MS of *The Canterbury Tales*
1411	Wyclif's books burned at Carfax
	Oxford purged of Lollardy
1413	Death of Henry IV; accession of Henry V
	Trial of Sir John Oldcastle for Lollard heresy
1414	Oldcastle's rebellion fails
	Council of Constance
	Alien priories suppressed
1414–17	*Lo, He That Can Be Cristes Clerc* (*Defend Us From All Lollardy*)
1415	Earl of Cambridge's anti-Lancastrian plot fails
	English defeat French at Agincourt
	Huss burned at the stake
	John Claydon burned as heretic
	Hoccleve's *Address to Oldcastle*
1417	End of Great Schism
	Oldcastle captured and executed
1420	Treaty of Troyes (Henry V recognized as heir of France)
	Henry V marries Catherine of Valois
1422	Death of Henry V; accession of Henry VI
1428	Arrest of Lollards in Kent
1429	Joan of Arc and the siege of Orleans
1431	Henry VI crowned king of France (Paris)
	Revolt at Abingdon

Chronology

Joan of Arc burned at Rouen

1436–37   *Libel of English Policy*

c1439   *Fasciculi zizaniorum* (MS Bodleian Library e Musaeo 86): anti-Lollard documents

1444   Peace negotiations with France

1447   Death of Humphrey, Duke of Gloucester

1450   Cade's Rebellion

Loss of Normandy

c1450   *God Speed the Plough*

Reginald Pecock's *Repressor of Over Much Blaming the Clergy* (anti-Lollard)

1461   Henry VI cedes Berwick to the Scots

Succession of Edward IV

1463   Truce with Scotland

1470–71   Readeption of Henry VI

1479   Plague throughout England

1481   War with Scotland

1483   Death of Edward IV; succession of Edward V; usurpation of Richard III

1485   Battle of Bosworth Field

Succession of Henry VII

1489   Tax revolt in Yorkshire

c1490   *Freers, Freers, Wo Ye Be*

Poems of Political Prophecy

Introduction

Middle English poems and documents of a political nature are closely linked with Latin and vernacular prophecies. Prophecies in this sense are predictions concerning kingdoms or peoples; and these predictions often have an eschatological or apocalyptic cast to them. At the same time they frequently resemble traditional laments or complaints against the times under the guise of visionary utterance.

The prophetic tradition in English derives largely from Geoffrey of Monmouth's *History of the Kings of Britain* (1136), book 7, the so-called "Prophecies of Merlin," which sets the stage for the books devoted to King Arthur. Merlin prophesied great political struggles leading to an apocalyptic decline in England and throughout the world: "In the twinkling of an eye the seas shall rise up and the arena of the winds shall be opened once again. The winds shall do battle together with a blast of ill-omen, making their din reverberate from one constellation to another." Merlin adduces *impossibilia* or *lusus naturae* as part of his prophecies: "In these days the oaks shall burn in the forest glades and acorns shall burgeon on the lime trees' boughs." Or: "Roots and branches shall change their places and the oddness of this will pass for a miracle."[1] Such impossibilities or *mirabilia* hark back to Nennius' *Historia Brittonum* and Celtic sources; and the combination of mystic symbolism and animal imagery for humans survives into later political verse such as *When Rome Is Removed* (printed below), *Richard the Redeless*, or *Ther Is a Busch That Is Forgrowe*, on the fall of Richard II (printed below). And both Wales and Scotland figure prominently in English prophecies — in references to Caernarvon, Welsh birthplace of Edward II, to Thomas of Erceldoune, Scots visionary, or to Roxburgh, Bannockburn, or Berwick. Shakespeare's Hotspur, referring to the Welshman Owen Glendower, speaks derisively of "the dreamer Merlin and his prophecies" as "a deal of skimble-skamble stuff" (III.i).

Prophetic statements based on the formula "When [some event] happens, then [something else] will result" became the staple of the later tradition. This is the form

---

[1] Quotations are from Geoffrey of Monmouth, *History of the Kings of Britain*, trans. Lewis Thorpe (New York: Penguin, 1966), pp. 185, 177, and 184 respectively.

1

of the first prophecy printed in this section, *The Prophecy of Merlin* from Trinity College Dublin MS 516 (*Index* § 3986), which testifies that when certain dire phenomena occur — when lords rule wilfully, priests turn treacherous, robbery is condoned — "Then schal the lond of Albyon torne into confusioun!" Although this poem is cast in the future, it actually predicts events which contemporary moralists deplored, such as the rise of baronial power, the alleged perfidy of clerics, the openness of duplicity and hypocrisy, and the decline of sexual morality ("lechery callyd pryvé solace"). The emphasis on morality and the sense of apocalyptic doom inheres in the genre, as in the following fifteenth-century verse "scrap":

Wanne the hillus smoken,	*When; hills*
Thanne Babilon schal have an ende;	
But whan they brenne as tho fyyr,	*burn; fire*
Thanne eerthe schal henus weende;	*go hence (end)*
Whenne tho watres rennen hem froo,	*run away*
The pepul schal turne to eerthe ageyne;	
And yf ye bleden aboute over,	*bleed*
Alle men schul be slayne.[2]	

A similar construction appears near the opening of *Wynnere and Wastoure*, an early alliterative poem which influenced *Piers Plowman*:

When wawes waxen schall wilde and walles bene doun,	
And hares appon herthe-stones schall hurcle in hire fourme	*crouch; their nest*
And eke boyes of blode with boste and with pryde	*commoners*
Schall wedde ladyes in londe and lede hem at will,	
Thene dredful Domesdaye it draweth neghe aftir.[3]	

Siegfried Wenzel has identified the Dublin *Prophecy of Merlin* as what he terms a fourth version of Type B complaint lyrics ("The Prophecy"). Type B complaints, according to Wenzel, witness that "the old virtues have passed away, vices are now triumphant, what used to be prized highly is nowadays scorned, and the like." A fourth type of these complaint lyrics (exemplified by the Dublin prophecy) offers "a series of four evils" followed by "a prophetic final couplet." Most important, Wenzel

---

[2] Printed by Thomas Wright and J. O. Halliwell in *Reliquiae Antiquae* (London: Pickering, 1841), 1:166. *Index* § 4036.

[3] *Wynnere and Wastoure and The Parlement of the Thre Ages*, ed. Warren Ginsberg, (Kalamazoo: Medieval Institute Publications, 1992), lines 13–16, p. 13. *Index* § 3137.

considers these poems as not true prophecies — they do not so much predict future events as expose existing conditions — but rather complaint lyrics in the guise of prophecies.[4] He traces this version of prophecy to a lyric in *Fasciculus Morum* (*Index* § 3133), which he regards as older than the present lyric:

Sithyn law for wyll bygynnyt to slakyn,	*Since; begins to decline*
And falsehed for sleythe is i-takyn,	*prudence*
Robbyng and revyng ys holden purchas,	*looting; bargain*
And of unthewes is made solas —	*vices*
Engelonde may synge "alas, alas!"[5]	

Wenzel concludes: "It would . . . appear that genetically in all these cases the vaticinal form is a secondary development and formally less important than the 'when-then' formula" (p. 201). Wenzel's investigations, and his division of complaint lyrics into Type A and Type B (with four especially popular lyrics), are very valuable for unraveling the tangled relations among previously mislabeled poetic genres. But he perhaps too quickly denies political or ideological content to the poems by emphasizing genealogy (in Latin poems and in preaching manuals) and convention. The sources and analogues explain much but they do not explain everything. The Merlin prophecies belong in this volume if for no other reason than that they expose the complaint foundations of prophetic or political poems such as *When Rome Is Removed*, *John Ball's Letters*, or *Addresses of the Commons*. Prophetic and political poems are affiliated with complaint lyrics, and vice versa. The text of the present edition of the Dublin *Prophecy of Merlin* is based on F. J. Furnivall's careful transcription for the Chaucer Society and is checked against RHR's version: p. 121. I include the four-line lyric beginning "Longe berde herteles" to show the context of the prophecy (and see below, the Magdalene College *Prophecy of Merlin*).

---

[4] *Preachers, Poets, and the Early English Lyric* (Princeton: Princeton University Press, 1986), pp. 182, 194, 196, and 201. For a concurring view see V. J. Scattergood, *Politics and Poetry in the Fifteenth Century* (New York: Barnes and Noble, 1971), pp. 301–02 (characterizing the Dublin *Prophecy of Merlin*).

[5] *Verses in Sermons: Fasciculus Morum and Its Middle English Poems* (Cambridge: Mediaeval Academy of America, 1978), p. 178 (no. 40; *Index* § 3133). I have normalized the u/v spelling. See also *Preachers, Poets, and the Early English Lyric*, p. 195.

Similar to the Dublin version of *The Prophecy of Merlin* is an eight-line poem in Bodleian Library MS 6943 fol. 78*r* (*Index* § 3986),[6] a prophecy sometimes attributed to Chaucer. Several lines in the Bodleian lyric appear to be variants of the Dublin poem, but the Oxford verses also contain a couplet alluding to messianic predictions that link Christ and Arthur: "And whan the moon is on David stall, / And the kynge passe Arthures hall." This poem exemplifies the English prophetic tradition in that it combines murky, quasi-scriptural prediction with quasi-political complaint. The text of the present edition is based on an electrostatic copy of the Bodley MS and is checked against Skeat's text in the Oxford Chaucer, vol. 7, pp. lxxxi–lxxxii.

Included here is a third *Prophecy of Merlin* from Magdalene College Cambridge MS 1236 fol. 91*r*, which begins "When feythe fayleth in prestys sawys" (*Index* § 3943). This consists of two poems in the same scribal hand (separated by a gap in the manuscript), the second beginning "When Goneway shall on Curtays call" (*Supplement* § 3951.5). I print them together because the first lyric witnesses the "timeless" prophecy that Wenzel and others claim are in fact complaints, while the second, which seems to be affiliated with the first, offers more specific referents.[7] The first poem features the "Albeon/confusion" couplet; the second, more enigmatic, highlights the role of Celtic lands in bringing about that confusion: "Wallys," "Albeon Skottlonde," and "the rede Irlonde fox." The present edition is based on an excellent electrostatic print of the manuscript and is checked against Skeat's edition in the Oxford Chaucer (*Chaucerian and Other Pieces*, vol. 7, p. 450, the first of three "Sayings [of Chaucer] Printed by Caxton"). I have also checked "When Goneway shall on Curtays call" against RHR's partial (and error-ridden) transcription on pp. 316–17.

Also in the "When-Then" tradition falls *Thomas of Erceldoune's Prophecy*, a unique text from the well-known MS Harley 2253 (about 1330; *Index* § 3989). This poem claims to predict the end of the Scottish wars in answer to a question from the countess of Dunbar, wife of the Earl of March. Thomas of Erceldoune, sometimes identified as the son of Thomas the Rhymer, was a thirteenth-century Scots poet and seer; and his name became attached to several later prophecies (see those printed by Murray in EETS o.s. 61). The Harley *Prophecy* is in southern or south-midland

---

[6] Manuscript executed "1447–56" (Robbins, "Poems," p. 1636). § 3986 has been deleted in favor of an expanded § 3943 in *Supplement*.

[7] For other examples of "Type B" complaints juxtaposed with other lyrics, see *When Rome Is Removed* and lines 14–17 (beginning "Whenne lordis wol lose har olde lawys" [*Supplement* § 3943]) printed by E. C. and R. Fawtier in *The Bulletin of the John Rylands Library*, 5 (1919), 389.

dialect and betrays English not Scottish sympathies. And the poem is, like some other late products of the alliterative revival, semi-alliterative, sometimes lapsing into prose. The combination of internal rhyme through alliteration and anaphora on the word *when* gives the verse an incantatory impressiveness. The present text of *Thomas of Erceldoune's Prophecy* is based on a photostat of the British Library manuscript, checked against the editions of J. A. H. Murray for the EETS, of RHR, and of Turville-Petre. I have consulted and profited from Murray's translation of *Thomas of Erceldoune's Prophecy* (see p. lxxxvi).

The Magdalene College *Prophecy of Merlin* and *Thomas of Erceldoune's Prophecy* exhibit an interest in Scotland and Scottish-English political relations. Thomas of Erceldoune was regarded as a great oracle who not only could see into the future but could discern the inner structure, the political-spiritual content, of that future. This combination of politics and spirituality is true also of *Ercyldoun's Prophecy* (*Index* § 3762), a unique text in British Library MS Arundel 57, which contains other prophecies and the autograph text of *Ayenbite of Inwit*. *Ercyldoun's Prophecy* features a conversation between Thomas ("the minstrel") and King Alexander III of Scotland concerning the birth of Edward II of Caernarvon. In another "When/Then" construction Alexander learns that his reign will not succeed him (because he will leave no male heirs). The minstrel (Thomas) tells him that his pretensions to dynastic kingship will vanish "When Bannockburn is strewn with men's bones." Bannockburn was the decisive battle of 1314, when Robert Bruce and the Scots, though heavily outnumbered, defeated Humphrey de Bohun of Hereford, Aymer de Valence of Pembroke, Gilbert de Clare of Gloucester, and the forces of Edward II. Many English and Scottish prophetic poems refer to this debacle. Robbins dates this poem to either "about 1340" or "ca 1350" ("Poems," pp. 1526 and 1720 respectively). The text of *Ercyldoun's Prophecy* is based on a photostatic copy of the manuscript, which is checked against the editions of Wright and Halliwell and of Richard Morris for the Early English Text Society.

The final poem included in this section begins "Qwhen Rome is removyde into Inglande" (*Index* § 4008). This piece, also known as *The Second Scottish Prophecy*, offers a mélange of lyrics, including four lines on the Abuses of the Age (see *Index* § 4006) and a verse characterized elsewhere as *The Prophecie of Beid*. The poem exists in three states or versions, designated as A, B, and C, and is witnessed in twenty-one manuscripts. The present edition prints the best-known version (A) from Cambridge University Library MS Kk.1.5 (IV). The prophecy seems originally to have been Scottish, but the author of the Cambridge version altered the sympathies from Scottish to English. It features an allegory (based on symbols developed in Geoffrey of Monmouth's *Prophecies of Merlin*) of the Leopard (England) versus the Lion (Scotland), with the former triumphing over both the Lion and his "stepsons," the

5

Scottish lords, who were particularly unruly in the late fourteenth century. The political allegory apparently refers to events of the 1380s, which culminated in the battle of Otterburn (1388). The text of *When Rome Is Removed* is based on an electrostatic print of the Cambridge MS and is checked against the editions of J. Rawson Lumby for the Early English Text Society, of Haferkorn, and of RHR. The present text is one line shorter than that of RHR, who inserts a line from other manuscripts after line 8.

Select Bibliography

Manuscripts

Trinity College Dublin MS 516 fol. 115*r* (1450–75)

Oxford University, Bodleian Library MS 6943 fol. 78*r* (1447–56)

Cambridge University, Magdalene College MS 1236 fol. 91*r* (c. 1460)

British Library MS Harley 2253 fol. 127*r* (c. 1340)

British Library MS Arundel 57 fol. 8*v* (c. 1350)

Cambridge University MS Kk.1.5 [IV] fols. 33*r*–34*r* (1480–1500)

Previous Editions

Furnivall, F. J., ed. *Animadversions uppon the Annotacions and Corrections of Some imperfections of impressiones of Chaucers workes (sett downe before tyme, and nowe) reprinted in the yere of oure lorde 1598 sett downe by Francis Thynne*. Chaucer Society. 2nd Series 13. London: Trübner, 1876. [Version of the Dublin MS of *The Prophecy of Merlin* on p. xlvi.]

Gray, Douglas, ed. *The Oxford Book of Late Medieval Verse and Prose*. Oxford: Oxford University Press, 1988. [Bodley version of *The Prophecy of Merlin* on p. 22.]

Haferkorn, Reinhard, ed. "When Rome is Removed into England: Eine politische Prophezeiung des 14. Jahrhunderts." *Beiträge zur englischen Philologie* 19 (1932),

92–98. [A critical text, with variants from other versions and a translation into German on facing pages.]

Lumby, J. Rawson, ed., *Bernardus de cura rei familiaris with Some Early Scottish Prophecies.* EETS 42. London: N. Trübner, 1870. [Edition of "When Rome Is Removed" ("Ancient Scottish Prophecy, No. 2") on pp. 32–34.]

Morris, Richard, ed. *Dan Michel's Ayenbite of Inwyt, or, Remorse of Conscience.* EETS o.s. 23. London: N. Trübner, 1866. [*Ercyldoun's Prophecy.*]

Murray, J. A. H., ed. *The Romance and Prophecies of Thomas of Erceldoune.* EETS 61. London: N. Trübner, 1875. [Edition of *Thomas of Erceldoune's Prophecy* on pp. xviii–xix; valuable translation of "The Old Harleian Prophecy" on p. lxxxvi.]

Skeat, W. W., ed. *The Complete Works of Geoffrey Chaucer*, vol. 7: *Chaucerian and Other Pieces.* The Oxford Chaucer. Oxford: Clarendon, 1897. [Bodley version of *The Prophecy of Merlin* on pp. lxxxi–lxxxii.]

Turville-Petre, Thorlac, ed. *Alliterative Poetry of the Later Middle Ages: An Anthology.* Washington, D.C.: The Catholic University of America Press, 1989. [Edition of *Thomas of Erceldoune's Prophecy* on pp. 36–37, with valuable notes.]

Wright, Thomas and J. O. Halliwell. *Reliquiae Antiquae.* 2 vols. London: Pickering, 1841, 1843. 1:30. [Version of *Ercyldoun's Prophecy* in volume 1, p. 30.]

General Studies

Bestul, Thomas H. *Satire and Allegory in Wynnere and Wastoure.* Lincoln: University of Nebraska Press, 1974. [Discussion of political prophecies on pp. 59–65.]

Fawtier, E. C. and Fawtier, R. "From Merlin to Shakespeare: Adventures of an English Prophecy." *Bulletin of the John Rylands Library* 5 (1919), 388–92. [Prints John Rylands Library, Manchester Latin MS 210 (R. 39882), a longer version of a Merlin prophecy, and discusses its relations with others of the type.]

Pearsall, Derek. *Old English and Middle English Poetry.* London: Routledge, 1977. [Prophecies discussed on pp. 124–25.]

Scattergood, V. J. *Politics and Poetry in the Fifteenth Century*. New York: Barnes and Noble, 1971. [Brief discussion of Merlin prophecies as complaint lyrics on pp. 301–02; predictions by the dice on pp. 359–60. See also Scattergood's discussions of individual poems with prophetic qualities, including a poem on the battle of Shrewsbury: pp. 117–19.]

Taylor, Rupert. *The Political Prophecy in England*. New York: Columbia University Press, 1911. Rpt. New York: AMS Reprint, 1967. [Still valuable study, with summaries of material. No index but an extensive chapter outline of the dissertation on pp. xi–xx.]

Wenzel, Siegfried. *Preachers, Poets, and the Early English Lyric*. Princeton: Princeton University Press, 1986. [Analyzes prophecies as examples of Type B complaint lyrics. See pp. 193–203.]

————. *Verses in Sermons: Fasciculus Morum and Its Middle English Poems*. Cambridge, Mass.: The Mediaeval Academy of America, 1978. [Argues for the special contexts of Middle English lyrics within sermons based on the *Fasciculus Morum*, a handbook for preachers.]

Bibliography

Robbins, Rossell Hope. "XIII. Poems Dealing with Contemporary Conditions." *A Manual of the Writings in Middle English 1050–1500*. Vol. 5. Ed. Albert E. Hartung. New Haven: Connecticut Academy of Arts and Sciences, 1975. Pp. 1385–1536; 1631–1725 (bibliography). [Discusses *Prophecies of Merlin* (§§ 277, 278) on pp. 1520–21, bibliography p. 1716; *Thomas of Erceldoune's Prophecy* (§ 288) on page 1525, bibliography p. 1720; *Ercyldoun's Prophecy* (§ 289) on p. 1526, bibliography p. 1720; *When Rome Is Removed* (§ 285) on p. 1524, bibliography pp. 1718–19.]

The Prophecy of Merlin

(Trinity College Dublin MS 516 fol. 115r)

	When lordes wille is londes law,	*the law of the land*
	Prestes wylle trechery, and gyle hold soth saw, [1]	
	Lechery callyd pryvé solace,	*is called secret pleasure*
	And robbery is hold no trespace —	*held to be no crime*
5	Then schal the lond of Albyon torne into confusioun!	*(see note)*
	A M CCCC lx and on, few lordes or ellys noone.	*In 1461 [there are]*
	Longe berde herteles,	*i.e., An old man*
	Peyntede hoode wytles,	*foolish*
	Gay cote graceles,	*ill-mannered*
10	Maketh Engelond thrifles.	*worthless*

The Prophecy of Merlin

(Oxford University, Bodleian Library MS 6943 fol. 78r)

Prophecia Merlini doctoris perfecti

	Whane lordis wol leefe theire olde lawes,	*abandon*
	And preestis beon varyinge in theire sawes,	*teachings*
	And leccherie is holden solace,	*lechery is considered to be*
	And oppressyon for truwe purchace;	
5	And whan the moon is on David stall,	*David's stable (see note)*
	And the kynge passe Arthures hall,	*by-passes*
	Than is the lande of Albyoun	
	Nexst to his confusyoun.	*Near; its*

---

[1] *Priests intend treachery, and guile turns into figures of speech*

The Prophecy of Merlin

(Magdalene Coll. Cambridge MS 1236 fol. 91*r*)

	When feythe fayleth in prestys sawys,	*sayings*
	And lordys wyll be londys lawys,	*law of the land*
	And lechery is prevy solas,	*secret comfort*
	And robbery ys goode purchas:	*booty*
5	Than shall the londe of Albeon	*Britain*
	Be turned into confusion.	
	When Goneway shall on Curtays call,	*(see note)*
	Then Wallys shall rayke and hastely ryse;	*Wales; wander; rebel*
	Then Albeon Skottlonde shall to hem fall;	
10	Then waken wonders in every wyse.	*way*
	The rede Irlonde fox shall ryse with all	*(see note)*
	With glayvys grownde, and gare men to agryse [1]	
	To fell and fende oure fomen all;	*kill; thwart; enemies*
	Sevyn shall sytt in youre asyse.	*Seven; trial*

---

[1] *With sharpened swords, and men ready to terrorize*

Thomas of Erceldoune's Prophecy

(British Library MS Harley 2253 fol. 127*r*)

La countesse de Donbar demanda a Thomas de Essedoune quant la guere descoce prendreit fyn e yl la respoundy e dyt:

When man as mad a kyng of a capped man;   *a fool has been made a king*

When mon is levere othermones thyng then is owen; [1]

When Londyon ys forest, ant forest ys felde;   *and; field*

When hares kendles o the herston;   *give birth; hearthstone*

5 When wyt and wille werres togedere;   *war against one another*

When mon makes stables of kyrkes, and steles castles wyth styes; [2]

When Rokesbourh nys no burgh ant market is at Forweleye;   *Roxburgh; city*

When the alde is gan ant the newe is come that don notht;   *old; gone; nothing*

When Bambourne is donged wyth dede men;   *Bannockburn; manured; dead*

10 When men ledes men in ropes to buyen and to sellen;

When a quarter of whaty whete is chaunged for a colt of ten markes; [3]

When prude prikes and pees is leyd in prisoun;   *pride gallops; peace*

When a Scot ne may hym hude ase hare in forme that the Englysshe
    ne shal hym fynde; [4]

When rytht ant wrong ascenteth to-gedere;   *conspire*

15 When laddes weddeth lovedis;   *churls wed ladies*

When Scottes flen so faste that for faute of ship hy drouneth hem-selve: —[5]

Whenne shal this be? Nouther in thine tyme ne in myne.   *shall; Neither*

Ah comen and gon with-inne twenty wynter ant on.   *But [this] shall come to pass*

---

[1] *When [a] man would rather have the goods of another than his own*

[2] *When men make stables out of churches, and capture castles with ladders*

[3] *When a quarter of moldy (?) wheat is exchanged for a colt of ten marks*

[4] *When a Scot may not hide like a hare in its lair so that the English can't find him*

[5] *When Scots flee so fast that for lack of a ship they drown themselves*

Ercyldoun's Prophecy

(British Library MS Arundel 57 fol. 8*v*)

Thomas de Erseldoune, Escot et dysur, dit au rey Alisandre le paroles desuthdites, du rey Edward ke ore est, kaunt yl fust à nestre.

	To-nyght is boren a barn in Kaernervam,	*born; child; Caernarvon*
	That ssal wold the out ydlis ylcan.	*shall rule all the outer islands*
	The kyng Alesandre acsede,	*asked*
	Hwan sall that be? The menstral zede:	*When shall; minstrel said*
5	Hwan Banockesbourne is y-det myd mannis bonis; [1]	
	Hwan hares kendleth in hertth-stanes;	*give birth; hearth-stones*
	Hwan laddes weuddeth levedes;	*churls wed ladies*
	Hwan me ledeth men to selle wytth rapis; [2]	
	Hwan Rokysburth is no burth;	*Roxburgh; city*
10	Hwan men gyven an folu of twenti pound for an seme of hwete. [3]	

---

[1] *When Bannockburn is strewn with men's bones*

[2] *When men are led to market with ropes*

[3] *When men give a fool twenty pounds for a pack-horse load of wheat*

When Rome Is Removed

(Cambridge Univ. MS Kk.1.5 [IV] fols. 33r–34r)

	Qwhen Rome is removyde into Inglande,	*When; England*
	And the preste haffys the poppys power in hande,	*priest has; pope's*
	Betuix thre and sex — whoso wyll understande —	*Between three and six*
	Mekyll baret ande bale shall fall in Brutis lande. [1]	
5	When pryde is most in price, ande wyt is in covatyse,	*held most dear*
	Lychory is ryffe, and theffis has haldin thar lyff,	*Lechery; widespread; thieves*
	Holy Chirche is awlesse, and justicis ar lawlesse,	*irreverent*
	Bothte knychtis and knawys clede in on clething,	*knaves; the same dress*
	Be the yheris of Cryst, comyn and gone,	*By; years*
10	Fully nynty ande nyne (nocht one wone):	*nothing further*
	Then shall sorow be sett ande unsell,	*sorrow and unhappiness subside*
	Than shall Dame Fortowne turne hir whell.	*Fortune; wheel*
	Scho sall turne up that ar was doune,	*She shall; before*
	And than sall leawté ber the crowne.	*uprightness wield power*
15	Betweyne the cheyff of the somer and the sad winter,	*height; depths of*
	For the heycht of the heyte happyne sall wer;	*promise; heat; war*
	And everyche lorde shall austernly werk.	*every; harshly*
	Then shall Nazareth noy well awhile;	*suffer*
	And the Lilly so lele wytht lovelyche flouris	*loyal with lovely flowers*
20	For harmes of the hardé heyte sall hillyne his ledis,	
	Syne speyde hime at sped, and spawne in the wynter. [2]	
	All the Flowris in the Fyrth sall folow hime one.	*it (the Lily) alone*
	Tatcalders sall call on Carioun the noyus,	*Cadwalader; Conan the troublesome*

---

[1] *Much strife and misery shall occur in Brutus's land (England)*

[2] *Because of injuries from the strong heat shall hide its (the Lily's, i.e., the French) people, /
Afterwards they themselves will quickly thrive and multiply in the winter*

And than sall worthe up Wallys and wrethe othir landis, [1]

25   And erth on tyll Albany, if thai may wyne.   *spur on Scotland; succeed*

Herme wnto alienys, anever thai sall wakyne!   *Evil befall*

The Bruttis blude sall thame wakyne and bryttne wyth brandis of stell: [2]

Ther sall no bastarde blode abyde in that lande.

Then Albanattus the kene, kynde kynge offe erthe,   *Albanact; bold; natural; of*

30   Unto the Libert shall leng — leve yhe non othir. [3]

The Lyone, leder of bestis,

Shall lowte to the Libert and long hume wytht,   *bow; leopard; belong to him*

And shall stere hume at stryff be stremis of Humber. [4]

The stopsonys of the Lyonne, steryt up at ones,   *stepsons; lion; stirred up*

35   The Leoperde sall thame stryke doune, and stroy thame for ever.   *destroy them*

He sall thame kenly kersse, as Cryst has hume bydyne,   *boldly condemn; bid him*

And thus He sall thame doune dryff, ewyne to the ende.   *force down; even*

For thai luf nocht the Lylly nor the Libert lelle,   *love; Lily; loyal Leopard*

And thai halde to the hardé, happyn as it may,   *adhere; brave*

40   Ay to the tayle of somyr tyne hir lappis.   *destroy their clothing*

Wytht that sall a Libert be louse, when thai lest weyne.   *With; loosed; least think*

Ane Egle of the est, ande ane aventruse byrde,   *Eagle; daring bird*

Shall fande flowrys to fange in that fyrste sesoun;   *discover; gather*

Sterte to the stopsonys, stryke thame doune to-gether,   *Attack; stepsons*

45   To bynde bandis unbrokyne that salbe furthe broucht.   *shall be*

He sall hime garlandis gete of the gay flowrys

At in that sesoune spredis so fayre.   *That*

And all sall fawle the foulke that the freke strykis;   *fall; folk; warrior*

A sely northyrune flaw sall fadyne for ever. [5]

50   Herafter on othir syde sorow sall ryse,

The Barge of Bar-Jona bowne to the sonkyne,   *(see note)*

Secularis sall set thame in spiritual clothis   *Laymen*

And occupy thar offices, ennoyntyd as thai war.   *as if they were*

---

[1] *And then Wales shall rise up and assail other lands*

[2] *Evil [fall] on strangers, if ever they shall rouse! / The Brut's blood shall waken and slaughter them with swords of steel*

[3] *To the leopard shall belong — believe you nothing else*

[4] *And shall rouse himself to battle at the river Humber*

[5] *A paltry northern squall shall fade forever*

Thar tonsurys tak wytht turnamentis inowe,   *torments*

55   And trow tytyll of trouth that the strenth haldis.   *title; power*

     That salbe tene for to tell the tende of thar sorow   *shall be grief; tithe*

     That sall ourdryff the date doune to the boke.   *delay; period*

     This most betyde in the time — throw yhe forsuthe —   *happen; eye*

     Qwhen A B C may sett hume to wryte.   *themselves*

60   Anon efter M¹, evene to rewlle,   *one thousand; to measure level*

     Tre CCC in a sute semblyt to-gether,   *Three hundreds; group assembled*

     Ande syne, efter ane *l*, as the lyne askis,   *afterwards; fifty; requires*

     Tris X ande ane R enterly folowande: *Three tens; without exception*

     This is the dolorouse date — understande yhe the glose —   *you*

65   Wheroff whyll Merlyne melys in his bokis.   *speaks*

     Busk ye wyell, Berwyk, be blyth of this wordis,   *Prepare; well; glad; these*

     That Sant Bede fande in his buk of the byg bergh.   *conceived; book*

     The trew towne upon Twede wytht towrys fayre!   *(Berwick-upon-Tweed)*

     Thow sall releve to thi keng, that is the kende eyr.   *natural heir*

70   Ande othir burghys abowte, wytht thar brade wall,   *broad*

     Sall wytht the Lyoune be leffe ande longe for-ever.   *happy; belong*

Notes

The Prophecy of Merlin (Dublin MS)

5   *Albyon*. The legendary, antique name for Britain, as in Geoffrey of Monmouth's *History of the Kings of Britain*. The fool in *King Lear* quotes this or a related poem when he says: "Then shall the realm of Albion / Come to great confusion" (III.ii.85–86).

6   *A M CCCC lx and on*. RHR does not print this part of the poem, nor does he include the material I have here numbered 7–10 as if it were subjoined to the above six lines. The lyrics are separate poems, yet the thought seems to be related. The dating 1461 should be compared with "When Rome Is Removed" lines 60–63.

7–10   *Longe berde . . . thrifles*. These lines, which constitute a separate poem, are part of a catalogue genre that Siegfried Wenzel terms "Type A" complaint lyrics. Wenzel terms them a priamel, "in which a list of individual instances, the *abusiva*, leads to a 'particular point of interest or importance,' the 'evil things' of the last line" (*Preachers, Poets, and the Early English Lyric* [Princeton: Princeton University Press, 1986], p. 178). The "Type A" lyrics derive from *De duodecim abusivis* (the twelve abuses: seventh century, although attributed to Cyprian), a popular Latin treatise used extensively by medieval preachers; and Wenzel believes that many of these verses "derive from a native and oral tradition" (p. 181). See the discussion and many examples Wenzel provides in chapter 6. Lines 7–10 of the present lyric — which also appears in *The Brut* (Wenzel, p. 180) — resemble the moralizing "Abuses of the Age" lyrics, with their "world upside down" contents. RHR prints the following fragment attributed to "Aluredus king" (sayings of King Alfred) from the flyleaf of Trinity College Cambridge MS 108 (thirteenth-century):

> Ald man witles   *Old*
> yung man recheles

wyman ssameles	*shameless*
betere ham were lifles	*for them to be*

See RHR, p. 328, and the poem which this note glosses ("Bissop lorles, / Kyng redeles"): *Abuses of the Age, I* from British Library MS Harley 913 fol. 6v (*Index* § 1820). The "Proverbs of Alfred" (c. 1175, frequently edited) were an amorphous collection of gnomic sayings generically related to *The Distichs of Cato*. See S. O. Arngart, *The Proverbs of Alfred*, 2 vols. (Lund: Gleerup, 1942–55), and Derek Pearsall, *Old English and Middle English Poetry* (London: Routledge, 1977), pp. 77–79. The Proverbs of Alfred have also been edited by Richard Morris (EETS o.s. 49, 1872), W. W. Skeat (1907), J. Hall (1920), and Brandl and Zippel (2nd ed., 1927). For similar examples of "Abuses of the Age" verses, see *When Rome Is Removed* lines 5–9 and note to line 5; *The Letter of John Ball* (from Stow's *Annales*); Ball's Letter in the *Addresses of the Commons* from Henry of Knighton's *Chronicon*: lines 35–41.

The Prophecy of Merlin *(Bodley MS)*

Headnote: *Prophecia Merlini.* "The prophecy of the excellent, learned Merlin." This lyric appears in Oxford University Bodleian MS 6943 fol. 78r but is housed in the Ashmolean collection (MS Ashmole 59). See *Index* § 3986, *Supplement* § 3943.

1   *leefe.* So Skeat and Gray. Robbins, *Index* and *Supplement*, § 3986 transcribes *leefe* as *leese*. The MS can sustain either reading.

2   *beon.* So MS; Skeat, Gray *been.*

5   *David stall.* David's stable, a reference to Christ's birth in Bethlehem (city of David). Of the apocalyptic element in this poem Gray comments: "On the more intellectual prophetic tradition, reflected in the Joachimite dream of a *renovatio mundi*, compare M. Reeves, *The Influence of Prophecy in the Later Middle Ages* (Oxford, 1969)."

7   *Than is the.* Skeat's correction of MS *Þat is is.*

7–8   *Than is . . . his confusyoun.* The language and sentiments of this prophecy should be compared with a lyric (No. 40) from the *Fasciculus Morum* printed

17

by Wenzel (see above, Introduction to Political Prophecies, p. 8). In *Preachers, Poets, and the Early English Lyric*, Wenzel argues against the prophetic nature of the Merlin lyrics by pointing to the coincidences of phrasing in lyric no. 40 and the alleged prophetic poems and more generally to the debts they owe to the language of complaint.

The Prophecy of Merlin *(Magdalene Coll. MS)*

1   *When feythe fayleth.* Versions of this lyric — identified as "Chaucer's Proverbs" —were regularly printed in earlier editions of Chaucer. Richard Morris's edition contains the following lyric:

> Qwan prestis faylin in her sawes,
> And Lordis turnin Goddis lawes
> Ageynis ryght;
> And lecherie is holdin as privy solas,
> And robberie as fre purchas,
> Bewar than of ille!
> Than schall the Lond of Albion
> Turnin to confusion,
> As sumtyme it befelle.

As printed in *The Poetical Works of Geoffrey Chaucer*, rev. ed. (London: Bell, 1875), vol. 6, p. 307. Skeat prints a similar version of this poem from Caxton's edition of Chaucer, as the first one of the "Sayings" (or proverbs) of Chaucer:

> Whan feyth failleth in prestes sawes,
> And lordes hestes ar holden for lawes,
> And robbery is holden purchas,
> And lechery is holden solas,
> Then shal the lond of Albyon
> Be brought to grete confusioun.

See Skeat's *Complete Works of Geoffrey Chaucer*, vol. 7 (Oxford: Clarendon, 1897), p. 450.

4   *purchas.* Skeat glosses *purchas* as "bargain." It is that which is acquired.

7   *Goneway . . . Curtays.* Perhaps Gone-Away and Courtesy, allegorical figures of rudeness and politeness respectively. That is, when Rudeness calls upon Courtesy. Another possibility: Goneril and Cordelia from the King Lear story (Geoffrey of Monmouth, *History of the Kings of Britain* book 2, chapters 11–14).

7–14   *When Goneway . . . in youre asyse.* RHR prints five and one-half lines of this lyric in his notes to the Trinity College Dublin version of "When lordes wille is londes law." I supply variants from RHR's text in the notes below.

8   *Wallys.* Wales. The poet mentions three Celtic regions: Wales, Scotland (line 9), and Ireland (line 11).

9   *Albeon Skottlonde.* A pleonasm for Scotland or northern Britain.

11   *rede Irlonde fox.* So MS; RHR (in his partial transcription) *rede londe.* Perhaps a reference to Robert I "the Bruce" (reigned 1306–29), who had red hair and who was noted for his duplicity and self-serving policies. This cryptic line also perhaps alludes to the Battle of Bannockburn (1314). It might, however, refer to John Comyn the Red, who defeated Edward I's forces at Roslin in 1301. Robert Bruce murdered the Red Comyn during a parley at the Greyfriars' church, Dumfries, in 1306.

12   *glayvys grownde.* So MS; RHR *glaringe grounde.* RHR's transcription breaks off with these words.

Thomas of Erceldoune's Prophecy

Headnote: French reads, "The countess of Dunbar asked Thomas of Erceldoune when the Scots war should come to an end, and he replied and said." The Countess of Dunbar is probably Marjory, who surrendered Dunbar castle in 1296 (Turville-Petre). Both John Pinkerton and Sir Walter Scott believed that this Countess of Dunbar was Black Agnes, sister of Robert the Steward, who stoutly defended Dunbar castle in 1337 and of whom the Earl of Salisbury is reported to have said, when he besieged her castle for six months: "Came I early, came I late, I found Agnes at the gate." The poem and manuscript, however, were probably composed before Black Agnes's legendary defense.

1   *When man.* Murray translates: "When people have (*man has*) made a king of a capped man"; perhaps an allusion to Edward II. This line, and the poem's concept generally, anticipates Shakespeare's *King Lear*, especially the Fool's speech in III.ii (on which see *The Prophecy of Merlin* [Dublin MS], line 5 and note). Brandl puts quotation marks around lines 1–16, as if spoken by Thomas; 17a, by the Countess of Dunbar; and 17b–18, by Thomas.

3   *Londyon.* MS *londyonus* or *loudyonys*; Brandl *Londyon*; Turville-Petre *Loudyon*. This line may refer to Loudon Hill (Lothian) and its battle, 1307, when Robert Bruce defeated Aymer de Valence. Or it may refer to the city of London.

7   *Rokesbourh.* Roxburgh, one of the four boroughs of Scotland, which has a famous castle.

    Forweleye. MS and RHR *fforweleye*; Murray and Brandl *Forwyleye*. This place name has not been identified.

8   *don notht.* MS and RHR *don noþt*; Murray *don (or dou) noþt*; Brandl *dou noþt*.

9   *Bambourne.* The battle of Bannockburn, 1314, a stunning defeat for the English. Murray argues that the poem may have been composed "on the eve of the Battle of Bannockburn, and circulated under Thomas's name, in order to discourage the Scots and encourage the English in the battle" (EETS 61: xix). Murray also observes that "twenty wynter ant on" prior to 1314 was 1293, when Thomas was "still alive" (p. xix).

13   *When a Scot.* The syntax is difficult. Murray translates: "When a Scot cannot hide like a hare in form that the English shall not find him" (p. lxxxvi). The Scots were notorious for their abilities to vanish in battle and to escape detection. Brandl emends *forme* to *forwe* and reads *sal* for *shal*. See also *Wynnere and Wastoure* lines 12–13:

> When wawes waxen schall wilde and walles bene doun,
> And hares appon herthe-stones schall hurcle in hire fourme . . . .

For the text see *Wynnere and Wastoure*, ed. Warren Ginsberg (Kalamazoo: Medieval Institute Publications, 1992), p. 13.

15   *When laddes weddeth lovedis.* Social climbing was a common complaint in "Abuses of the Age" poetry. See also *Ercyldoun's Prophecy*, line 7; *Piers the Plowman's Crede*, lines 748–49 note; *The Plowman's Tale*, lines 301–08; and *Wynnere and Wastoure*, lines 14–15:

>   And eke boyes of blode with boste and with pryde
>   Schall wedde ladyes in londe and lede hem at will . . . .

Thomas Bestul comments: "The poet's disgust in *Wynnere and Wastoure* at men of inferior birth who marry their betters is a frequent topic of complaint, but the Harley prophecy (and other examples) show that it is expressed in the conventional diction of political prophecy" (*Satire and Allegory in Wynnere and Wastoure* [Lincoln: University of Nebraska Press, 1974], p. 61).

Ercyldoun's Prophecy

Headnote: "Thomas of Erceldoune, Scot and seer, said to King Alexander the following words, about King Edward who is now ruling, when he [Alexander] was still alive." Alexander = Alexander III of Scotland (1249–86); Edward = Edward II of England (r. 1307–27). Morris reads *auestre* for *à nestre*.

1   *Kaernervam.* Caernarvon, in northwestern Wales (Gwynedd), where Edward II was born as the first English Prince of Wales (Edward I's unsuccessful attempt to placate the Welsh). Alexander III of Scotland died in 1286 without leaving a male heir, which caused a crisis of succession in Scotland. Edward I defeated John Balliol in July 1296, annexed Scotland to England, and carried the Stone of Destiny from Scone to Westminster Abbey. Brandl puts quotation marks around lines 1–2, as if Thomas were speaking; 4a, in the voice of Alexander; and 5–10, as Thomas's reply.

2   *That . . . ylcan.* Trans.: "Who shall rule the outer islands each one." The line seems to refer to Alexander's hopes for retaining the kingship in his family (see note to line 1). I am indebted to Paul F. Schaffner and Hugh P. Campbell for help translating this line.

5   *Banockesbourne.* The Battle of Bannockburn, 21 June 1314, a great victory for the Scots, a crushing defeat for Edward II. See also *Thomas of Erceldoune's Prophecy*, note to line 9.

6–7   *Hwan hares . . . levedes.* See *Thomas of Erceldoune's Prophecy,* lines 4, 15. Morris: *wenddeþ* for *weuddeth* but with the note *weddeþ?*

9   *Rokysburth.* See *Thomas of Erceldoune's Prophecy,* note to line 7.

10   *Hwan men . . . seme of hwete.* This seems to be a variant on *Thomas of Ercel-doune's Prophecy,* line 11. The idea in both instances is that a time will come when ordinary folk will strike impossibly bad bargains. Morris reads *foln* for *folu.* In his transcription for the EETS, Morris includes lines which I do not find on fol. 8*v:* "E. ssel. uordo. P. thorȝ. viȝt and strengþe of al Miȝt. Er M. þri croked xl. alle bi hoked. Ssel diuerse an daunce þet neuir wes .y. mad. ine fronce."

When Rome Is Removed

This poem is found in three versions, with fragments quoted elsewhere, in eighteen manuscripts. Version A, which is the version printed here, is found in seven manuscripts, with fragments in five others. See RHR, p. 312. RHR suggests that "the original prophesy was apparently Scottish in sympathy; the Camb. text, however, changes the attitude to favor the English" (p. 314). The date of the original is probably c. 1375–80.

1   The opening line perhaps alludes to Geoffrey of Monmouth, in his *Prophesies of Merlin,* where he foretells: "Religion shall be destroyed a second time and the sees of the primates will be moved to other places" (trans. Thorpe, p. 172). Certainly the tone of the opening lines is apocalyptic, and the "removal" of Rome to England more a curse than a blessing. *ROMA* is sometimes mocked in the later fourteenth century as an acrostic for greed: *Radix omnia malorum avaritia;* and English vernacular complaints often dispraise the Vatican's imperious avarice.

2   *And the preste haffys the poppys power in hande.* The implication seems to be that, given the backing of a corrupt Rome, the English priesthood will behave dictatorially as each priest, in that day, plays pope. It is *remotely* conceivable that some of the fifteenth-century versions of the prophecy used it against Lollardy, the sense of the opening lines implying that when the Vatican is ignored (removed), and each man is a priest and each priest a pope, then strife and sorrow ensue, the land becomes lawless, the Church disrespected, etc. The solution to the riddle depends upon how one understands it.

3 *Betuix thre and sex.* Between three and six: a reference to throws of the dice (a conventional way of announcing a prophecy). Some manuscripts of this prophecy, including BL Sloane 2578 (Haferkorn, p. 155), include diagrams of the dice. For an example of a poem "by the dice," see RHR, p. 120.

 wyll. So RHR; MS *wyll~*, Lumby *wylle.*

 whoso wyll understande. The poet enigmatically addresses those readers in the know, a characteristic device of prophetic satire. The effect is not unlike that of the Gospel writer of Mark who speaks of Jesus' parable of the sower as a deliberate obfuscation whereby those who know will, hearing, hear and, seeing, see, while those who don't understand will be excluded (Mark 4:9–12).

4 *baret*, from OFr *barat* = "strife," "contention," "fighting"; also "trouble," "sorrow." See, for example, *Sir Gawain and the Green Knight*, line 21: "Bolde bredden þerinne, baret þat lofden" (ed. Tolkien and Gordon).

 Brutis lande. Brutus or Brut — great grandson of Aeneas — was the eponymous founder of Britain in Geoffrey of Monmouth's *History of the Kings of Britain* and in later chronicle histories of England. See also the opening lines of *Sir Gawain and the Green Knight.*

5 *When pryde.* Here begins a version of a five-line lyric on the Abuses of the Age: "When pride is most in prise / And couetus most wise" (*Index* § 4006). Haferkorn renders the half-line as "*an envye wyth couetyse.*" Wenzel, citing *Index* §§ 2356, 3133, 3943, 4005.5, 4006, and 4008, has identified these verses as a version of the "Type B" complaint lyric; and he tracks the thread to *John Ball's Letter* (*Index* § 1791). See *Preachers, Poets, and the Early English Lyric*, pp. 196–97.

6 *haldin thar lyff.* "? escape hanging" (RHR).

8 *Bothte.* Haferkorn omits.

9 Haferkorn and RHR insert a line — "Godis fleysh and his blode swore in hethinge" — which appears in all the other MSS. Lumby omits it from his transcription of the Cambridge MS.

10   *Fully nynty ande nyne.* Perhaps an oblique numerological allusion to the parable of the lost sheep, which the Church nowadays ignores, but which in the final year will be found (see Matt. 18:11–14; Luke 15:1–7).

      nocht one wone. Haferkorn glosses as "nothing further, nothing beyond that" (p. 119).

11   *sorow . . . unsell.* MS *settande.* Lumby reads *settande* as a present participle: "setting, waning, disappearing," with *unsell* as adjectival ("unhappy"), which may be correct. RHR reads *sett* as a past participle: "circumscribed."

12   *Than.* So MS and Lumby (*Þan*); RHR *Þen.*

      hir. So MS and Lumby; RHR *her.* Haferkorn reads: *And sone Dame Fortun wyth here whele / Shall turne [all] vp that ere was down.* All other manuscripts, except for the Cambridge MS, read *wyth* for *turne.*

15   I follow Haferkorn and RHR in placing a break between lines 15 and 16, although the MS contains no such division; nor does Lumby make a break. Haferkorn assigns formal divisions to lines 1–15 (I), 16–51 (II), 52–59 (III), 60–66 (IV), 68–73 (V). Beginning line 15 the poet reproduces material known as *The Prophecy of Bede.* Prophecies were attached to the name of Bede the Venerable as well as to Merlin, Thomas the Rymer, and Thomas of Erceldoune. See "The Prophecie of Beid" (inc. "Betwixt the chiefe of Summer & the said Winter"), in *The Whole Prophecies of Scotland, England, France, Ireland and Denmarke* (Edinburgh: A. Hart, 1617 [STC 17842]), pp. A5r–A6v; and *The Prophisies of Rymour, Beid, and Marlyng*, Appendix II of *The Romance and Prophecies of Thomas of Erceldoune*, ed. James A. H. Murray, EETS o.s. 61 (London: Trübner, 1875), pp. 52–61, especially lines 445–end. Murray's edition is a collation of versions in BL MS Lansdowne 762 and Bodleian MS Rawlinson C. 813. I am indebted to George H. Brown for help with *The Prophecy of Bede.*

17   *And everyche . . . werk.* Haferkorn: *And all euerwic londe ernystly [shall] be wrocht.*

18   *Nazareth noy well awhile.* RHR quotes Haferkorn: "Christus in anger will turn away and let the evil in the world have its course for a time." Most MSS read *newly* for *noy well.* *awhile.* MS *A while.*

19   *the Lilly so lele.* ? France, which was Scotland's ally through much of the mid- to later-fourteenth century.

20–21   Perhaps the point is that the Lily (France) goes into hiding as the French suffer from English attacks in the summer, but replenishes itself (*hime*) during the winter.

20   *ledis.* Haferkorn *leuys.*

21   *at sped.* Haferkorn *to spred.*

22   *All the Flowris in the Fyrth.* "In May, 1385, Jean de Vienne, Admiral of France, arrived in the Forth with ships of war, arms and plate armour, fifty thousand francs and 'all the flower of chivalry'" (John Prebble, *The Lion in the North* [London: Secker and Warburg, 1971], p. 129). The point may be that the Scots follow the French (the Lily) in their policies against the English oppressors.

23   *Tatcalders . . . Carioun.* Tatalders (Cadwallader, d. 689), profligate last king of Britain in Geoffrey's *History of the Kings of Britain.* The Anglo-Saxons defeated him, and he fled to Brittany; when he longed to regain his lost kingdom, an angelic voice forbade him to return. Cariown (Conan, or Conanus Meridiadocus) struggled to become king of Britain after the death of his uncle, Octavius, and defeated Maximianus in battle. Later he conquered the Franks in Brittany, ruling in Armorica. Geoffrey of Monmouth's *Prophecies of Merlin* include this prediction: "Cadwallader shall summon Conanus and shall make an alliance with Albany. Then the foreigners shall be slaughtered and the rivers will run with blood" (trans. Thorpe, p. 175). On this, see Rupert Taylor, *The Political Prophecy in England* (New York: Columbia University Press, 1911), pp. 44–45. For the *b* half-line Haferkorn reads: *on Kynon the nobyll.*

24   *and wrethe other landis.* Haferkorn: *and worshipe here londes.*

25   *And erth . . . wyne.* Haferkorn: *[And] inheryt in-to Albany at here own wyll.*

27   *wakyne.* So MS and RHR; Lumby *waykne.*

28   *that lande.* Haferkorn: *this londe.*

Libert. Leopard, symbol of England in this poem. Lions have long been assoc-
iated with England in English heraldry: "Gules, three lions passant-gardant in
pale, Or" (Julian Franklyn, *Shield and Crest: An Account of the Art and Science
of Heraldry* [New York: Sterling, 1960], p. 90). This device can be seen in
fourteenth- and fifteenth-century depictions of royalty. But the lions of English
heraldry have sometimes been identified as leopards: *lion-léopardé.* Edward III
minted gold coins in 1344 called "gold leopards" (*leopardi auri*). See Franklyn,
Shield and Crest, pp. 90–91; Gerard J. Brault, *Early Blazon: Heraldic Termin-
ology in the Twelfth and Thirteenth Centuries with Special Reference to Arthurian
Literature* (Oxford: Clarendon, 1972), s.v. *lion passant* (pp. 231–32); Thomas
Woodcock and John Martin Robinson, *The Oxford Guide to Heraldry* (Oxford:
Oxford University Press, 1988), Appendix A: "The Royal Arms of Great
Britain," pp. 187–89. The royal banner, including fleurs-de-lys and lions pas-
sant-gardant in alternating panels, appears in depictions of Richard II's career
(Froissart's *Chroniques*, British Library MS Royal 18 E.1, fol. 175*r*). For another
leopard (=Edward, Duke of York), see "When the cocke in the Northe," line
13 (RHR, p. 115). Referring to *The Cock in the North*, Rupert Taylor says: "The
hero is clearly the Lion. In other predictive poems of this same collection the
Lion is invariably used as a heraldic symbol for the King of Scotland." Later on
Taylor observes: "The Lion was used for several generations of Scottish Kings.
When it was found necessary to distinguish it from other lions, it was called the
Red Lion, as in the *Rymour Prophecy* in *The Whole Prophecy*. Similarly, though
less frequently, the Leopard was used for the English Kings, perhaps only for
the first three Edwards" (*The Political Prophecy in England*, p. 76, note 53, pp.
113–14). In *The Prophecy of John of Bridlington* (mid-fourteenth century) occurs
the following gloss to the sixth chapter: "*Conjunget flores deliciarum*, scilicet
armorum Franciae, *cum leopardis* regni Angliae. . . . Et illi *flores deliciarum
conjuncti cum leopardis* demonstrant annos posteriores guerrarum, scilicet quod
erunt magna bella et multa annis sequentibus inter Anglicos et Gallicos"
(Wright, *PPS* 1:148). In medieval symbolism generally the leopard represents
"sin, cruelty, the Devil, and the Antichrist" (leopard *in malo*; see George
Ferguson, *Signs and Symbols in Christian Art* [New York: Oxford University
Press, 1954], p. 21); but the leopard was often interchanged with the lion in
heraldry as a noble, royal beast. The Lyone (line 31), or Scotland, will be
subservient to the Leopard, or England. Geoffrey's *Prophecies of Merlin* fore-
casts the following: "The Lion of Justice shall come next, and at its roar the
towers of Gaul shall shake and the island Dragons tremble. In the days of this
Lion gold shall be squeezed from the lily-flower and the nettle, and silver shall

flow from the hoofs of lowing cattle" (trans. Thrope, p. 174). I am indebted to Steven C. Perkins for help with this reference. Haferkorn reads *lyly* for *Libert*.

31   *The Lyone*. In the MS there is a word scratched out after *Lyone*; Lumby includes ellipses after *bestis*. For this line Haferkorn reads: *The lyon, leder of all [and] lord of all this bestys.*

32   *Libert*. Haferkorn *lyly*.

34   *stopsonys*. So MS. Lumby and RHR emend to *stepsonys* (also in line 44). For the b half-line Haferkorn reads: *stordy of hem-sylf.*

35   *The Leoperde . . . for ever*. Haferkorn: *They shall be steryde a stounde and sterte vp at onys, / Son strike down the bestys and strye hem for euer.*

36–37   *He sall . . . to the ende*. The sense here is difficult. Haferkorn: *They shall kyndely kerue that Criste hath forbede, / And thus [shall] thos dere dryue in-to the ende.* The sense of the Cambridge manuscript seems opposite to this, however, where he (the Leopard) condemns them (the stepsons) "as Christ has bidden him to do, / And thus Christ [or perhaps the leopard] shall drive them down, even to the end." The point of this apocalyptic vision seems to cast Christ in the role of judge rather than as a pacifier, who destroys the stepsons (border people who are neither English or Scottish?), perhaps as Christ condemns the Laodicians in Apocalypse 3:14–19.

38   *thai*. The stepsons.

        nor the Libert lelle. Haferkorn: *ne the lyon*.

39   *And thai . . . hardé*. Haferkorn: *Ffor they shull hold to the herte.*

41   *Wytht that . . . louse*. Haferkorn: *But they shull lyghtly be lowsyd.*

45   *unbrokyne*. Haferkorn: *[brykyll]*.

46   *gete*. RHR's emendation; Lumby *[gather]*.

48   *fawle*. So RHR; MS and Lumby *fawlo*. For this line Haferkorn reads: *But all shall faile at the freke traystys.* It is possible that *fawle = falewen*, "fade," "grow

pale," as in the frequent moral refrain "al sal falewi þi grene." See *English Lyrics of the XIIIth Century*, ed. Carleton Brown (Oxford: Clarendon, 1932), p. 17, and Brown's Glossary s.v. *falewi*.

49   RHR: "Apparently corrupt (*sely* = insignificant). Other MSS. full, fell. Compare *Whole Prophecie* ('Merling saies in his booke'): 'And an fellowne flaw shall fall soone after.' Also Geoffrey of Monmouth, *HRB* vii: 'Tunc exsurget in illum aquilo; et flores quos zephyrus procreavit eripiet.'" Haferkorn reads: *A fell northryn flaw shall fadyn hem for euer.*

50   *Herafter.* So MS (*Heraft~*) and Lumby; RHR *Hereafter.*

51   *The Barge . . . sonkyne.* Trans. "The Church is ready to sink." RHR, after Lumby, emends MS *sonkyne* to *senkyne* and comments: "Other MSS. syr Bariona . . . bounde to be sonkyn. The barge of Simon Peter, the son of John (Matt. 16.17; John 1.42), i.e., the Church." For *Bar-Jona* the MS, Lumby, and RHR read *bariona.* Christ says: "Beatus es Simon Bar Iona" (Matt. 16.17). Lumby explains: "'The barge of Barjona' is 'the vessel of the Papacy'" (Glossary).

52   *Secularis.* Apparently laymen rather than secular clergy.

53   *ennoyntyd.* So MS and Lumby; RHR *ennoynted.*

55   *And . . . haldis.* Trans. "And those who hold the power believe they own the title of truth."   *trouth.* So MS and Lumby; RHR *trouthe.*

61   *sute.* So RHR (preserving the alliteration); MS and Lumby *fute.*

63   RHR comments: "Five texts read R, one V, one VII, and the others 2 (i.e., 1382). Haferkorn (p. 129) suggests the Arabic '2' was read as a medium length 'r.' As the prophecy was recopied, other years were substituted, e.g., 1387, 1482, 1535. The B version is dated 1480, although Haferkorn thinks this best preserves the original Scottish prophecy. A late variant of C is dated 1642." The Cambridge text seems to indicate 1382 or 1385. Lumby in a marginal note reads "one thousand three hundred and eighty-R."

64   *understande.* So RHR; MS and Lumby *under.*

65   *Merlyne . . . his bokis.* A reference to Geoffrey of Monmouth's *Prophecies of Merlin* in his *History of the Kings of Britain* and the prophetic tradition deriving from it.

66   *Berwyk.* Berwick-upon-Tweed, an important border town. Berwick surrendered to England in 1333, after the battle of Halidon Hill, when Edward Balliol, supported by Edward III of England, defeated David Bruce. In the 1380s the English-Scottish wars began at Berwick. The wars arose when James, Earl of Douglas opposed Robert II, Richard II's choice for king of Scotland. Richard and John of Gaunt invaded Scotland in 1385, but they were defeated by the Scots and their French allies. But in the summer of 1388 Henry Hotspur and the English forces defeated the Scots and killed the Douglas at the battle of Otterburn. Henry VI of England ceded Berwick to Scotland in 1461; and in 1463 a long truce was established between the kingdoms.

67   *fande.* Lumby in a marginal note paraphrases lines 66–71: "Berwick! Be glad of these words that Bede *found*; thou shalt be true to thy king, the Lion, for ever." RHR suggests the translation "devised" for *fande* (Glossary).

68   *trew.* So MS and Lumby; RHR *trewe.*

69   *releve.* Haferkorn *be-left.*

71   *be leffe.* So MS and RHR; Lumby *beleff*, Haferkorn *be-leue.*

Anticlerical Poems and Documents

Introduction

Protest against political institutions found greatest expression in anticlerical literature: poems and treatises attacking friars, the papacy, Lollards, or religious in general. Satirists and writers of complaint literature — often clerics themselves — deplored the manifest gap between professed ecclesiastical ideals and the too often sordid realities of religious orders and their detractors.

Middle English anticlerical literature derives from a rich tradition of Latin writings on the Investiture Controversy of the eleventh and twelfth centuries and from the later interest in clerical reform as embodied, for example, in estates satire. Earlier writers in the Latin tradition include Peter Damian, Benzo of Alba (who attacked Pope Gregory VII), Serlo of Wilton, Bernard of Morval, Walter Map, Hugo of Orléans, Walter of Châtillon, the Archpoet of Cologne, Gerald of Wales, Nigel Wireker, and the author of the *Apocalypse of Golias*. It is perhaps not sufficiently appreciated that the extensive so-called "goliardic" corpus of verse is concerned less with "wine, women, and song" (in Symonds's celebrated phrase) than with satirical attacks on clerical abuses and contempt of the world.[1] "Golias," who indicts himself through his words, anticipates Jean de Meun's Faussemblant and Chaucer's Pardoner as much as Gargantua or Pantagruel.

Anticlerical literature in England was also much influenced by the vicious quarrels between the secular masters and the mendicants at the University of Paris in the mid-thirteenth century. The secular faculty resented the strong (and growing) fraternal influence in the university; and William of St-Amour virtually inaugurated the antifraternal tradition with his influential treatise *De periculis novissorum temporum* (On the dangers of the latemost times), written in 1256.[2] In this treatise, which attempts

---

[1] Jill Mann, "Satiric Subject and Satiric Object in Goliardic Literature," *Mittellateinisches Jahrbuch* 15 (1980), 63–86.

[2] Matthew Paris had prepared the way in his *Chronica Majora* (1247) by attacking the ostentation of mendicant convents and by calling them the "modern Pharisees." And he called the friars "no longer fishers of men, but of coins." See W. R. Thomson, "The Image of the Mendicants in the Chronicles of Matthew Paris," *Archivum Franciscanum Historicum* 70 (1977), 3–34, at 20. For William and his treatise, see M.-M. Dufeil, *Guillaume de Saint-Amour et la*

to expose the friars as the "many antichrists" of 1 John 2:18 as well as the "lovers of themselves" of 2 Timothy 3 and the "false prophets" of Matthew 24, William draws parallels with the scriptural "last times" or the "consummation of the world" and his own time. He chronicles the forty-one "signs" which distinguish the "true apostles" from the "pseudo-apostles." Jean de Meun imported William's extremist prophecy into his section of *Le Roman de la Rose*, a poem Geoffrey Chaucer says he translated. Viewed in one way, then, the anticlerical literature of the later Middle Ages may be seen as documenting the predicted end of the world. Seen in another way, as it also should be, the attack on friars — the antifraternal tradition — merely refocuses the anticlerical tradition of the "goliard poets" and clerical reformists of the late eleventh and twelfth centuries. Antifraternal writers sharpened the portrait of a society in spiritual disarray; and the friars would become a favorite target of estates satirists, joining the traditional hierarchy of pope, bishop, archdeacon, dean, parson, vicar, monk of *The Apocalypse of Golias*. In this way Chaucer's Friar Huberd takes his place alongside the courtly Prioress, the hunt-loving Monk, the studious Clerk, and the ideal Parson of the General Prologue to *The Canterbury Tales*.

English anticlerical writers of the thirteenth and fourteenth centuries attacked the new orders in complaint and satire. They regarded the very novelty as both a break with traditional Christianity and as a portent of the end of the world. A poem from Harley MS 2253 — which begins "Qui vodra à moi entendre" — portrays "un Ordre novel," a new order, that combines all the alleged worst aspects of the traditional orders. This is "le Ordre de Bel-Eyse" (the Order of Fair Ease), which encourages frequent meals and drinking (points from Sempringham and Beverly), fine clothes (Hospitalers), meat three times daily (regular canons), drunkenness (Benedictines), fraternization with nuns (secular canons), lewd "praying" with nuns on the floor and private visitation cells (Cistercians), luxury accommodations when traveling (Franciscan friars), horseback riding (Dominican friars), and material enhancement (Austin friars).[3] *The Order of Fair Ease* adopts the outrageous pose of "bishop Golias" and anticipates the carnal pleasures of *The Land of Cokaygne*, an often-printed Middle English poem from Harley MS 913 fols. 3r–6v.[4]

The first anticlerical poem in this collection is a unique lyric against friars from British Library MS Cotton Cleopatra B. ii fols. 63v–65r beginning "Preste, ne monke, ne yit chanoun" (*Index* § 2777), which RHR (following Wr) dates to 1382. (The

---

polémique universitaire parisienne, 1250–1259 (Paris: Picard, 1972), especially pp. 253–56.

[3] See Wr, *PSE*, pp. 137–48, and Isabel S. T. Aspin, ed., *Anglo-Norman Political Songs* (Oxford: Blackwell, 1953), pp. 130–42.

[4] Printed by RHR pp. 121–27; *Index* § 762.

foliation differs from the traditional paging since the manuscript was recently refoliated.) Rhyming *aaabcccbdede* in 180 semi-alliterating lines, this piece begins as mock encomium and features a vigorous portrait of the mendicant orders as vagrant pedlars and tricksters; and as in *PPC* and *JU*, this lyric links the four orders to Caym (Cain): Carmelites, Austins, Jacobins (Dominicans), and Minorites. Another antifraternal poem from the same MS (fol. 65*v*) follows, this one beginning "Of thes Frer Mynours me thenkes moch wonder" (*Index* § 2663, also of 1382). This forty-two line poem, with semi-alliterating verses rhyming *aaaabb* (in stanzas), attacks the Franciscan order for its alleged tendencies to dramatize Minorite piety by making false analogies between modern-day friars and Christ. Joseph Grennen explains the "overriding message" of this lyric as an attack on friars: "for their distortions, lies, heresy, pride, cupidity, and above all hypocrisy, the friars will be 'brent' — consigned to the flames, not as the self-regarding myth in which they see themselves in the role of Elijah in the fiery chariot would have it, but to the flames of hell-fire."[5] The lyric has a refrain (*bb*) beginning "With an O and an I," a formula (exploited in other poems) which has not been convincingly explained. The present texts of both poems are based on a photographic reproduction of the British Library manuscript, which is checked against the editions of Wr, Cook (who reprints Wr's texts), Heuser (for "Of thes Frer Mynours"), RHR, Grennen, and Krochalis and Peters.

Next are two antifraternal poems from St. John's College Cambridge MS 195 (fol. 1*v* and 1*v*-2*r* = flyleaves) beginning "Thou That Sellest the Worde of God" (*Index* § 3697), in three six-line stanzas rhyming *aabccb*; and "Allas, what schul we freris do" (*Index* § 161), in nine four-line stanzas rhyming *abab*. The first poem professes to be an outspoken layman's attack on simoniac clergy — those who sell God's word. The narrator singles out the friars as especially blameworthy and bids them to appear only when summoned. The second lyric purports to be an aggrieved friar's rejoinder to "Thou That Sellest." The narrator reveals his anxieties about laymen's access to Scripture. Mary and Richard Rouse have collected accusations against friars to the effect that they conspired to keep secular clergy away from books of Scripture; and they argue that these charges may reflect actual fourteenth-century conditions.[6] The

---

[5] "The 'O and I' Refrain in Middle English Poems: A Grammatology of Judgment Day," *Neophilologus* 71 (1987), 620–21.

[6] "The Franciscans and Books: Lollard Accusations and the Franciscan Response" (1987), rpt. in *Authentic Witnesses: Approaches to Medieval Texts and Manuscripts*, ed. Mary A. Rouse and Richard H. Rouse (Notre Dame: University of Notre Dame Press, 1991), pp. 409–24. They cite and quote from *JU*, *Fifty Heresies and Errors of the Friars* (1384?), *How Religious Men Should Keep Certain Articles*, *Of Clerks Possessioners*, the prologue to the *Floretum* (1384–96), and the *Opus Arduum* (1389–90); and they trace such charges to FitzRalph's *Defensio Curat-*

present texts are based upon an electrostatic print of the Cambridge MS, which is checked against the versions of Utley, RHR, and Person; and I adopt several of Utley's and RHR's readings, notably Utley's reading of line 3 of "Thou That Sellest." Utley and RHR entitle "Thou That Sellest" *The Layman's Complaint*, believing that "Allas! What Schul We Freris Do" (which they entitle *The Friar's Answer* after a marginal inscription) responds directly to it. Browne and Wells suggest that "Thou That" and "Allas, What Schul" were part of the same poem; but Utley argues that they are separate poems, that the author of the former "belonged to the reforming party," and that "his purpose was similar to that of the fourteenth century author of Pierce the Ploughmans Crede." Person likewise says: "That the scribe . . . regarded them as a single poem might be inferred from the absence of any break in the MS. and the fact that the title to the latter part has been supplied in the margin by a later hand. . . . In any event, since each of the parts has more meaning in juxtaposition with the other than by itself, it is probably just as safe to look upon it as a sort of dialogue, a plaint and response reminiscent of Chaucer's *Fortune*."[7] If RHR and Person are correct, these poems provide further evidence for a tradition of satirical paired poems (like *FDR* and *UR* or Chaucer's *Friar's* and *Summoner's Tales*).[8]

---

orum (see quote on p. 413). The Franciscan William Woodford, in his *Responsiones ad Quaestiones LXV* (Oxford Bodley 703, fols. 41–57), acknowledged that regular clergy withheld books from secular clergy: "For all such have libraries to keep their books in, whether works on Holy Scripture or on other subjects, which are closed up so that seculars are excluded, for the most part" (p. 416). He observed that restricting access to books was the rule rather than the exception in monastic libraries; that theft was a problem (so books were often chained to library stacks); and that books must be available for use by regular clergy (see p. 418).

[7] Francis L. Utley, "The Layman's Complaint and The Friar's Answer," *Harvard Theological Review* 38 (1945), 143; Henry A. Person, *Cambridge Middle English Lyrics* (Seattle: University of Washington Press, 1953), p. 79.

[8] On the paired poems see the Introductions to *FDR* and *UR* in *Six Ecclesiastical Satires*, ed. Dean. Another telling example of this paired genre may be found in the *Epistola Jesu Christi ad Prelatos*, a supposed response to Peter Ceffons of Clairvaux's *Epistola Luciferi ad Cleros*, a mid-fourteenth century satiric attack on the clergy. But the alleged refutation is as anticlerical in its way as is the *Epistola Luciferi*. For the *Epistola Luciferi* in Middle English (from Huntington Library HM 114 fols. 319r–325v), see Robert R. Raymo, "A Middle English Version of the *Epistola Luciferi ad Cleros*," in *Medieval Literature and Civilization: Studies in Memory of G. N. Garmonsway*, ed. D. A. Pearsall and R. A. Waldron (London: Athlone Press, 1969), pp. 233–48. Raymo includes the Latin *Epistola* below the Middle English text.

Introduction

Scattergood doubts that the author of "Allas, What Schul We Freris Do" could be a friar because of certain disparaging remarks.[9]

These paired lyrics are followed by a forty-two line macaronic, antifraternal poem in a unique text of about 1490 from Trinity College Cambridge MS 1148 fol. 58v beginning "Freers, freers, wo ye be, *ministri malorum*" (*Index* § 871). As in so much antifraternal literature, the anonymous author of "Freers, Freers" traces the evils that friars do to their demonic connections. Friars are not merely wicked, they are said to inherit Lucifer's seven deadly sins when the rebel angels fell from heaven. They have a special mission or ministries to deceive, do violence, trick, and grasp. They are greedy for money but also for sex. Scattergood observes that the circumstances of this poem's preservation — it was "evidently copied out by William Womyndham, Canon of Kyrkeby 'super Algam'" — reveals the "bad feeling which existed between the secular clergy and the friars."[10] The text of this edition is based on an electrostatic reproduction of the manuscript and checked against the editions of Wr (for *PPS*, reprinted in *Reliquiae Antiquae*) and RHR. On the model of the manuscript, Wr in *Reliquiae Antiquae* prints the Latin half-lines as continuous with the English half-lines and not, as in Wr (*PPS*), RHR, or the present edition, as subjacent.

Samples of Wycliffite or Lollard writings come next: selections from the General Prologue to *The Wycliffite Bible*; and the Prologue to and chapters 3–5 of *The Lanterne of Light*. Wycliffites were the followers of John Wyclif (*Doctor Evangelicus*, died 1384), the Oxford master and controversialist, who formulated influential doctrines on ecclesiastical endowments, on the papacy and church hierarchy, and on theological issues, including transubstantiation. His attacks on clerical abuses found a wide audience in England and on the continent; and until 1382 John of Gaunt protected him from prelates who wished to suppress his more extreme formulations. For most of his career, though, Wyclif was regarded as a first-rank realist philosopher and teacher, with well-known students including Nicholas Hereford, John Aston, Philip Repyngdon, and John Purvey. But he ventured often and trenchantly into polemics after the fashion of Richard FitzRalph, archbishop of Armagh and author of *De paupertate Salvatoris* (On the Lord's Poverty, 1356: a treatise on lordship and dominion), and of *Defensio curatorum* (The Defense of Curates, 1357: a sermon

---

[9] V. J. Scattergood, *Politics and Poetry in the Fifteenth Century* (London: Blandford, 1971), p. 248.

[10] *Politics*, p. 246.

35

attacking friars).[11] His adherents, the so-called Lollards or Wycliffites, were for the most part craftsmen, and they, after Wyclif, "opposed the subjection of the English church to Rome, the temporal rule of the clergy, the doctrine of transubstantiation, clerical celibacy, the consecration of physical objects, masses for the dead, pilgrimages, and the veneration of images."[12] The English term *Lollard* (Lat. *Lollardus*) — first recorded use in 1382 — may derive from the Dutch *lollaert*, mumbler of prayers. Some medieval English writers deliberately confused *Lollard* with *loller*, lazy vagabond, idler, loafer, and sometimes with Latin *lolia*, tares, weeds. The word quickly became a term of abuse signifying a religious zealot;[13] and weeds, probably as a result of the parable of the sower (Matt. 13), became a metaphor for Lollards, as in Chaucer's *Man of Law's Epilogue*, when the Shipman (or, perhaps, the Wife of Bath) complains that the Parson (a possible "Lollere," according to the Host) "wolde sowen som difficulte, / Or springen cokkel in our clene corne" (II.1183–84). Sometimes known as *bretheren*, *bible men*, or *known men*, the Lollards developed Wyclif's controversial ideas into a political agenda which denounced the established church as hopelessly flawed and prelates (including the pope) as agents of Satan and Antichrist. Some of Wyclif's ideas about church temporalities found expression in the Peasants' Revolt of 1381; and later chroniclers, such as Thomas Walsingham and Henry Knighton, censured Wyclif as an instigator of the Rising. Whether Wyclif had any connection with the Peasants' Revolt is unclear; but in 1382, at the Blackfriars council in London, Wyclif's opponents at Oxford, induced by William Courtenay, archbishop of Canterbury, condemned ten Wycliffite propositions as heretical and fourteen as erroneous. After 1382 it could be dangerous to be associated with Wyclif's ideas, although Lollard political views enjoyed wide support in certain regions and even in parliament until about 1414–15. After 1401 prelates could seek out and consign heretics to the secular branch for burning according to the edict *De haeretico comburendo*. In 1409 archbishop Thomas Arundel issued his *Constitutions*,

---

[11] John Trevisa translated the *Defensio curatorum*. See the edition of A. J. Perry: EETS o.s. 167 (London: Oxford University Press, 1925), pp. 39–93.

[12] Steven Ozment, *The Age of Reform 1250–1550* (New Haven: Yale University Press, 1980), p. 210.

[13] See Hudson, *The Premature Reformation* (Oxford: Clarendon, 1988), pp. 2–4. The word *Lollard* was also applied to German heretics in the early fourteenth century. A cleric in Liège wrote, in 1309: "Eodem anno quidam hypocritae gyrovagi, qui Lollardi sive Deum laudantes vocabantur, per Hannoniam et Brabantiam quasdam mulieres nobiles deceperunt." (In that year deceitful wanderers, who are called Lollards or praisers of God, beguiled some noble women in Hainault and Brabant), *Dictionnaire de théologie catholique* (Paris: Letouzey and Ané, 1926), 9.1: col. 911.

which enjoined the possession or reading of unauthorized scriptural translations, which prohibited unlicensed preaching in English, and which remained as law until 1529;[14] and in 1411 a book-burning of Wyclif's writings occurred at Carfax while the chancellor of Oxford University looked on. Persecution of the Lollards only intensified after Sir John Oldcastle, a Lollard knight (and prototype for Shakespeare's Falstaff), tried to incite a rebellion against King Henry V in January, 1414. When Oldcastle refused to abjure his heresy in a trial, the king imprisoned him in the Tower. Oldcastle managed to escape, and he called for a general rebellion; but it failed miserably when Henry learned details of the plot (see below, "Lo, He That Can Be Cristes Clerc").[15] After this revolt, the Lollard movement suffered persecution from the secular arm as well as from the clergy, since the rebellion exposed a threat to the crown. Yet many manuscripts of the Lollard Bible and other Lollard writings survive, attesting to the strength of conviction of these lay craftsmen and women who would be preachers.

The Wycliffite Bible — a translation which influenced the King James version and the only complete Bible in English prior to Miles Coverdale's vernacular Bible of 1535 — is a feat of scholarship and a labor of love carried out under difficult circumstances, since clerical authorities discouraged books in English and especially vernacular Scripture. The translators of this English Bible are anonymous, but it is thought that Wyclif's Oxford disciples and colleagues played a central role — men such as Nicholas Hereford, William Middleworth, John Purvey, and perhaps even John Trevisa.[16] It exists in at least two states, an earlier and a later version.[17] The first

---

[14] Arundel's *Constitutions* are printed in English translation in *The Acts and Monuments of John Foxe*, ed. Stephen Reed Cattley, vol. 3 (London: Seeley, 1837), 242–48. By Foxe's reckoning, the seventh constitution is that "no man, hereafter, by his own authority translate any text of the Scripture into English or any other tongue, by way of a book, libel, or treatise; and that no man read any such book, libel, or treatise, now lately set forth in the time of John Wickliff, or since, or hereafter to be set forth, in part or in whole, privily or apertly [openly], upon pain of greater excommunication, until the said translation be allowed by the ordinary of the place, or, if the case so require, by the council provincial. He that shall do contrary to this, shall likewise be punished as a favourer of error and heresy" (p. 245).

[15] The most accurate contemporary account of Oldcastle's problems with authorities is Walsingham's. For the story in Latin with facing English translation and explanation, see *Gesta Henrici Quinti*, ed. and trans. Frank Taylor and John S. Roskell (Oxford: Clarendon, 1975), chapter 1 and Appendix 1.

[16] David C. Fowler, "John Trevisa and the English Bible," *Modern Philology* 58 (1960), 81–98; Hudson, *The Premature Reformation*, pp. 395–98. Fowler mounts a plausible though circumstantial case that scholars of Queen's College, Oxford — who for four years resisted the election of Thomas Carlisle, a northerner, as provost (1376) — were in an excellent position to serve as translators based on a list of books returned to the provost, a list that includes Higden's

version, markedly literal and dependent upon Vulgate diction, was completed about 1390; the later, more idiomatic version was completed about 1395. The Lollards and Wyclif, who may have supervised the earlier version, undertook these translations to make Scripture available to lay persons (including women), a decision with political ramifications (see "Allas, What Schul We Freris Do" and "Lo, He That Can Be Cristes Clerc").[18] The Prologue author explains that clerics have appropriated Holy Scripture, depriving "simple" (plain) and "lewid" (lay) folk — not terms of opprobrium — of its knowledge and power:

> For though covetouse clerkis ben woode by simonie, eresie, and manye othere synnes, and dispisen and stoppen Holi Writ as myche as thei moun, yit the lewid puple crieth aftir Holi Writ, to kunne it, and kepe it, with greet cost and peril of here lif. For these resons and othere, with comune charité to save alle men in oure rewme, whiche God wole have savid, a symple creature hath translatid the Bible out of Latyn into English.

The Prologue, printed from Forshall and Madden's edition of the later version and which dates from 1395–96, has often been attributed to John Purvey, and it demonstrates the care with which Lollards attempted to discriminate between literal and figurative interpretations of Scripture. Laurence Muir has written of the General Prologue:

> The connection of the Wyclyfite versions with the Lollard movement is little apparent in the Biblical text, but rather in the General Prologue, appearing in some of the manuscripts. This Prologue constitutes an introduction to the books of the Old Testament, and it includes statements of the Lollard views about the translating and

---

Polychronicon (which Trevisa translated), a Bible, and two commentaries of Nicholas of Lyra (often cited by the author of the General Prologue). For the list of twenty-four books, see p. 94. There is evidence of other translations made in the late fourteenth and early fifteenth centuries. See Henry Hargreaves, "The Wycliffite Versions," in *The Cambridge History of the Bible*, ed. G. W. H. Lampe, vol. 2 (Cambridge: Cambridge University Press, 1969), 389–90.

[17] Some of the manuscripts that Forshall and Madden identified as belonging to the Earlier Version have been subsequently identified as intermediary stages between the EV and the LV. For an even-handed summary of the state of present scholarship on these controversial issues, see Hudson, *The Premature Reformation*, pp. 239–40.

[18] See also *Chronicon Henrici Knighton*, ed. J. R. Lumby, Rolls Series 92 (1895), 2:151–52.

reading of Scripture. In addition it includes an enlightened set of principles for translating, principles it exemplified and justified by the revisions themselves.[19]

In a segment from chapter 13 (printed below) the Prologue author complains about proposed curricular changes at Oxford University which would make study of divinity and Scripture even more difficult. "This semith uttirly the develis purpos," he laments, "that fewe men either noon schulen lerne and kunne Goddis lawe."[20] He believes the masters at Oxford foster errors to the detriment of "symple men" and men "of good wille." He is scrupulous about rendering ("resolving") Latin into English "openli," that is, clearly and accurately. He wants to translate as literally and faithfully as he can, but he acknowledges, with well-chosen examples, that literal translations sometimes result in sentences that are "derk and douteful" (unclear and ambiguous). His program is to honor Jerome's inspired Latin but to make the English accessible to "symple" and "lewid" people like himself; and he even hopes (or at least originally "purposid"), "with Goddis helpe," to "make the sentence [meaning] as trewe and open in English as it is in Latyn, either more trewe and more open than it is in Latyn" — a bold if not scandalous claim. Assertions like these brought down the wrath of clerical authority, including statutes forbidding translation of Scripture (1407, 1409) and the destruction of Wycliffite Bibles and Lollard writings. The *Statutes of the Realm* rebuke Lollard literacy and unauthorized schooling: "They make unlawful conventicles and confederacies, they hold and exercise schools, they make and write books, they do wickedly instruct and inform people."[21]

The author of the General Prologue writes in Latinate periods, with Latinate diction and word order, as in this sentence opening: "But it is to wite that Holy Scripture . . . ." This awkward construction (in English) imitates the common Latin construction *Est scire*. Also noticeable is the author's concern with literal understanding,

---

[19] "Translations and Paraphrases of the Bible, and Commentaries," in *A Manual of the Writings in Middle English 1050–1500*, vol. 2, ed. J. Burke Severs (New Haven: The Connecticut Academy of Arts and Sciences, 1970), 403.

[20] For a spirited and learned defense of translating Scripture into English, see C. F. Bühler's edition of "A Lollard Tract," *Medium Aevum* 7 (1938), 167–83. The anonymous author of this treatise points out that better access helps promote the faith and that this is why Jerome translated the Bible into Latin. He also cites precedent for Scripture in English, including Bede the Venerable, King Alfred, and Richard Rolle. The sentiments of this document agree closely with those of John Trevisa in his *Dialogue Between a Lord and a Clerk upon Translation*, which serves as something like a preface to the *Polychronicon*.

[21] Margaret Aston, *Lollards and Reformers: Images and Literacy in Late Medieval Religion* (London: Hambledon Press, 1984), p. 198.

as he frequently supplies alternate words or phrases to help explain a concept (with *either* = or and *either . . . either* = either . . . or). Forshall and Madden, through their punctuation, made every effort to preserve the periodic nature of the prose style; and they relied heavily on semicolons. Although I base the present text on Forshall and Madden, I often ·alter their punctuation for better sense; and I have compared Forshall and Madden's version with that in *The True Copye of a Prolog Wrytten about Two C. Yeres Paste by J. Wycklife* (R. Crowley, 1550; STC 25588), and with that of Anne Hudson in *Selections from English Wycliffite Writings* (chapter 15 only).

The Lanterne of Light, an anonymous treatise which dates from the early fifteenth century (probably between 1409 and 1415), is one of the most important and influential witnesses to Lollard writings. Unlike so many Lollard writings, which cannot be dated with any precision, *The Lanterne of Light* appears independently in documents of inquisition against a London currier named John Claydon, who was summoned before Henry Chichele, archbishop of Canterbury, on charges of heresy on 17 August 1415. The specific charge was possession of books in English, including a volume "bound in red leather, of parchment, written in a good English hand, called the *Lanterne of Light*."[22] Claydon, who could not read, had the book copied by John Gryme, scribe; and Claydon's servants acknowledged that they had heard it read aloud in Claydon's house. The Archishop asked four friars to examine the book, and they drew up a list of fifteen errors, including: "That the bishop's license, for a man to preach the word of God, is the true character of the beast, i.e. Antichrist; and therefore simple and faithful priests may preach when they will, against the prohibition of that Antichrist, and without license" (§ 3); and "That the Court of Rome is the chief head of Antichrist, and the bishops be the body; and the new sects (that is, the monks, canons and friars), brought in not by Christ, but damnably by the pope, be the venemous and pestiferous tail of Antichrist" (§ 4).[23] Claydon was burned as a heretic on 10 September 1415 at Smithfield.

The prose style of *The Lanterne of Light*, especially in its generous quotations from Scripture (sometimes reminiscent of Chaucer's *Parson's Tale*), is vigorous and engaging not to mention polemical.[24] The author at the outset establishes a crisis atmosphere — an increase in the world's wickedness (a commonplace of the exordium:

---

[22] *The Lanterne of Li3t*, ed. Lilian M. Swinburn, EETS o.s. 151 (London: Kegan Paul, 1917), p. viii. For corroboration of Swinburn's dating of the treatise and a retelling of Claydon's story with its implications for Lollardy, see Hudson, *The Premature Reformation*, pp. 13, 211–14.

[23] As quoted in Swinburn's edition (from Foxe's *Actes and Monuments*), p. ix.

[24] Hudson characterizes it as "Lollard and indeed of the radical wing of Lollardy" (*The Premature Reformation*, p. 213).

senium mundi) — and then tackles the important issue of the nature of Antichrist. He divides Antichrist into his general and specific qualities. Among the former the author mentions that Antichrist generally opposes Christ and commits six sins against the Holy Ghost; among the specific qualities, Antichrist consists of those who promulgate laws contrary to Christ. Antichrist has three parts and five conditions or launches five "assaults" on humans. The present text of the selections from *The Lanterne of Light* is based on an excellent electrostatic print of the Harley manuscript and is checked against Swinburn's edition.

The last work included in this section is an anti-Lollard poem in 152 lines from British Library MS Cotton Vespasian B. xvi. fol. 2v–3r (*Index* § 1926), which begins, "Lo, he that can be Cristes clerc" and which has as its refrain variants of "For lewde lust of Lollardie." RHR titles this poem *Defend Us From All Lollardy* and dates it "after mid 1414 and before end of 1417" (p. 331). It focuses on Sir John Oldcastle, a Lollard knight prominent in the failed revolt of 1414 (often called "Oldcastle's rebellion"); and it depicts Sir John as a corrupt knight-turned-cleric who not only betrays the king and parliament but also leads his followers into spiritual perdition through heretical interpretations of Scripture. The author of this lyric portrays Oldcastle as a shameful traitor to his class in trying to pass himself off as an ecclesiastic, "To bable the Bibel day and night" (line 27). The Lollards who took part in the rebellion apparently wanted to separate the clergy from their temporalities but also to kill the king ("the chief of chivalrie," Henry V), his brothers, and high prelates and magnates of the realm. When the rebellion miscarried, Oldcastle went into hiding; and the poem seems to have been written before his execution in 1417. This lyric is notable for its elaborate metaphor comparing Sir John to a castle that has gone to ruin (unabashed wordplay on Sir John's name). Other writers — including John Hardyng in his verse *Chronicle*, Thomas Hoccleve, and the author of the *Liber Metricus* of Elmham (Rolls Series 1858) — denounced Oldcastle and his ill-fated rebellion. The text for the present edition is based on a (sometimes illegible) photostatic copy of the manuscript, which is checked against the editions of Wright (*PPS*) and of RHR. The manuscript's scribe has laid out the text with about eight stresses to the line, in staves of four lines each headed by a paraph (¶).

Select Bibliography

Manuscripts

British Library MS Cotton Cleopatra B. ii fols. 63*v*–65*r* (1382)

Cambridge University, St. John's College MS 195 fols. 1*v* and 1*v*–2*r* (1425)

Cambridge University, Trinity College MS 1144 fol. 58*v* (c. 1490)

British Library MS Harley 2324 fols. 1*v*–4*r*, 5*v*–20*v* (1409–15)

British Library MS Cotton Vespasian B. xvi. fol. 2*v* (1450–60)

British Library MS Harley 3362 fol. 47*r* (1475–1500)

Previous Editions

Preste, Ne Monke, Ne Yit Chanoun (MS Cotton Cleopatra)

Cook, Albert S., ed. *A Literary Middle English Reader*. Boston: Ginn, 1915. ["Preste, ne monke": pp. 361–64: lines 1–84 only; "Of thes Frer": pp. 364–65. Reprint of Wr.]

Krochalis, Jeanne and Edward Peters, eds. *The World of Piers Plowman*. Philadelphia: University of Pennsylvania Press, 1975. [Pp. 103–08.]

Robbins, Rossell Hope, ed. *Historical Poems of the XIVth and XVth Centuries*. New York: Columbia University Press, 1959. [Pp. 157–62.]

Of Thes Frer Mynours (MS Cotton Cleopatra)

Heuser, W. "With an O and an I." *Anglia* 27 (1904), 283–319. [Definitive early study, with textual editions, of Middle English and Anglo-Latin "O and I" refrain poems. "Of Thes Frers" is printed on pp. 302–03.]

Grennen, Joseph E. "The 'O and I' Refrain in Middle English Poems: A Grammatology of Judgment Day," *Neophilologus* 71 (1987), 614–25. [Text on p. 620.]

Krochalis, Jeanne and Edward Peters, eds. *The World of Piers Plowman*. Philadelphia: University of Pennsylvania Press, 1975. [Pp. 108–10.]

RHR, pp. 163–64.

Wright, Thomas. *Political Poems and Songs*. Rolls Series 14.1. 2 vols. London: Longman, Green, 1859, 1861. [Poem in volume 1, pp. 268–70.]

Thou That Sellest and **Allas, What Schul We Freris Do** (St. John's College MS)

Person, Henry A., ed. *Cambridge Middle English Lyrics*. Seattle: University of Washington Press, 1953. [The two poems on pp. 41–43.]

RHR, pp. 166 and 166–68.

Utley, Francis L. "The Layman's Complaint and The Friar's Answer." *Harvard Theological Review* 38 (1945), 140–47. [Prints the poems with important commentaries.]

Freers, Freers, Wo Ye Be (Trinity College MS)

RHR, pp. 164–65.

Wright, Thomas. *Political Poems and Songs*. Rolls Series 14.1. 2 vols. London: Longman, Green, 1859, 1861. ["Freers, freers" appears in II, 249–50.]

The Wycliffite Bible: General Prologue

Forshall, Josiah. and Frederic Madden, eds. *The Holy Bible, Containing the Old and New Testaments, with the Apocryphal Books, in the Earliest English Versions Made from the Latin Vulgate by John Wycliffe and His Followers*. 4 vols. Oxford: Oxford University Press, 1850. Rpt. New York: AMS Press, 1982. [Prologue in vol. 1. Outdated in certain ways but still the most accessible edition of the Wycliffite Bible.]

The True Copye of a Prolog Wrytten about Two C. Yeres Paste by J. Wycklife. R. Crowley, 1550. [STC 25588; UMI Reel 10370.]

Hudson, Anne, ed. *Selections from English Wycliffite Writings* (Cambridge: Cambridge University Press, 1978). [Prints chapter 15 on pp. 67–72; valuable notes on pp. 173–77.]

Pollard, Alfred W., ed. *Fifteenth Century Prose and Verse*. London: A. Constable, 1903. Rpt. New York: Cooper Square, 1964. [Prints a modernized version of chapter 15, based on Forshall and Madden, on pp. 193–99.]

The Lanterne of Light (Harley MS)

Swinburn, Lilian, ed. *The Lanterne of Liȝt*. EETS o.s. 151. London: Kegan Paul, 1917. [Standard edition with Notes and Glossary.]

Lo, He That Can Be Cristes Clerc (MS Cotton Vespasian)

RHR, pp. 152–57.

Wright, Thomas. *Political Poems and Songs*. Rolls Series 14.1. 2 vols. London: Longman, Green, 1859, 1861. ["Lo, He" in II, 243–47.]

General Studies

Aston, Margaret. *England's Iconoclasts*. Volume 1: *Laws Against Images*. Oxford: Clarendon, 1988. [Studies the Lollard opposition to religious images and their use in religious institutions.]

———. "Lollardy and Sedition, 1381–1431." *Lollards and Reformers: Images and Literacy in Late Medieval Religion*. London: Hambledon, 1984. Pp. 1–47.

Bennett, J. A. W. "Wyclif and the Wycliffite Writers." *Middle English Literature*. Ed. Douglas Gray. Oxford: Clarendon, 1986. Pp. 335–46. [Good, brief general introduction to the subject.]

Bühler, Curt F. "A Lollard Tract: On Translating the Bible into English." *Medium Ævum* 7 (1938), 167–83.

Gradon, Pamela. "Langland and the Ideology of Dissent." *Proceedings of the British Academy* 66 (1980), 179–205. [Concludes that *Piers Plowman*, while it shares many points with Wycliffite or Lollard writings, should be considered a satiric, visionary poem rather than a theoretical work offering the ideology of dissent. Valuable for demonstrating the commonplace nature of much of late fourteenth-century anticlericalism.]

Greene, Richard L. "A Middle English Poem and the 'O-and-I' Refrain-Phrase." *Medium Ævum* 30 (1961), 170–75. [Traces the "O and I" to Dante's *Inferno* 24.97–102.]

Introduction

Grennen, Joseph E. "The 'O and I' Refrain in Middle English Poems: A Grammatology of Judgment Day." *Neophilologus* 71 (1987), 614–25. [Argues that the "O" and "I" letters in *Of Thes Frer Mynours* are "grammatological" and not "idiophonic" and that they may be traced to *oculi* and *ictu* in the phrase "twinkling of an eye" (1 Cor. 15:52).]

Hargreaves, Henry. "The Wycliffite Versions." *The Cambridge History of the Bible*. Ed. G. W. H. Lampe. Cambridge: Cambridge University Press, 1969. II, 387–415.

Hudson, Anne. *Lollards and Their Books*. London: Hambledon Press, 1985. [A convenient gathering of her previously published essays on Lollard issues.]

———. *The Premature Reformation: Wycliffite Texts and Lollard History*. Oxford: Clarendon, 1988. [A major book by the acknowledged expert on Lollardy at the present time. Hudson revises conventional wisdom on the Lollards and their project.]

Lindberg, Conrad. "Reconstructing the Lollard Versions of the Bible." *Neuphilologische Mitteilungen* 90 (1989), 117–23. [Discusses four versions of the Wycliffite Bible: the original, the interlinear, the earlier, and the later versions. Focuses on Judges to argue the case.]

Mann, Jill. *Chaucer and Medieval Estates Satire: The Literature of Social Classes and the General Prologue to The Canterbury Tales*. Cambridge: Cambridge University Press, 1973. [Authoritative study of the tradition of estates satire keyed to Chaucer's pilgrims.]

Osberg, Richard H. "A Note on the Middle English 'O & I' Refrain." *Modern Philology* 77 (1980), 392–96.

Peter, John. *Complaint and Satire in Early English Literature*. Oxford: Clarendon, 1956. [The seminal work distinguishing medieval satire from complaint.]

Rouse, Mary A., and Richard H. "The Franciscans and Books: Lollard Accusations and the Franciscan Response." *From Ockham to Wyclif*. Ed. Anne Hudson and M. Wilks. Studies in Church History: Subsidia 5 (Oxford: Oxford University Press, 1987), 369–84. Reprinted in *Authentic Witnesses: Approaches to Medieval Texts and Manuscripts*. Ed. Mary A. Rouse and Richard H. Rouse (Notre Dame: University of Notre Dame Press, 1991), pp. 409–24. [They argue that Lollard accusations that the Franciscans kept books away from laymen reflect actual late fourteenth-century conditions, since even the Franciscan William Woodford acknowledged that regular clergy kept books under lock.]

Scase, Wendy. *Piers Plowman and the New Anticlericalism*. Cambridge Studies in Medieval Literature 4. Cambridge: Cambridge University Press, 1989. [Argues that there was a new, all-encompassing anticlericalism in the fourteenth century which differed from traditional oppositions to clerical abuses. Contains important treatments of Richard FitzRalph, mendicancy, lordship, and dominion.]

Scattergood, V. J. *Politics and Poetry in the Fifteenth Century*. London: Blandford, 1971. [See especially chapter 7: "Religion and the Clergy." VJS discusses "Thou that sellest" on pp. 246–47; "Allas, What Schul We Freris Do" on pp. 247–48; "Freers, Freers" on pp. 245–46; and "Lo, He" on pp. 252, 255, 257, and 262.]

Tucker, Samuel Marion. *Verse Satire in England Before the Renaissance*. New York: Columbia University Press, 1908; rpt. New York: AMS, 1966. [See chapters 2 and 3 for material on the Latin and English traditions of satire and complaint. This study has been largely superseded by Peter's *Complaint and Satire in Early English Literature*.]

Bibliographies

Hargreaves, Henry. "John Wyclif and Wyliffite Writings." *The New Cambridge Bibliography of English Literature*. Gen. ed. George Watson. Vol. 1. Cambridge: Cambridge University Press, 1974. Cols. 491–96.

Muir, Laurence. "IV. Translations and Paraphrases of the Bible, and Commentaries." *A Manual of the Writings in Middle English 1050–1500*. Vol. 2. Gen. ed. J. Burke Severs. (New Haven: The Connecticut Academy of Arts and Sciences, 1970), 381-409, 534–52. [See especially "Wyclyfite Versions," pp. 402–03, 547–50.]

Robbins, Rossell Hope. "XIII. Poems Dealing with Contemporary Conditions." *A Manual of the Writings in Middle English 1050–1500*. Vol. 5. Gen. ed. Albert E. Hartung. Vol. 5 (New Haven: The Connecticut Academy of Arts and Sciences, 1975), 1385–1536, 1631–1725. [Discusses *Preste, Ne Monke, Ne Yit Chanoun* (§ 100) on pp. 1443–44, bibliography pp. 1672–73; *Of Thes Frer Mynours* (§ 101) on pp. 1444–45, bibliography p. 1673; *Thou That Sellest* (§ 102) on p. 1445, bibliography pp. 1673–74; *Allas, What Schul We Freris Do* (§ 103) on p. 1445, bibliography p. 1674; *Freers, Freers, Wo Ye Be* (§ 105) on p. 1445, bibliography p. 1674; *Lo, He That Can Be Cristes Clerc* (§ 120) on pp. 1452–53, bibliography p. 1679.]

Preste, Ne Monke, Ne Yit Chanoun

[*The Orders of Cain* (1382)]

(British Library MS Cotton Cleopatra B.ii fols. 63*v*–65*r*)

	Preste, ne monke, ne yit chanoun,	*canon*
	Ne no man of religioun,	
	Gyfen hem so to devocioun[1]	
	As done thes holy frers.	*do; friars*
5	For summe gyven ham to chyvalry	*devote themselves; chivalry*
	Somme to riote and ribaudery;	*debauchery; coarse jesting*
	Bot ffrers gyven ham to grete study,	
	And to grete prayers.	
	Who-so kepes thair reule al,	*Whoever observes their entire rule*
10	Bothe in worde and dede,	
	I am ful siker that he shal	*certain*
	Have heven blis to mede.	*heaven's bliss as reward*
	Men may se by thair contynaunce	*countenance*
	That thai are men of grete penaunce,	
15	And also that thair sustynaunce	*nourishment*
	Simple is and wayke.	*insufficient*
	I have lyved now fourty yers,	
	And fatter men about the neres	*buttocks*
	Yit sawe I never than are these frers,	
20	In contreys ther thai rayke.	*where; wander about*
	Meteles so megre are thai made,[2]	
	And penaunce so puttes ham doun,	
	That ichone is an hors-lade	*each one; horse load*
	When he shall trusse of toun.	*leave town*

---

[1] *Give themselves so [wholeheartedly] to worship*

[2] *They become so gaunt through lack of food*

25   Allas, that ever it shuld be so,
     Suche clerkes as thai about shuld go,
     Fro toun to toun by two and two,   *in pairs*
       To seke thair sustynaunce!
     By God that al this world wan,   *redeemed*
30   He that that ordre first bygan,
     Me thynk certes it was a man   *I think for sure*
       Of simple ordynaunce.   *rule of life*
         For thai have noght to lyve by,[1]
         Thai wandren here and there,
35   And dele with dyvers marcerye,   *merchandise*
         Right as thai pedlers were.   *peddlars*

     Thai dele with purses, pynnes, and knyves,
     With gyrdles, gloves for wenches and wyves;   *belts*
     Bot ever bacward the husband thryves   *adversely*
40   Ther thai are haunted till.[2]
     For when the gode man is fro hame,   *away*
     And the frere comes to oure dame,
     He spares nauther for synne ne shame   *neither*
       That he ne dos his will.   *Until he accomplishes*
45   If thai no helpe of houswyves had,
         Whan husbandes are not inne,
         The freres welfare were ful bad,
          For thai shuld brewe ful thynne.   *fare poorly*

     Somme frers beren pelure aboute,   *carry rich fur*
50   For grete ladys and wenches stoute,
     To reverce with thair clothes withoute —
       Al after that, thai ere —   *are*
     For somme vaire, and somme gryse,   *(see note)*
     For somme bugee and for somme byse.
55   And also many a dyvers spyse   *spice*
       In bagges about thai bere.
         Al that for women is plesand   *to; pleasing*

---

[1] *Because they have nothing with which to gain their living*

[2] *"Where they are accustomed to go" (RHR)*

48

	Ful redy certes have thai.	
	But lytel gyfe thai the husband	
60	That for al shal pay.	

	Trantes thai can and many a jape;	*Trentals; tricks*
	For somme can with a pound of sape	*soap*
	Gete him a kyrtelle and a cape,	*mantle*
	And somwhat els therto.	*something; in the bargain*
65	Wherto shuld I othes swere?	*Why; swear oaths*
	Ther is no pedler that pak can bere	*peddlar; pack*
	That half so dere can sell his gere	*profitably; wares*
	Then a frer can do.	
	For if he gife a wyfe a knyfe	
70	That cost bot penys two,	*only twopence*
	Worthe ten knyves, so mot I thryfe,	
	He wyl have er he go.[1]	

	Ich man that here shal lede his life,	*Each*
	That has a faire doghter or a wyfe,	*daughter*
75	Be war that no frer ham shryfe,	*confess them*
	Nauther loude ne still.	*(see note)*
	Thof women seme of hert ful stable,	*Though; heart*
	With faire byhest and with fable	*promises*
	That can make thair hertes chaungeable	*[friars]*
80	And thair likynges fulfille.	*pleasures*
	Be war ay with the lymitour,	*(see note)*
	And with his felawe bathe;	*companion also*
	And thai make maystries in thi bour,	
	It shal turne the to scathe.[2]	

	Were I am a man that hous helde,	*a householder*
85	If any woman with me dwelde,	
	Ther is no frer bot he were gelde	*unless; castrated*
	Shuld com with-in my wones.	*house*

---

[1] *He will receive [in return], before he departs [from the wife], / The worth of ten knives, so may I prosper*

[2] *If they make "masteries" in your bedroom, / You shall be harmed by it*

	For may he til a woman wynne	*to; gain access*
90	In priveyté, he wyl not blynne	*cease*
	Er he a childe put hir with-inne —	
	And perchaunce two at ones!	
	Thof he loure under his hode,	*Though; look sad*
	With semblaunt quaynte and mylde,	*countenance genteel*
95	If thou him trust, or dos him gode,	*do good for him*
	By God, thou art bygylde.	*duped*

	Thai say that thai distroye synne,	
	And thai mayntene men moste ther-inne;	
	For had a man slayn al his kynne,	
100	Go shryve him at a frere,	*confess*
	And for lesse then a payre of shone	*shoes*
	He wyl assoil him, clene and sone,	*absolve; fully*
	And say the synne that he has done	
	His saule shal never dere.	*soul; harm*
105	It semes sothe that men sayne of hame	*true; them*
	In many dyvers londe,	
	That that caytyfe cursed Cayme	*wretch; Cain*
	First this ordre fonde.	*established*

	Nou se the sothe whedre it be swa,	*Now observe; truth whether*
110	That frere Carmes come of a k,	
	The frer Austynes come of a,	
	Frer Iacobynes of i,	
	Of M comen the frer Menours.	
	Thus grounded Caym thes four ordours,	
115	That fillen the world ful of errours	
	And of ypocrisy.	*hypocrisy*
	Alle wyckednes that men can tell	*cite*
	Regnes ham among;	*reigns among them*
	There shal no saule have rowme in hell,	*soul; room*
120	Of frers ther is such throng.	

	Thai travele yerne and bysily	*labor eagerly*
	To brynge doun the clergye;	
	Thai speken therof ay vilany,	*always*
	And therof thai done wrong.	*do*

125   Whoso lyves oght many yers   *Whoever lives for any length of time*
       Shall se that it shal fall of frers   *befall*
       As it dyd of the Templers
          That wonned here us among.   *who lived*
          For thai held no religioun
130   Bot lyved after lykyng;   *according to their desires*
          Thai were distroyed and broght adoun
          Thurgh ordynaunce of the kyng.

       Thes frers haunten a dredful thing,   *practice*
       That never shal come to gode endyng:
135   O frer for eght or nyen shal synge,   *One; eight; nine*
          For ten or for elleven.
       And when his terme is fully gone,
       Conscience then has he none,
       That he ne dar take of ychone   *each one*
140   Markes sixe or seven.
          Suche annuels has made thes frers
             So wely and so gay,   *adroit*
          That ther may no possessioners   *(see note)*
          Mayntene thair array.   *match; dress*

145   Tham felle to lyve al on purchace   *It was their lot to live wholly on begging*
       Of almes geten fro place to place;   *alms gathered*
       And for all that tham holpen has   *for those who have helped them*
          Shuld thai pray and syng.
       Bot now this londe so negh soght is
150   That unnethe may prestes seculers   *scarcely*
       Gete any service for thes frers.   *on account of*
          And that is wondre thing.
             This is a quaynt custome   *bizarre*
             Ordeyned ham among,
155   That frers shal annuel prestes bycome
             And so-gates selle ther song.   *in this manner*

       Ful wysely can thai preche and say,   *preach; talk*
       Bot as thai preche, no thing do thai.
       I was a frere ful many a day,
160   Therfor the sothe I wate.   *I know the truth*

Bot when I sawe that thair lyvyng
Acordyd not to thair prechyng,
Of I cast my frer clothing *Off*
   And wyghtly went my gate. *quickly; way*
165   Other leve ne toke I none
       Fro ham when I went,
       Bot toke ham to the devel ychone, *each one*
       The priour and the covent.

Out of the ordre thof I be gone, *though*
170 Apostata ne am I none; *I'm not an apostate*
Of twelve monethes me wanted one,
   And odde days nyen or ten. *nine*
Away to wende I made me boun, *ready*
Or tyme come of professioun, *Before*
175 I went my way thurghout the toun
   In syght of many men.
     Lord God that with paynes ill *hard*
       Mankynde boght so dere, *redeemed*
     Let never man after me have will *the will*
       For to make him frere. *to become*

Of Thes Frer Mynours

[*On the Minorites* (1382)]

(British Library MS Cotton Cleopatra B.ii fol. 65v)

Of thes Frer Mynours me thenkes moch wonder,		*Minorites*
That waxen are thus hauteyn, that som tyme weren under.[1]		
Among men of Holy Chirch thai maken mochel blonder;		*cause great confusion*
Nou He that sytes us above, make ham sone to sonder.		*sits; them soon to disperse*
5 With an O and an I, thai praysen not Seynt Poule,		
Thai lyen on Seyn Fraunceys, by my fader soule.[2]		

First thai gabben on God, that all men may se,   *sneer at; see*
When thai hangen him on hegh on a grene tre   *high; green tree*
With leves and with blossemes that bright are of ble,   *hue*
10 That was never Goddes Son, by my leuté.   *faith*
      With on O and an I, men wenen that thai wede,   *suppose; rage*
      To carpe so of clergy, thai can not thair Crede.[3]

Thai have done him on a croys fer up in the skye,   *placed; cross*
And festned on him wyenges, as he shuld flie.   *wings as though*
15 This fals feyned byleve shal thai soure bye,[4]
On that lovelych Lord so forto lye.   *lovely*
      With an O and an I, one sayd ful still,
      Armachan distroy ham, if it is Goddes will.   *Richard Fitzralph*

---

[1] *That have grown so proud, who once were humble*

[2] *They lie about Saint Francis, on my father's soul*

[3] *To disparage clerics [when they themselves] don't know their Creed*

[4] *For this false, mistaken belief they shall pay dearly*

Ther comes one out of the skye in a grey goun,   *habit*
20   As it were an hog-hyerd hyand to toun.   *swineherd hastening*
Thai have mo goddes then we, I say by Mahoun,   *Mohammed*
All men under ham, that ever beres croun.   *them; wears a crown*
    With an O and an I, why shuld thai not be shent?   *ruined*
    Ther wantes noght bot a fyre, that thai nere all brent![1]

25   Went I forther on my way in that same tyde,   *time*
Ther I sawe a frere blede in myddes of his syde,
Bothe in hondes and in fete had he woundes wyde,   *feet*
To serve to that same frer, the pope mot abyde.
    With an O and an I, I wonder of thes dedes,
30   To se a pope holde a dische whyl the frer bledes.

A cart was made al of fyre, as it shuld be;
A grey frer I sawe ther-inne, that best lyked me.   *pleased me*
Wele I wote thai shal be brent, by my leauté.   *know; burned; faith*
God graunt me that grace that I may it se.
35   With an O and an I, brent be thai all,   *burned*
    And all that helpes therto, faire mot byfall![2]

Thai preche all of povert, bot that love thai noght,   *preach; poverty*
For gode mete to thair mouthe the toun is thurgh soght.[3]
Wyde are thair wonnynges and wonderfully wroght;[4]
40   Murdre and horedome ful dere has it boght.[5]
    With an O and an I, ffor six pens er thai fayle,
    Sle thi fadere, and jape thi modre, and thai wyl the assoile![6]

---

[1] *I.e., They require only a fire for all of them to be burned*

[2] *And may all those who help [the burning] prosper*

[3] *The town is ransacked for good food for their mouths*

[4] *Spacious are their dwellings and beautifully constructed*

[5] *Murder and villainy have paid dearly for (the great houses)*

[6] *[For sixpence they will] Slay your father and seduce your mother, and they will confess you*

Thou That Sellest the Worde of God

[*The Layman's Complaint*]

(St. John's College Cambridge MS 195 fol. 1*v*)

	Thou that sellest the Worde of God,	
	Be thou berfot, be thou schod,	*barefoot; shod*
	Cum nomore here.	*Come*
	In principio erat Verbum	*In the beginning was the Word*
5	Is the Worde of God, all and sum,	*some*
	That thou sellest, lewed frere.	*ignorant friar*
	Hit is cursed symonie	*It*
	Ether to selle or to bye	*Either; buy*
	Ony gostly thinge.	*Any spiritual*
10	Therfore, frere, go as thou come,	
	And hold the in thi hows at home	*thee; thy house*
	Til we the almis brynge.	*bring thee alms*
	Goddis lawe ye reverson,	*God's; reverse*
	And mennes howsis ye persen,	*penetrate*
15	As Poul berith wittnes.	*bears witness*
	As mydday develis goynge abowte,	*devils going*
	For money lowlé ye lowte	*you bow low*
	Flaterynge boythe more and lesse.	*both*

Allas, What Schul We Freris Do

[*The Friar's Answer*]

(St. John's College Cambridge MS 195 fols. 1v-2r)

	Allas, what schul we freris do	*shall; friars*
	Now lewed men kun Holy Writ?	*laymen know*
	Alle abowte whire I go	*wherever*
	Thei aposen me of it.	*argue against; with*
5	Then wondrith me that it is so,	*I wonder*
	How lewed men kan alle wite.	*know; wisdom*
	Sertenly we be undo	*Certainly; undone*
	But if we mo amende it.	*Unless we may remedy [the situation]*
	I trowe the devel browght it aboute	*believe; Devil*
10	To write the Gospel in Englishe;	
	For lewed men ben nowe so stowt	*ignorant; arrogant*
	That thei geven us neyther fleche ne fishe.	
	When I come in-to a schope	*shop*
	For to say In principio,	
15	Thei bidine me "goo forth lewed poppe,"[1]	
	And worche and win my silver so.	*work*
	Yif I saie hit longoth not	*If I say it is not appropriate*
	For prestis to worche where thei go,	*labor*
	Thei leggen for hem Holy Writ	*adduce; themselves*
20	And sein that Seint Polle did soo.	*say; Paul*

---

[1] *They command me to "go away, [you] illiterate priest"*

56

Than thei loken on my nabete,   *habit*
And sein, "Forsothe withoutton othes,   *say; oaths*
Whether it be russet, blakk, or white,
It is worthe alle oure werynge clothes."

25   I saye, "I, not for me,
Bot for them that have none."
Thei seyne, "Thou havist to or thre.   *say; two*
Geven hem that nedith therof oone."

Thus oure disseytis bene aspiede   *deceits are detected*
30   In this maner and mani moo;   *more [ways]*
Fewe men bedden us abyde   *ask us to stay*
But hey fast that we were goo.[1]

If it goo forthe in this maner,   *things proceed*
It wole doen us myche gyle.   *cause us much harm*
35   Men schul fynde unnethe a frere   *scarcely one*
In Englonde within a whille.

---

[1] *"But they hasten us (on) quickly, so that we might be gone" (RHR)*

Freers, Freers, Wo Ye Be

(Trinity College Cambridge MS 1144 fol. 58*v*)

	Freers, freers, wo ye be,	*woe be to you*
	ministri malorum!	*ministers of evil*
	For many a mannes soule brynge ye	
	ad penas inffernorum	*to the pains of hell*
5	Whan seyntes ffelle ffryst ffrom heven,	*first*
	quo prius habitabant,	*who originally dwelt [there]*
	In erthe leyfft tho synnus seven	*(see note)*
	et ffratres communicabant.	*and consigned them to the friars*
	Folness was the ffryst ffloure	*Foulness; first blossom*
10	*quem ffratres pertulerunt,*	*which the friars perfected*
	For folnes and fals derei	*violence*
	multi perierunt.	*many perish*
	Freers, ye can weyl lye,	*lie*
	ad ffalandum gentem	*to deceive people*
15	And weyl can blere a mannus ye	*fool; eye*
	pecunias habentem.	*to get money*
	Yf thei may no more geytte,	*get*
	fruges petunt isti,	*they seek the first-fruits*
	For folnes walde thei not lette,	*would; cease*
20	*qui non sunt de grege Cristi.*	*who are not of Christ's flock*
	Lat a ffreer off sum ordur,	*of some order*
	tecum pernoctare	*spend the night with you*
	Odur thi wyff or thi doughtor	*Either*
	hic vult violare;	*he will want to violate*
25	Or thi sun he weyl prefur,	*son; will abduct*
	sicut ffurtam ffortis.	*like a strong thief*
	God gyffe syche a ffreer peyn	*give; pain*
	in inferni portis!	*at the gates of hell*

	Thei weyl assayle boyth Jacke and Gylle,	*will accost*
30	licet sint predones,[1]	
	And parte off pennans take hem tylle,	
	qui sunt latrones.	*who are thieves*
	Ther may no lorde of this cuntré	*country*
	sic edifficare	*build in this way*
35	As may thes ffreers, were thei be,	*wherever*
	qui vadunt mendicare.	*who go about begging*
	Mony-makers I trow thei be,	*Counterfeiters*
	regis proditores,	*traitors to the king*
	Therffore yll mowyth thei thee,	*For this may they ill prosper*
40	*ffalsi deceptores.*	*false deceivers*
	Fader ffyrst in Trinité,	
	ffilius atque fflamen.	*Son and Holy Ghost*

Omnes dicant Amen.   *Let all say Amen*

---

[1] *Lines 30–31: Although they are [normally] just petty thieves / who help themselves to the penance money*

59

The Wycliffite Bible: From the Prologue

From Cap. XII [Literal and Allegorical Interpretation of Scripture]

But it is to wite that Holy Scripture hath iiij. undirstondingis: literal, allegorik, moral, and anagogik. The literal undirstonding techith the thing don in deede, and literal undirstonding is ground and foundament of thre goostly undirstond-ingis, in so myche as Austyn, in his *Pistle to Vincent,* and othere doctouris seyn,

5   oonly bi the literal undirstonding a man may argue agens an adversarie. Allegorik is a goostly undirstonding that techith what thing men owen for to bileeve of Crist either of Hooly Chirche. Moral is a goostly undirstonding that techith men what vertues thei owen to sue and what vices thei owen to flee. Anagogik is a goostly undirstonding that techith men what blisse thei schal have in hevene. And

10   these foure undirstondingis moun be taken in this word *Jerusalem*; forwhi to the literal undirstonding it singnefieth an erthly citee, as Loundoun, either such another; to allegorie it singnefieth Hooly Chirche in erthe, that fightith agens synnes and fendis; to moral undirstondinge it singnefieth a Cristen soule; to anagogik it singnefieth Hooly Chirche regnynge in blisse either in hevene, and

15   tho that ben therinne. And these thre goostly undirstondingis ben not autentik either of beleeve no but tho ben groundid opynly in the text of Holy Scripture, in oo place other other; either in opin resoun that may not be distroied; either whanne the Gospelris either other apostlis taken allegorie of the Eelde Testa-ment, and confeermyn it (as Poul in the Pistle to Galat. in iiij.° c°. preveth) that

20   Sara, the free wijf and principal of Abraham, with Isaac hir sone, singnefieth bi

---

1 it . . . wite, one should learn; **iiij. undirstondingis,** four interpretations. **2 anagogik,** anagogic (see note); **in deede,** in fact. **3 foundament,** foundation; **goostly,** spiritual. **4 in so myche as,** in so far as; **Austyn,** St. Augustine; **Pistle,** letter; **Vincent,** Vincentius, Donatist bishop of Cartennae (Ténès); **doctouris,** learned clerics. **5 agens,** against. **6 owen,** ought. **7 either,** or. **8 owen to sue,** should try to emulate. **10 moun be taken,** may be observed; **forwhi,** because. **11 singnefieth,** signifies. **11–12 either . . . another,** or another such (city). **12 to allegorie,** allegorically. **15 tho,** those. **16 no but . . . ben,** unless they are; **opynly,** patently. **17 in oo . . . other,** in one place or another; **opin resoun,** plain argument; **dis-troied,** refuted. **17–18 either whanne,** or when. **18 taken,** use. **18–19 Eelde Testament,** Old Testament.

60

allegorie the Newe Testament and the sones of biheeste; and Agar, the hand mayde, with hir sone Ismael, signefieth bi allegorie the Elde Testament and fleschly men that schulen not be resseyved in to the eritage of God with the sones of biheeste, that holden the treuthe and freedom of Cristis Gospel with
25   endeles charité. Also Holy Scripture hath many figuratif spechis, and as Austyn seith in the iij. book *Of Cristen Teching*, that autouris of Hooly Scripture usiden moo figuris — that is, mo fyguratif spechis — than gramariens moun gesse, that reden not tho figuris in Holy Scripture. It is to be war, in the bigynnyng, that we take not to the lettre a figuratif speche, for thanne, as Poul seith, the lettre sleeth
30   but the spirit, that is, goostly undirstonding, qwykeneth; for whanne a thing which is seid figuratifly is taken so as if it be seid propirly, me undirstondith fleschly; and noon is clepid more covenably the deth of soule than whanne undirstonding, that passith beestis, is maad soget to the fleisch in suynge the lettre.

Whatever thing in Goddis word may not be referrid propirly to onesté of
35   vertues neither to the treuthe of feith, it is figuratyf speche. Onestee of vertues perteyneth to love God and the neighebore; treuthe of feith perteyneth to knowe God and the neighebore. Hooly Scripture comaundith no thing no but charité, it blamith no thing no but coveitise; and in that manere it enfoormeth the vertues either goode condiscouns of men. Holy Scripture affirmith no thing no
40   but Cristen feith bi thingis passid, present, and to comynge, and alle these thingis perteynen to nursche charité, and make it strong, and to overcome and quenche coveitise. Also it is figuratijf speche, where the wordis maken allegorie, ether a derk lycnesse either parable. And it is figuratyf speche in i.° c.° of Jeremye: "To day I have ordeyned thee on folkis and rewmys, that thou draw up bi the roote,
45   and distroie, and bylde, and plaunte." That is, that thou drawe out elde synnes,

21 **sones of biheeste,** sons of promise (virtuous pagans and Christians). 21-22 **Agar . . . mayde,** Hagar, the handmaiden. 23 **fleschly,** carnal; **resseyved,** received; **eritage,** heritage. 25 **figuratif spechis,** figures of speech (figural language); 26 *Of Cristen Teching, De doctrina Christiana (On Christian Doctrine)*; **autouris,** authors. 26–27 **usiden moo,** used more. 27 **gramariens . . . gesse,** grammarians can think of. 28 **It . . . war,** One should be careful. 29 **take . . . lettre,** don't interpret literally; **sleeth,** slays. 30 **qwykeneth,** gives life. 31 **propirly . . . fleschly,** in itself (i.e., literally), I interpret in a carnal manner. 32 **clepid . . . deth,** called more fittingly the death. 33 **passith . . . suynge,** surpasses that of beasts, is made subject to the carnal interpretation in following. 34 **onesté,** decorum, honesty. 35 **neither,** nor. 37 **no but,** except. 38 **blamith . . . coveitise,** condemns only avarice; **enfoormeth,** helps fashion. 39 **condiscouns,** conditions, qualities. 40 **to comynge,** future. 41 **nursche,** foster. 42–43 **ether . . . either,** either a shadowy likenesse or. 44 **rewmys,** kingdoms. 45 **bylde,** build; **elde synnes,** old sins.

and distroie circumstaunces either causis of thoo, and bylde vertues, and plaunte goode werkis and customys. Alle thingis in Holy Scripture that seemyn to unwijse men to be ful of wickidnesse agens a man himself either agens his neighebore ben figuratyf spechis, and the prevytees, either goostly undirstondinges, schulden be 50 sought out of us, to the feeding either keping of charité. Such a reule schal be kept in figuratif spechis, that so longe it be turned in mynde bi diligent consideracioun, til the expownyng either undirstonding be brought to the rewme of charité; if eny speche of Scripture sounneth propirly charité, it owith not to be gessid a figuratif speche; and forbeedith wickidnesse, either comaundith profyt 55 either good doynge, it is no figuratyf speche; if it seemith to comaunde cruelté, either wickidnesse, either to forbede prophit, either good doinge, it is a figuratijf speche. Crist seith: "If ye eten not the flesch of mannis Sone and drinke not His blood, ye schulen not have lijf in you." This speche semith to comaunde wickidnesse either cruelté, therfore it is a figuratif speche, and comaundith men to 60 comune with Cristis passioun, and to kepe in mynde sweetly and profitably, that Cristis flesch was woundid and crucified for us. Also whanne Hooly Scripture seith, "If thin enemy hungrith, feede thou hym, if he thurstith, geve thou drinke to hym," it comaundith benefice, either good doinge. Whanne it seith, "Thou schalt gadere togidere coolis on his heed," it seemith that wickidnesse of yvel 65 wille is comaundid. This is seid bi figuratijf speche, that thou undirstonde that the coolys of fijer ben brennynge weylyngis, either moornyngis of penaunce, bi whiche the pride of hym is mad hool, which sorwith that he was enemy of a man that helpith and relevith his wrecchidnesse. Also the same word either the same thing in Scripture is taken sumtyme in good, and sumtyme in yvel, as a lyoun 70 singnefieth sumtyme Crist and in another place it singnefieth the devyl. Also sour dough is set sumtyme in yvel, where Crist seith, "Be ye war of the sour dough of Farisees, which is ypocrisie"; sour dough is sett also in good, whanne Crist seith, "The rewme of hevenes is lyk sour dough," etc. And whanne not oo thing aloone

46 **either . . . thoo,** or their causes. **47 werkis,** works; **unwijse,** unwise. **49 pryvetees,** hidden (understandings). **50 feeding either keping,** nourishing or sustenance. **51–52 consideracoun,** contemplation. **52 expownyng,** explanation. **53 sounneth,** promote. **53–54 owith . . . gessid,** should not be supposed. **54 forbeedith,** (and if it) discourages. **54–55 either comaundith . . . doynge,** (it) either commands (spiritual) profit or good actions. **58 lijf,** life. **62 thurstith,** thirsts. **64 gadere . . . heed,** gather together coals on his head. **65 that thou undirstonde,** so that you should understand. **66 coolys . . . weylyngis,** coals of fire are burning wailings; **moornyngis of,** sorrow in. **67 mad hool,** made whole. **69 taken . . . yvel,** understood sometimes in a good sense, sometimes in an evil sense. **72 Farisees,** Pharisees.

but tweyne, either mo, ben feelid either undirstonden, bi the same wordis of
75 Scripture, though that it is hid, that he undirstond that wroot it is no perel, if it
may be prevyd bi othir placis of Hooly Scripture that ech of tho thingis acordith
with treuthe. And in hap the autour of Scripture seith thilk sentense in the same
wordis which we wolen undirstonde; and certys the Spirit of God, that wroughte
these thingis bi the autour of Scripture, bifore sigh withoute doute, that thilke
80 sentense schulde come to the redere, either to the herere — yhe, the Holy Goost
purveyde — that thilke sentence, for it is groundid on trewthe, schulde come to
the redere, either to the herere, forwhi what myghte be purveyed of God largiliere
and plentyvousliere in Goddis spechis than that the same wordis be undirstonden
in manye maners, whiche maners, either wordis of God, that ben not of lesse
85 autorité, maken to be preved. Austin in iij. book *Of Cristen Teching* seith al this
and myche more, in the bigynnyng therof. Also he whos herte is ful of charité
conprehendith, withouten any errour, the manyfoold abundaunce and largest
teching of Goddis Scripturis, forwhi Poul seith, "The fulnesse of lawe is charité,"
and in another place, "The ende of lawe," that is, the perfeccioun (either filling)
90 of the lawe, "is charité of clene herte, and of good conscience, and of feith not
feyned"; and Jhesu Crist seith, "Thou schalt love thi Lord God of al thin herte,
and of al thi soule, and of al thi mynde, and thi neighebore as thi-self, for in
these twey comaundementis hangith al the lawe and prophetis."

*

From Cap. XIII [Dangerous curricular changes at Oxford University]

Thes worldly foolis schulden wite that hooly lijf is a launterne to bringe a man
95 to very kunnynge, as Crisostom seith, and the drede and love of God is the
bigynning and perfeccioun of kunnyng and wijsdom; and whanne these fleschly
apis and worldly moldewerpis han neither the bigynnyng of wijsdom, neither

74 **tweyne,** two; **feelid,** perceived. 75 **it . . . perel,** there is no danger (of misinterpretation).
76 **prevyd,** tested. 77 **in hap . . . autour,** perhaps the author. 79 **bifore sigh,** foresaw. 80
redere . . . herere, reader . . . hearer; **yhe,** indeed. 81 **purveyde,** saw beforehand; **that thilke,**
that that (same). 82–83 **purveyed . . . plentyvousliere,** foreseen by God more broadly and
universally. 85 **Austin . . . Teching,** St. Augustine in the third book of *On Christian
Doctrine.* 88 **forwhi,** which is why. 89 **filling,** fulfillment. 90 **clene,** pure. 91 **of . . . herte,**
with all your heart. 93 **twey,** two. 95 **very kunnyng,** true knowledge. 97 **apis,** apes;
moldewerpis, moles (lit. "earth-throwers").

desyren it, what doon thei at Hooly Scripture, to schenschipe of hemself and of othere men? As longe as pride and coveitise of worldly goodis and onouris is
100 rootid in her herte, thei maken omage to Sathanas, and offren to him bothe bodi and soule, and al her witt and fynding. Such foolis schulden thenke that wijsedom schal not entre into an yvel willid soule, neither schal dwelle in a body soget to synnes; and Jhesu Crist seith that the Fadir of hevene hijdith the prevytees of Hooly Scripture fro wijse men and prudent, that is wijse men and prudent to the
105 world, and in her owne sight, and schewith tho to meke men; therfore worldly foolis, do ye first penaunce for youre synnes, and forsake pride and coveitise, and be ye meke, and drede ye God in alle thingis, and love Him over alle other thingis, and youre neigheboris as youre self; and thanne ye schulen profite in stodie of Hooly Writ. But alas, alas, alas! The moost abomynacoun that ever was
110 herd among Cristen clerkis is now purposid in Yngelond, bi worldly clerkis and feyned religiouse, and in the cheef universitee of oure reume, as manye trewe men tellen with greet weylyng. This orrible and develis cursednesse is purposid of Cristis enemyes and traytouris of alle Cristen puple, that no man schal lerne dyvynité, neither Hooly Writ, no but he that hath doon his fourme in art, that is,
115 that hath comensid in art, and hath ben regent tweyne yeer aftir. This wolde be ix. yeer either ten bifore that he lerne Hooly Writ aftir that he can comunly wel his gramer, though he have a good witt and traveile ful soore, and have good fynding ix. either x. yeer aftir his gramer. This semith uttirly the develis purpos, that fewe men either noon schulen lerne and kunne Goddis lawe. But God seith
120 bi Amos, on thre greete trespasis of Damask and on the iiij., "I schal not converte him"; where Jerom seith, the firste synne is to thenke yvelis, the ij. synne is to consente to weyward thoughtis, the iij. synne is to fille in werk, the iiij. synne is to do not penaunce aftir the synne, and to plese himself in his synne. But Damask is interpretid drinkynge blood, either birling blood. Lord, whether Oxun-
125 ford drinke blood and birlith blood, bi sleeinge of quyke men and bi doinge of

98 schenschipe of hemself, (the) ruination, disgrace of themselves. **99 onouris,** honors. **100 omage,** homage. **101 fynding,** discoveries. **102 soget,** susceptible. **103 hijdith,** hides. **105 tho,** such matters. **109 stodie,** study; **abomynacoun,** abomination. **110 herd,** heard; **purposid in Yngelond,** intended in England. **111 feyned,** false; **cheef universitee,** i.e., Oxford. **112 weylyng,** wailing; **orrible,** horrible. **113 traytouris,** traitors; **puple,** people. **114 fourme,** classes (form). **115 comensid,** received a Master's degree; **tweyne yeer aftir,** for two years afterward. **116 ix. yeer,** nine years. **116–17 can . . . gramer,** knows generally his grammar. **117 traveile ful soore,** work very hard. **118 fynding,** support. **121 Jerom,** St. Jerome (author of the Vulgate Bible); **ij.,** second. **122 iij.,** third; **iiij.,** fourth. **124 birling,** pouring out; **whether,** (tell me) whether. **125 birlith,** poured out; **quyke,** living.

sodomye, in leesinge a part of mannis blood, wherbi a chijld myte be fourmed, deme thei that knowen; and wher Oxunforde drinke blood of synne, and stirith othere men of the lond to do synne bi booldnesse off clerkis, deme thei justly that seen it at iye and knowen bi experiens. Loke now wher Oxunford is in thre
130 orrible synnes and in the fourthe, on which God restith not til He punsche it. Sumtyme children and yunge men arsistris weren devout and clene as aungels in comparisoun of othere; now men seyn thei ben ful of pride and leccherie, with dispitouse oothis, needles and false, and dispising of Goddis heestis. Sumtyme cyvylians and canonistris weren devout and so bisy on her lernyng that they
135 tooken ful litil reste of bed; now men seyn that thei ben ful of pride and nyce array, envye, and coveitise, with leccherie, glotonie, and ydilnesse. Sumtyme dyvynys weren ful hooly and devout, and dispisiden outtirly the world, and lyveden as aungels in meeknesse, clennesse, sovereyn chastité, and charité, and taughten treuly Goddis lawe in werk and word; now, men seyn, thei ben as deligat
140 of hir mouth and wombe, and as coveitouse as othere worldly men, and flateren, and maaken leesingis in preching, to eschewe bodyly persecuscoun, and to gete benefices. The firste grete synne is generaly in the université, as men dreden and seen at iye; the ij. orrible synne is sodomye and strong mayntenaunce thereof, as it is knowen to many persones of the reume, and at the laste parlement. Alas,
145 dyvynys, that schulden passe othere men in clennesse and hoolynesse, as aungels of hevene passen freel men in vertues, ben moost sclaundrid of this cursed synne agens kynde! The iij. orrible synne is symonie, and forswering in the semble hous, that schulde be an hous of rightfulnesse and hoolynesse, where yvelis schulde be redressid; this symonie with portenauncis thereof is myche worse and more abom-
150 ynable than bodily sodomye. Yit on these thre abomynacouns God wolde gra-

126 **leesinge,** losing; **chijld . . . fourmed,** child might be educated. 127 **wher,** (or tell me) whether; **stirith,** stirs up. 128–29 **deme . . . experiens,** they judge justly who have seen it with their eyes and have known it through experience. 130 **punsche,** punish. 131 **Sumtyme,** At one time; **arsistris,** masters of arts (*arceters*). 133 **dispitouse oothis,** spiteful oaths. 134 **cyvylians,** experts in civil law; **canonistris,** experts in canon law; **so bisy . . . lernyng,** so eager for their studies. 135–36 **nyce array,** foolish dress. 136 **ydilnesse,** idleness. 137 **dyvynys,** theologians (divines); **outtirly,** utterly. 138 **lyveden,** lived (their lives); **clennesse,** purity. 139 **deligat,** greedy. 140 **wombe,** stomach. 141 **maaken leesingis,** make lies; **eschewe . . . persecuscoun,** avoid bodily persecution. 143 **at iye,** with their eyes; **ij. orrible,** second horrible. 145 **passe,** surpass. 146 **freel,** frail. 146–47 **sclaundrid . . . kynde,** afflicted by this cursed sin against nature. 147 **iij.,** third; **forswering . . . semble hous,** swearing falsely in the assembly house. 149 **portenauncis,** appurtenances, accessories.

ciously converte clerkis if thei wolden do very penaunce, and geve hem hooliche
to vertues. But on the iiij. most abomynacoun purposid now to letten Cristen
men — yhe, prestis and curatis — to lerne freely Goddis lawe til thei han spendid
ix. yeer either x. at art, that conprehendith many strong errouris of hethene men
155   agens Cristen bileeve, it seemith wel that God wole not ceese of venjaunce til it
and othere ben punschid soore; for it seemith that worldly clerkis and feyned
relygiouse don this, that symple men of wit and of fynding knowe not Goddis
lawe, to preche it generaly agens synnes in the reume. But wite ye, worldly clerkis
and feyned relygiouse, that God bothe can and may, if it lykith Hym, speede
160   symple men out of the universitee, as myche to kunne Hooly Writ as maistris in
the université; and therfore no gret charge, though never man of good wille be
poisend with hethen mennis errouris ix. yeer either ten, but evere lyve wel and
stodie Hooly Writ, bi elde doctouris and newe, and preche treuly and freely agens
opin synnes, to his deth. See therfore what Jerom seith on Amos. God bifore
165   seith yvels to comynge, that men heere, and amende hemself, and be delyvered
fro the perel neighinge, either if that thei dispisen, thei ben punschid justiliere;
and God, that bifore seith peynes, wole not punsche men that synnen but that
thei be amendid. Jerom seith this in the ende of the j. book of Amos. God, for
His greet mercy, graunte that clerkis here the greet venjaunce manasid of God,
170   and amende hemself treuly, that God punsche not hem; for if thei amenden not
hemself, thei ben eretikis maad hard in her synnes. But see what Jerom seith
agens eretikis and in comendinge of Hooly Scripture. He seith thus on Amos:
"Eretikis that serven the wombe and glotonye ben clepid rightfully fattest kyin,
either kyin ful of schenschipe." "We owen to take Hooly Scripture on thre man-
175   eris. First, we owen undirstonde it bi the lettre and do alle thingis that ben
comaundid to us therinne; the ij. tyme bi allegorie, that is, goostly undirstonding;

151 **very,** true; **hooliche,** wholly. 152 **iiij.,** fourth; **letten,** impede. 153 **yhe,** namely. 153–54
spendid . . . art, spent nine or ten years studying the arts. 154 **hethene,** heathen. 155
bileeve, belief; **ceese of venjaunce,** cease from vengeance; **it,** i.e., the nine or ten year study
of arts. 156 **punschid soore,** severely punished. 158 **wite ye,** know this. 161 **no gret charge,**
[it is] no great matter. 162 **hethen mennis,** heathen men's. 164 **Jerom,** St. Jerome. 165
yvels to comynge, evils to come. 165–66 **delyvered . . . neighinge,** rescued from the ap-
proaching danger. 166 **justiliere,** with greater justice. 167–68 **but . . . amendid,** if they
mend their ways. 168 **j. book,** first book. 169 **here,** heed; **manasid of,** threatened by. 171
eretikis . . . synnes, heretics hardened in their sins. 173 **kyin,** cattle, kine. 174 **schenschipe,**
destruction; **owen,** ought. 174–75 **on thre maneris,** in three ways. 175 **bi the lettre,**
literally. 176 **the ij. . . . allegorie,** second time allegorically; **goostly,** spiritual.

and in the iij. tyme bi blisse of thingis to comynge." Jerom seith this in the ij. book on Amos, and in iiij. c°. of Amos. Natheles for Lyre cam late to me, see what he seith of the undirstonding of Holy Scripture. He writith thus on the ij.

180 prologe on the Bible: "Joon seith in v. c°. of Apoc. 'I sygh a book written withinne and withouteforth in the hond of the sittere on the trone'; this book is Holy Scripture, which is seid writen without forth as to the literal undirstonding and withinne as to the prevy and goostly undirstonding." And in the j. prologe he declarith iiij. undirstondingis of Hooly Writ in this manere: "Holy Writ hath this

185 specialté, that undir oo lettre it conteyneth many undirstondingis; for the principal autour of Hooly Writ is God Himself, in whose power it is not oonly to use wordis to singnifie a thing as men don, but also He usith thingis singnefied bi wordis to singnefie other thingis; therfore, bi the singnyfying bi wordis is taken the literal undirstonding (either historial) of Holy Scripture, and bi the singne-

190 fying which is maad bi thingis is taken the prevy either goostly undirstonding, which is thre maneres — allegorik, moral (either tropologik), and anogogik. If thingis singnefied bi wordis ben referrid to singnefie tho thingis that owen to be bileeved in the Newe Testament, so it is taken the sense of allegorik. If thingis ben referrid to singnefie tho thingis whiche we owen to do, so it is moral sense

195 either tropologik. If thingis ben referrid to singnefie tho thingis that scholen be hopid in blisse to comynge, so it is anagogik sense. The lettre techith what is doon; allegorie techith what thou owist for to bileeve; moral techith what thou owist for to do; anagogic techith whedir thou owist to go. And of these iiij. sensis (either undirstondingis) may be set ensaumple in this word *Jerusalem*. For bi the

200 literal undirstonding Jerusalem singnefieth a cyté that was sumtyme the cheef citée in the rewme of Jude; and Jerusalem was foundid first of Melchisedech, and aftirward it was alargid and maad strong bi Salomon. Bi moral sense it singnefieth a feithful soule, bi which sense it is seid in lij. c. of Isaie, 'Rise thou, rise thou, sette thou Jerusalem.' Bi sense allegorik it singnefieth the Chirche fightinge

205 agens synnes and feendis, bi which sense it is seid in xxj. c°. of Apoc: 'I sigh the hooly citée newe Jerusalem comynge doun fro hevene, as a spouse ourned to hire housbonde.' Bi sence anagogik it singnefieth the Chirche rengninge in blisse; bi

178 **Natheles for Lyre,** Nevertheless, since Nicholas of Lyra, author of important postils on Scripture. 180 **sygh,** saw. 181 **withouteforth,** on the outside. 183 **prevy,** hidden; **j. prologe,** first prologue. 185 **oo,** a single. 193 **the sense . . . allegorik,** in the allegorical (i.e., typological) sense. 197 **thou owist . . . bileeve,** you should believe. 198 **whedir . . . go,** where you should end up. 199 **may . . . ensaumple,** an example may be made. 200 **sumtyme,** at one time. 201 **Jude,** Judaea. 202 **alargid,** enlarged. 205 **sigh,** saw. 206 **ourned to,** adorned for. 207 **rengninge,** reigning.

this sence it is seid in iiij. c°. to Galat.: 'Thilke Jerusalem which is above, which is oure modir, is free'; and as ensaumple is set in oo word, so it might be set in
210 oo resoun, and as in oon, so and in othere." Lire seith al this in the firste prologe on the Bible.

*

Cap. XV [Translating Scripture from Latin into English]

For as myche as Crist seith that the Gospel shal be prechid in al the world, and Davith seith of the postlis and her preching, "The soun of hem yede out into ech lond, and the wordis of hem yeden out into the endis of the world"; and eft
215 Davith seith, "The Lord schal telle in the Scripturis of puplis, and of these princis that weren in it," that is, in Holi Chirche. And as Jerom seith on that vers: "Hooly Writ is the scripture of puplis, for it is maad that alle puples schulden knowe it." And the princis of the Chirche that weren therinne ben the postlis that hadden autorité to writen Hooly Writ, for bi that same that the
220 postlis writiden her scripturis bi autorité and confermynge of the Hooly Goost, it is Hooly Scripture, and feith of Cristen men, and this dignité hath noo man aftir hem, be he nevere so hooly, never so kunnynge, as Jerom witnessith on that vers. Also Crist seith of the Jewis that crieden Osanna to Him in the temple that, though thei weren stille, stoonis schulen crie, and bi stoonis He undirstondith
225 hethen men that worshipiden stoonis for her goddis. And we Englische men ben comen of hethen men, therfore we ben undirstonden bi thes stonis, that schulden crie Hooly Writ; and as Jewis, interpretid knowlechinge, singnefien clerkis that schulden knouleche to God bi repentaunce of synnes and bi vois of Goddis heriyng, so oure lewide men, suynge the corner ston Crist, mowen be singnefied
230 bi stonis, that ben harde and abydinge in the foundement. For, though covetouse clerkis ben woode by simonie, eresie, and manye othere synnes, and dispisen and stoppen Holi Writ as myche as thei moun, yit the lewid puple crieth aftir Holi Writ, to kunne it, and kepe it, with greet cost and peril of here lif.

For these resons and othere, with comune charité to save alle men in oure

209 **modir,** mother. 212 **myche,** much. 213 **Davith . . . preching,** David says of the apostles and their preching; **the soun . . . out,** their voices went out. 214 **eft,** again. 215 **puplis,** peoples. 222 **kunnynge,** knowledgeable. 229 **heriyng,** praise; **suynge,** clinging to. 230 **foundement,** foundation. 230–31 **covetouse . . . woode,** greedy clerks are mad. 232 **stoppen,** block access to; **moun,** may.

235   rewme whiche God wole have savid, a symple creature hath translatid the Bible
out of Latyn into English. First, this symple creature hadde myche travaile, with
diverse felawis and helperis, to gedere manie elde Biblis, and othere doctouris
and comune glosis, and to make oo Latyn Bible sumdel trewe; and thanne to
studie it of the Newe, the text with the glose, and othere doctouris as he mighte
240   gete, and speciali Lire on the Elde Testament, that helpide ful myche in this
werk. The thridde tyme to counseile with elde gramariens and elde dyvynis of
harde wordis and harde sentencis, hou tho mighten best be undurstonden and
translatid. The iiij. tyme to translate as cleerli as he coude to the sentence, and
to have manie gode felawis and kunnynge at the correcting of the translacioun.
245   First it is to knowe that the best translating is out of Latyn into English to
translate aftir the sentence and not oneli aftir the wordis, so that the sentence be
as opin (either openere) in English as in Latyn and go not fer fro the lettre; and
if the lettre mai not be suid in the translating, let the sentence evere be hool and
open, for the wordis owen to serve to the entent and sentence and ellis the
250   wordis ben superflu either false. In translating into English, manie resolucions
moun make the sentence open, as an ablatif case absolute may be resolvid into
these thre wordis, with covenable verbe, *the while, for, if,* as gramariens seyn; as
thus: *the maistir redinge, I stonde* mai be resolvid thus, *while the maistir redith, I
stonde,* either *if the maistir redith,* etc. either *for the maistir,* etc. And sumtyme it
255   wolde acorde wel with the sentence to be resolvid into *whanne* either into *aftir-
ward*; thus, *whanne the maistir red, I stood,* either *aftir the maistir red, I stood.* And
sumtyme it mai wel be resolvid into a verbe of the same tens, as othere ben in
the same resoun, and into this word *et* (that is, *and* in English); as thus, *arescent-
ibus hominibus prae timore,* that is, *and men shulen wexe drie for drede.* Also
260   a participle of a present tens either preterit, of actif vois eithir passif, mai be
resolvid into a verbe of the same tens and a conjunccioun copulatif; as thus,
dicens, that is, *seiynge,* mai be resolvid thus: *and seith* eithir *that seith.* And this
wole, in manie placis, make the sentence open, where to Englisshe it aftir the

235 **symple creature,** humble person. 237 **felawis . . . Biblis,** colleagues and helpers, to
gather together many old Bibles. 237–38 **doctouris . . . glosis,** doctors of the Church and
ordinary glosses (scriptural commentaries). 238 **sumdel,** somewhat. 240 **Lire,** Nicholas of
Lyra. 241 **dyvynis,** theologians. 242 **harde,** difficult. 243 **iiij.,** fourth; **sentence,** meaning.
245 **it is . . . knowe,** one should know. 247 **opin (either openere),** plain (or plainer). 248
suid, followed. 249 **and ellis,** otherwise. 250 **superflu,** superfluous. 251 **ablatif . . .
absolute,** see note. 252 **covenable,** appropriate. 255 **acorde,** harmonize. 256 *red,* read.
257 **tens,** tense. 259 *wexe drie,* become dry. 263 **open,** clear; **to Englisshe it,** to translate
it into English.

word wolde be derk and douteful. Also a relatif, which mai be resolvid into his

265 antecedent with a conjunccioun copulatif; as thus, *which renneth, and he renneth.*
Also whanne oo word is oonis set in a reesoun, it mai be set forth as ofte as it
is undurstonden either as ofte as reesoun and nede axen. And this word *autem*
either *vero* mai stonde for *forsothe* either for *but*, and thus I use comounli; and
sumtyme it mai stonde for *and*, as elde gramariens seyn. Also whanne rightful

270 construccioun is lettid by relacion, I resolve it openli. Thus, where this reesoun,
Dominum formidabunt adversarij ejus, shulde be Englisshid thus bi the lettre, *the
Lord hise adversaries shulen drede*, I Englishe it thus bi resolucioun, *the adversar-
ies of the Lord shulen drede him*; and so of othere resons that ben like. At the
bigynnyng I purposide, with Goddis helpe, to make the sentence as trewe and

275 open in English as it is in Latyn, either more trewe and more open than it is in
Latyn; and I preie, for charité and for comoun profyt of Cristene soulis, that if
ony wiys man fynde ony defaute of the truthe of translacioun, let him sette in the
trewe sentence and opin of Holi Writ, but loke that he examyne truli his Latyn
Bible, for no doute he shal fynde ful manye Biblis in Latyn ful false, if he loke

280 manie, nameli newe. And the comune Latyn Biblis han more nede to be cor-
rectid, as manie as I have seen in my lif, than hath the English Bible late trans-
latid; and where the Ebru, bi witnesse of Jerom, of Lire, and othere expositouris,
discordith fro oure Latyn Biblis, I have set in the margyn, bi maner of a glose,
what the Ebru hath, and hou it is undurstondun in sum place. And I dide this

285 most in the Sauter, that of alle oure bokis discordith most fro Ebru; for the
Chirche redith not the Sauter bi the laste translacioun of Jerom out of Ebru into
Latyn, but another translacioun of othere men, that hadden myche lasse kunnyng
and holynesse than Jerom hadde; and in ful fewe bokis the Chirche redith the
translacioun of Jerom, as it mai be previd bi the propre orignals of Jerom,

290 whiche he gloside. And where I have translatid as opinli or opinliere in English
as in Latyn, late wise men deme, that knowen wel bothe langagis and knowen wel
the sentence of Holi Scripture. And where I have do thus or nay, ne doute — thei
that kunne wel the sentence of Holi Writ and English togidere and wolen tra-

264 **derk,** obscure. 265 ***renneth,*** runs. 267 **nede axen,** is required. 270 **lettid by relacion,**
impossible because of the context; **openli,** unambiguously. 273 **ben like,** are similar. 274
purposide, intended. 279–80 **loke . . . newe,** examines many (Bibles), especially recent
ones. 281 **late,** recently. 282 **Ebru,** Hebrew. 282–83 **Jerom . . . fro,** St. Jerome, of
Nicholas of Lyra, and [of] other expositors, disagrees with. 285 **Sauter, that,** Psalms, which;
discordith . . . Ebru, diverges most from the Hebrew version. 290–91 **where . . . deme,**
whether I have translated as clearly or more clearly in English than the Latin, let wise men
judge. 291 **langagis,** languages. 292 **ne doute,** (let there be) no doubt.

295

300

305

310

315

vaile, with Goddis grace, theraboute — moun make the Bible as trewe and as opin, yea, and opinliere, in English than it is in Latyn. And no doute to a symple man, with Goddis grace and greet travail, men mighten expoune myche openliere and shortliere the Bible in English than the elde greete doctouris han expounid it in Latyn, and myche sharpliere and groundliere than manie late postillatouris, eithir expositouris, han don. But God, of His grete merci, geve to us grace to lyve wel and to seie the truthe in covenable manere, and acceptable to God and His puple, and to spille not oure tyme, be it short be it long at Goddis ordynaunce. But summe, that semen wise and holi, seyn thus: if men now weren as holi as Jerom was, thei mighten translate out of Latyn into English, as he dide out of Ebru and out of Greek into Latyn, and ellis thei shulden not translate now, as hem thinkith, for defaute of holynesse and of kunnyng. Though this replicacioun seme colourable, it hath no good ground, neither resoun, neithir charité forwhi this replicacioun is more agens Seynt Jerom and agens the firste LXX. translatouris, and agens Holi Chirche, than agens symple men, that translaten now into English. For Seynt Jerom was not so holi as the apostlis and evangelistis, whos bokis he translatide into Latyn, neither he hadde so highe giftis of the Holi Gost as thei hadden; and myche more the LXX. translatouris weren not so holi as Moises and the profetis, and speciali Davith, neither thei hadden so greete giftis of God as Moises and the prophetis hadden. Ferthermore Holi Chirche appreveth not oneli the trewe translacioun of meene Cristene men, stidefast in Cristene feith, but also of open eretikis, that diden awei manie mysteries of Jhesu Crist bi gileful translacioun, as Jerom witnessith in oo prolog on Job and in the prolog of Daniel. Myche more late the chirche of Engelond appreve the trewe and hool translacioun of symple men, that wolden for no good in erthe, bi here witing and power, putte awei the leste truthe — yea, the leste lettre either title — of Holi

294 **theraboute,** at it (i.e., studying Latin and English and translating). 296 **expoune,** explain. 297 **shortliere,** more quickly, or, perhaps, concisely. 298 **myche . . . groundliere,** with greater acumen and grounding; **late postillatouris,** recent exegetes. 301 **spille . . . long,** not waste our time, whether it be short or long. 305 **hem thinkith,** they think; **defaute . . . kunnyng,** lack of holiness and of knowledge. 305–06 **replicacioun . . . colourable,** argument seems plausible. 306 **forwhi,** because. 307–08 **LXX. translatouris,** translators of the Septuagint (Greek) version. 310 **neither . . . so,** nor had they such. 314 **meene,** unsophisticated; **stidefast,** steadfast. 316 **gileful,** cunning, fraudulent. 317 **late,** recently; **appreve,** authorized. 318–19 **bi . . . power,** i.e., knowingly and deliberately. 319 **putte awei,** omit, neglect; **leste,** least; **leste lettre,** most trivial letter.

320   Writ that berith substaunce either charge. And dispute thei not of the holynesse
       of men now lyvynge in this deadli lif, for thei kunnen not theron, and it is
       reservid oneli to Goddis doom. If thei knowen any notable defaute bi the trans-
       latouris either helpis of hem, lete hem blame the defaute bi charité and merci
       and lete hem nevere dampne a thing that mai be don lefulli, bi Goddis lawe, as
325   weeryng of a good cloth for a tyme either riding on an hors for a greet journey,
       whanne thei witen not wherfore it is don; for suche thingis moun be don of
       symple men, with as greet charité and vertu as summe that holden hem greete
       and wise kunnen ride in a gilt sadil either use cuyssyns and beddis and clothis of
       gold and of silk, with othere vanitées of the world. God graunte pité, merci, and
330   charité, and love of comoun profyt, and putte awei such foli domis, that ben
       agens resoun and charité. Yit worldli clerkis axen gretli what spiryt makith idiotis
       hardi to translate now the Bible into English, sithen the foure greete doctouris
       dursten nevere do this? This replicacioun is so lewid that it nedith noon answer
       no but stillnesse eithir curteys scorn; for these greete doctouris weren noon
335   English men, neither thei weren conversaunt among English men neither in caas
       thei kouden the langage of English, but thei ceessiden nevere til they hadden
       Holi Writ in here modir tunge, of here owne puple. For Jerom, that was a Latyn
       man of birthe, translatide the Bible bothe out of Ebru and out of Greek, into
       Latyn, and expounide ful myche therto. And Austyn and manie mo Latyns ex-
340   pouniden the Bible for manie partis, in Latyn, to Latyn men, among whiche thei
       dwelliden, and Latyn was a comoun langage to here puple aboute Rome and
       biyondis; and on this half, as Englische is comoun langage to oure puple, and yit
       this day the comoun puple in Italie spekith Latyn corrupt, as trewe men seyn that
       han ben in Italie. And the noumbre of translatouris out of Greek into Latyn
345   passith mannis knowing, as Austyn witnessith in the ij. book *Of Cristene Teching*,
       and seith thus: "The translatouris out of Ebru into Greek moun be noumbrid,
       but Latyn translatouris either thei that translatiden into Latyn, moun not be

320 either charge, or weight. **321 deadli,** mortal; **for . . . theron,** for they know nothing
about it. **323 either . . . hem,** or anything which might aid them. **324 lefulli,** licitly. **325
weeryng of,** wearing. **326 witen . . . wherfore,** don't know why. **328 gilt . . . cuyssyns,** golden
saddle or use cushions. **330 foli domis,** foolishness. **331–32 idiotis hardi,** ignorant people
bold. **333 dursten . . . do,** never dared to do; **replicacioun . . . lewid,** rejoinder is so
ignorant. **334 no but . . . scorn,** only silence or polite scorn. **335 neither . . . weren,** and
neither were they. **335–36 neither . . . kouden,** nor did they at all know. **336–37 ceessiden
. . . tunge,** never ceased until they had [translated] Holy Scripture into their mother tongue.
343 this day, today; **trewe,** honest. **345 passith mannis,** surpasses man's. **346 moun be
noumbrid,** may be numbered (counted).

noumbrid in ony manere." For in the firste tymes of feith, ech man, as a Greek book came to him and he semyde to him-silf to have sum kunnyng of Greek and

350 of Latyn, was hardi to translate; and this thing helpide more than lettide undurstonding, if rederis ben not necligent, forwhi the biholding of manie bokis hath shewid ofte eithir declarid summe derkere sentencis. This seith Austyn there. Therfore Grosted seith that it was Goddis wille that diverse men translatiden, and that diverse translacions be in the Chirche; for where oon seide derkli, oon

355 either mo seiden openli. Lord God — sithen at the bigynnyng of feith so manie men translatiden into Latyn, and to greet profyt of Latyn men, lat oo symple creature of God translate into English, for profyt of English men! For if worldli clerkis loken wel here croniclis and bokis, thei shulden fynde that Bede translatide the Bible and expounide myche in Saxon that was English either comoun

360 langage of this lond in his tyme; and not oneli Bede but also King Alvred, that foundide Oxenford, translatide in hise laste daies the bigynning of the Sauter into Saxon, and wolde more if he hadde lyved lengere. Also Frenshe men, Beemers, and Britons han the Bible and othere bokis of devocioun and of exposicioun translatid in here modir langage. Whi shulden not English men have the same in

365 here modir langage I can not wite — no but for falsnesse and necgligence of clerkis either for oure puple is not worthi to have so greet grace and gifte of God, in peyne of here olde synnes? God for His merci amende these evele causis, and make oure puple to have, and kunne, and kepe truli Holi Writ to lijf and deth! But in translating of wordis equivok — that is, that hath manie significa-

370 cions under oo lettre — mai lightli be pereil; for Austyn seith in the ij. book *Of Cristene Teching* that if equivok wordis be not translatid into the sense (either undurstonding) of the autour, it is errour. As in that place of the Salme, *the feet of hem ben swifte to shede out blood*, the Greek word is equivok to *sharp* and *swift*; and he that translatide *sharpe feet* erride, and a book that hath *sharpe feet*

375 is fals and mut be amendid. As that sentence *unkynde yonge trees shulen not geve*

---

349 he semyde . . . kunnyng, he seemed (in his own mind) to have some knowledge. **350 was hardi,** made bold. **351 rederis,** readers. **352 derkere sentencis,** more difficult (obscure) meanings. **353 Grosted,** Robert Grosseteste, bishop of Lincoln. **358 loken . . . bokis,** scrutinize their chronicles and books. **359 expounide,** explicated. **360 King Alvred,** King Alfred was once thought to have founded Oxford University. **361 Sauter,** the Psalms. **362 wolde . . . lengere,** would have [translated] more if he had lived longer; **Beemers,** Bohemians. **363 exposicioun,** exegesis. **364 modir langage,** mother tongue. **364–65 Whi . . . wite,** I can't think why Englishmen should not have the same [translations] in their mother tongue. **369 equivok,** equivocal, ambiguous. **372 Salme,** Psalm. **375 mut,** must.

depe rootis owith to be thus: *plauntingis of avoutrie shulen not geve depe rootis.* Austyn seith this there. Therfore a translatour hath greet nede to studie wel the sentence both bifore and aftir, and loke that suche equivok wordis acorde with the sentence; and he hath nede to lyve a clene lif, and be ful devout in preiers,

380   and have not his wit ocupied about worldli thingis, that the Holi Spiryt, autour of wisdom, and kunnyng, and truthe, dresse him in his werk, and suffre him not for to erre. Also this word *ex* signifieth sumtyme *of*, and sumtyme it signifieth *bi*, as Jerom seith; and this word *enim* signifieth comynli *forsothe* and, as Jerom seith, it signifieth *cause thus, forwhi*; and this word *secundum* is taken for *aftir*,

385   as manie men seyn, and comynli it signifieth wel *bi* eithir *up*, thus *bi youre word* either *up youre word*. Manie such adverbis, conjuncciouns, and preposiciouns ben set ofte oon for another, and at fre chois of autouris symtyme; and now tho shulen be taken as it acordith best to the sentence. Bi this maner, with good lyvyng and greet travel, men moun come to trewe and cleer translating, and trewe

390   undurstonding of Holi Writ, seme it nevere so hard at the bigynnyng. God graunte to us alle grace to kunne wel, and kepe wel Holi Writ, and suffre joiefulli sum peyne for it at the laste! Amen.

376 *avoutrie,* adultery. **379 clene,** pure. **381 dresse,** guide. **385** *up,* upon. **389 travel,** labor, pains. **390 seme . . . hard,** although it seem ever so hard.

The Lanterne of Light

(British Library MS Harley 2324 fols. 1v–4r, 5r–20v)

This is the prolog

God that is good in Him-silf, faire in Hise aungelis, merveilouse in Hise seintis, and merciful upon synners: have merci on us now and ever, and gyve us grace to holde the weye of truthe in thise daies of greet tribulacioun. For now manye that semeden to have be stable in vertu fallen from her holi purpose, dredyng losse of worldli goodis and bodili peyne, as Crist seith (Mat. xxiv°): *Quoniam habundabit iniquitas, refrigescet caritas multorum.* That is to seie: "The greet plenté and habundaunce of wickidnesse schal kele or make coolde the charité of many." For now the devel hath marrid this world bi his leeftenaunt Anticrist that men ben born aboute in diverse doughtis, as wawis of the see, wrechidli dividid in wonderful opyniouns, iche neighbore with othir. But, Seint Poul sett oon acorde in al Cristendom, and seith (Eph. iv°): *Unus dominus, una fides, unum baptisma.* That is to seie: "Ther is but oo Lord that alle men schulden drede and love; oo Feith that alle men schulden bileve withouten chaungyng; oo Baptem or Cristendom that alle men schulden kepe withouten defouling." Alas, hou is this oonhed or unité broken, that men unrulid walken aftir her lustis, as beestis in the corne! Certis, the wickid man that Crist spekith of hath done this dede (Matt. xiii°): *Inimicus homo superseminavit zizania.* That is to seie: "The enemy of God hath sowen taaris upon the seed" of Jesu Crist. This wickid man is Anticrist, that clowtith his lawis as roten raggis to the clene cloth of Cristis Gospel, and wakith in malise as Judas childe whilis Symon slep-ith and takith noon hede. O thou wickid man! Is ther ony othir that may save soulis than Crist Jesu? God seith bi the mouthe of Moyses (Deut° xxxii°): *Per-cuciam et ego sanabo et non est qui de manu mea possit eruere.* That is to seie: "I

4 **semeden,** seemed. 5 **dredyng,** fearing. 7 **habundaunce,** abundance; **kele,** cool. 8 **leef-tenaunt,** lieutenant. 9 **doughtis,** doubts; **wawis . . . see,** waves of the sea. 10 **wonderful,** wonder-provoking; **iche,** each. 11 **sett oon acorde,** made an agreement. 14 **Baptem,** baptism. 15 **oonhed,** oneness. 18 **sowen taaris,** sown tares (weeds). 19 **clowtith,** patches; **roten raggis,** filthy rags. 20 **malise,** malice; **Judas,** Judas's; **whilis Symon,** whilst Simon Peter. 21 **takith noon hede,** pays no attention.

75

schal smyt, and I schal heele, and ther is non that mai skape fro myn hand."

25 Who hath the keies of Davith to opyn hevene gatis, and thanne noon othir closith to close, and thanne noon othir opyneth? Seint Jon seith (Apoc. iii°): *Sanctus et verus habet clavem David qui aperit et nemo claudit, claudit et nemo aperit.* That is to seie: "Holi and trewe Crist Jesu hath the keie of Davith the whiche opineth and noon othir closith, closith and thanne noon othir opineth"

30 — who dingeth doun and thanne no man rerith; who rerith, and thanne no man dingeth doun. Job seith (xii°): *Si destruxerit nemo est qui edificet; si incluserit hominem nullus est qui apariat.* That is to seie: "Whanne the Lord God hath distroied, ther may noon othir bijlde; and whanne the Lord God stressith a man in the prisoun, ther mai noon othir delyver him" ne quite him from hise

35 boondis. And therfore in the vertu of this name Jesu stondith al mannes salvacioun, as it is writen (Actus iv°): *Nec enim aliud nomen est sub celo datum hominibus unde oporteat nos salvos fieri.* Seint Petir seith: "Ther is noon othir name undir hevene gyven to men but this name Jesu, in the whiche it bihoveth us to be made saaf," for oonli in vertu of this name cometh remyssioun of synnes, as

40 it is writen (Luc. xxiiii°): *Oportebat predicari in nomine eius penitenciam et remissionem peccatorum in omnes gentes.* That is to seie: "It bihoved to be prechid among alle folkis penaunce and remissioun of synnes in the name of Jesu." Art not thou thanne a wickid man, a foultid schepard, a cruel beest, the sone of perdicioun and Anticrist him-silf that pretendist in thee and in thi membris to

45 bynde and lose, to blesse and curse, biside this name Jesu? Peple withouten noumbre, folowyng thee and thi divided lawis, ben dividid from Crist Jesu, and gon with thee blyndlingis to helle for everemore. And this is greetli to sorow, so ferforthe that Crist makith mornyng therupon and seith (Jon v°): *Ego veni in nomine Patris mei et non accepistis me; si alius venerit in nomine eius illum acci-*

50 *pietis.* That is to seie: "I have comen in the name of my Fadir, and ye have not taken me; whanne anothir cometh in his owene name, him ye schal take." And this is Anticrist, as Seint Jon Crisostum seith upon this Gospel (Mat. xi°): *Tu es qui venturus es, an alium expectamus.* For who that wole not resceyve Crist, in peyne of synne he is compellid and constreyned to resceyve Anticrist. Therfore

---

24 smyt, smite; **heele,** heal; **skape,** escape. **25 keies of Davith,** keys of David; **hevene,** heaven's. **25–26 thanne . . . opyneth,** i.e., such that no one else may close them (heaven's gates) and no one else may open them. **30 dingeth,** strikes; **rerith,** raises up. **33 bijlde,** build; **stressith,** incarcerates. **34 quite,** release. **35 vertu,** power. **39 saaf,** saved. **43 foultid schepard,** foolish shepherd. **44–45 membris . . . lose,** followers to bind and loose. **47 blyndlingis,** blind men. **47–48 so ferforthe,** to such an extent. **48 makith mornyng,** grieves.

55   in this tyme of hidouse derknes somme seeken the lanterne of light, of the whiche spekith the prophete (Ps. cxviii): *Lucerna pedibus meis verbum tuum.* That is to seie: "Lord, Thi word is a lanterne to my feet." For as fer as the light of this lanterne schineth, so fer derkness of synne and cloudis of the fendis temptaciouns vanischen awey and moun not abide. And algatis whanne the lanterne

60   lightneth into the hert, it purgeth and clensith from corrupcioun; it swagith and heelith goostli soris. As the wise man seith (Sap. xvi°): *Neque herba neque malagma sanavit illos, sed omnipotens sermo tuus, Domine, qui sanat universa.* That is to seie: "Neithir herbe ne plaistir hath helid hem, but Lord Thi mighti Word that heelith alle thingis." For Lord whanne Thou diedist upon the Cros, Thou

65   puttidist in Thi Word the spirit of lijf, and gavest to it power of quickenyng bi Thin owene preciouse blood, as Thou Thi-silf seist (Jon. vi°): *Verba que ego locutus sum vobis spiritus et vita sunt.* That is to seie: "The wordis that I speke to yow, thei ben spirit and lijf."

What is Anticrist in general with .VI. condiciouns

Capitulum .iii^m.

    To speke in general, that is in moost in comune, Anticrist is every man that

70   lyveth agen Crist, as Seint Jon seith (Jon. ii°): *Nunc autem sunt multi antichristi.* That is to seie: "Forsothe, now ben manye anticristis." And therfore seith Seint Austin, "Who that lyveth contrarie to Crist, he is an anticrist, be thou withynne, be thou withoute"; and thou lyve contrarie to Crist, thou arte but chaff, of the whiche chaff Crist (Mat. iii°): *Paleas autem conburet igni inextinguibli.* That is to

75   seie: "Forsothe the chaff schal brenne with fire that mai not be quenchid"; for it schal brenne and never quenche, and the soule that is chaff schal evere suffre and never die. As the prophete seith (Isaie. ix°): *Omnis violenta predacio cum tumultu et omne vestimentum commixtum sanguine erit in combustionem et cibus ignis.* That is to seie: "Every proud soule that risith in swelling agens his God

80   and every-bodi that is defoulid in glotonye and in leccherie schal be in to sweyl-

---

55 hidouse, hideous. **59 moun,** may; **algatis,** especially. **60–61 swagith . . . soris,** relieves and heals spiritual wounds. **63 plaistir,** healing plaster. **65 lijf,** life; **quickenyng,** giving life. **70 agen,** contrary to. **71–72 Seint Austin,** St. Augustine. **73 and,** if. **76 brenne,** burn. **80 glotonye . . . leccherie,** gluttony . . . lechery (deadly sins). **80–81 sweyling,** burning.

ing, and mete of the fire." As if he schulde seie, The bodi and the soule damp-
ned schullen feed and norische the fire, the whiche schal evere brenne hem with
moost grevous peyne.

Six synnes ther ben agen the Holi Goost that turned the wrecchid soule in to
85 this chaff. But the philosophur seith: *Nullum malum vitatur nisi cognitum.* That
is to seie: "Ther is non yvel fled but if it be knowen"; and therfore we schullen
name hem in this litil tretise for the more lernyng of smale undirstondars.

The firste of thise synnes is presumpcioun. That is highe bolnyng of the spirit
withouten drede of Goddis rightwisenesse; and of this synne al manere malice
90 and wickidnes cacchith roote that regneth among mankynde in lewid or in
lerned. For the wise man seith (Ecc. i°): *Qui non timet non poterit justificari.* "He
that dredith not, he mai not be made rightwise." Forsothe in whom so that this
synne of presumpcioun hath noo lordschipe, in him the devel is overcomen; for
it is writen (Ecc. xv°): *Qui timet Deum faciet bona.* "He that dredith the Lord
95 schal do good thingis." And therfore seith the Holi Goost (Ecc. xxvii°): *Si non in
timore Domini tenueris te instanter, cito subvertetur domus tua.* That is to seie:
"But if thou holde the bisili in the drede of the Lord, thin hous schal soone be
turned upsodoun"; that is, thi bodi and thi soule schullen be turned from God
into the fendis service.

100 The secounde synne is desperacioun othir wanhope, that is, overe litil triste on
the merci of God. Seint Austin seith: *Amare et timere sunt due janue vite.* "Drede
of Goddis rightwisenesse and hope of Goddis merci ben twoo gatis of lijf," for
bi hem we entren here in to grace, and aftir in to blisse. As the prophete seith
(Ps. cxlvi): *Bene placitum est Domino super timentes eum, et in eis qui sperant*
105 *super misericordia eius.* "It is wel plesid unto the Lord upon hem that dreden
Him, and in hem that tristen on His mercy." And agenwarde, presumpcioun and
disperacioun ben twoo gatis of deeth, bi the whiche men entrien in to synne and
cumbraunce, and aftir in to the peyne of helle withouten ende. Seint Jon techith
us loore agen this synne, and seith (Jon ii°): *Filioli mei, hec scribo vobis ut non*
110 *peccetis, sed et si quis peccaverit advocatum habemus apud patrem Jesum Christum*
justum et ipse est propiciacio pro peccatis nostris. Non pro nostris tantum sed pro
tocius mundi. "Mi litil sones, thise thingis I write unto you, that ye synne not in

81 **mete of,** food for. **81–82 dampned,** damned. **86 fled,** avoided. **87 smale undirstondars,**
slow learners. **88 bolnyng,** swelling, arrogance. **89 rightwisenesse,** righteousness. **97 But
if . . . drede,** Unless you earnestly fear. **98 upsodoun,** upside down. **100 wanhope,** despair;
overe . . . on, too little trust in. **105 It is . . . hem,** The Lord is well pleased with them.
106 agenwarde, on the other hand. **107 entrien,** enter. **108 cumbraunce,** affliction.

the synne of dispeire; but if it be so that ony of us have synned, we have avoket anenst the Fadir Jesu Crist, oure just Lord, and He is the mercy-asker for oure

115 synnes, not oonli for oure synnes but also for the synnes of al the world." Jesu is for to seie a Saviour in oure tung, for He hath plenté of medicyn to save all mankynde if thei wolde take this medicyn and be saaf. For Gregor seith: *Se ipsum interimit qui precepta medici observare non vult.* "He sleeth him-silf that wole not kepe the biddingis of his leche."

120 The thridde synne is obstinacioun or hardnes of herte, the whiche wole not be contrit for conpunccioun neithir be made softe with pité, ne mevid with preiours ne thretingis, and settith nought bi betingis. It is unkynde agen good dedis, unfeithful to counseils, feeris and wood in doomes, unschamefast in foule thingis; neithir feerful in perelis, neithir manful in manhod; foolhardi agens God,

125 forgetil of tyme that is passid, necligent in tyme that is present, not purveiyng for tyme that is to cum. And schortli for to seie, this is that synne that neithir dredith God ne schameth man. Thus seith Seint Bernard (v. distinccioun iiii°). A medicyn for this hard herte techith Lincoln where he seith (diccio cvl): *Cor durum debet conteri in mortarialo petrino gravi pila. Mortarialum sunt vulnera*

130 *Christi, pila ex timore pene peccati.* "An harde herte wolde be braied in a morter with an hevi pestel. This morter is the bodi of Crist, hoolid or woundid in His passioun; this pestel is the drede of dampnacioun, that folowith aftir this synne." Thanne thus thou obstinat man, thou endurid man in synne, thou hard hertid wrecche. Neighe thou to the bodi of Crist, and for drede of dampnacioun, con-

135 forme thee to Cristis passioun.
The fourthe synne is fynali inrepentaunt, that is, he that wole never do verri penaunce but contynueli ledith his lijf aftir the desiris of his fleische, overcomen with the fende and the fals world. For no man doth verry penaunce to God but he that fulli leveth that synne, for the whiche he suffrith penaunce, thus seith

---

113-14 avoket anenst, advocate with. **117 saaf,** saved. **118 sleeth,** slays. **119 biddingis . . . leche,** doctor's orders. **120 thridde,** third; **obstinacioun,** obstinacy; **herte,** heart. **121 contrit,** contrite; **conpunccioun,** compunctions. **121-22 mevid . . . thretingis,** moved by prayers or threats. **122 settith . . . betingis,** cares nothing about beatings; **It,** i.e., such a one; **unkynde,** unnatural. **123 feeris . . . doomes,** fierce and mad in judgments; **unschamefast,** without shame. **124 neithir . . . neithir,** neither . . . nor; **perelis,** perils. **125 forgetil,** forgetful. **125-26 purveiyng . . . cum,** looking ahead to the times that are to come. **130 braied,** ground up. **131 hevi,** heavy. **133 endurid . . . synne,** inured to sin. **134 Neighe thou,** Approach. **136 fynali inrepentaunt,** ultimate impenitence. **136-37 verri penaunce,** true penitence. **137 ledith . . . fleische,** leads his life according to the desires of his flesh. **139 leveth,** abandons.

140   Seint Austin. But for thei holden it miche worschipe to write her names in the
erthe, thei maken a feyned schrifte to a prest, and taken part of sacramentis; thei
bilden chirches with other ournmentis, and fynden prestis to rede and syng; thei
releven the pore nedi, and menden placis that ben perilous; but stille thei lien
harde, congelid as froost, in oolde custum of synne. To thise unrepentaunt men

145   spekith Gregor moost scharpli in hise Pastorals upon this tixte (Mat. vi°): *Nonne
anima plus est quam esca, et corpus plus quam vestimentum?* "Whethir is not the
lijf more than mete, and the bodi more than clothe?" Upon this seith this doc-
tour: *Qui cibum vel vestem pauperibus largitur et anime vel corporis iniquitate
polluitur quod magis est contulit culpe quod minus est contulit justicie, sua dedit*

150   *Deo, se ipsum diabolo.* "He that gyveth mete or clothe to the pore nedi and is
pollutid or defoulid in wickidenesse of bodi and of soule, that thyng that is
moost he gyveth to synne, that thing that is leest he gyveth to rightwisenesse;
hise goodis he gyveth to God, him-silf to the devel, for he settith more prijs bi
worldli richesse than he doth bi the bodi or the soule, and loveth moost that

155   God loveth leest, wherfore his love is turned to hate. God hath govun to man
fyve preciouse giftis. The leest of alle is worldli goodis. Betir than thise is man-
nes bodi, that God hath dowid with kyndeli strengthis and grauntid in resoun to
use this world, him-silf to chastise, cloothe, and feede. Aboven thise tweyne is
mannes soule, that berith Goddis ymage and his licknes. Lord, what profite were

160   it to wynne this world and putt peirement to this soule? And the bodi is a wlat-
ful careyn whanne the soule is goo therfro. But Goddis grace passith thise thre;
for where this failith, no wisdam availith. Loke thise ben not mys-dispendid,
neithir worche oony thing biside ther ordir, but that thei strecche alle to oo
ende: to wynne the fifthe, that is the blisse of hevene for evere. Thou that

165   chaungist this ordir upsodoun, Seint Poul axith this questioun of the (Ro. ii°):
An divicias bonitatis eius et paciencie et longanimitatis contempnis? Ignoras quon-

---

140 miche worschipe, great honor. **141 feyned schrifte,** pretended confession; **taken . . .
sacramentis,** take part in [the] sacraments. **142 ournmentis,** adornments; **rede,** read. **143
releven . . . nedi,** relieve the needy poor. **145 tixte,** text. **146–47 Whethir . . . lijf,** Is not
life. **147 mete,** food; **clothe,** clothing. **152 moost,** most important. **153 settith . . . bi,** sets
a higher value on. **154 that,** what. **155 govun,** given. **157 dowid . . . kyndeli,** endowed with
natural. **158 tweyne,** two (i.e., worldly goods and man's body). **159 that berith . . . licknes,**
which bears God's image and likeness. **160 putt peirement to,** jeopardize. **160–61 wlatful
. . . therfro,** foul carcass when the soul has departed from it. **162 Loke . . . mys-dispendid,**
Watch out that these not be ill-spent. **163 biside ther ordir,** outside their [proper] order.
163–64 oo ende, a single goal. **165 chaungist . . . upsodoun,** reverses this order; **axith,**
asks; **the,** thee.

iam benignitas Dei ad penitenciam te adducit, secundum autem duriciam tuam et cor impenitens thesaurizas tibi iram in die ire et revelacionis justi judicii Dei qui reddet unicuique secundum opera eius. "Whethir dispisist thou the richessis of the

170 goodnes and pacience and longabiding of thi God? Knowist thou not that the goodnes of God ledith othir dryveth thee to penaunce? Forsothe, aftir thin hardnes and thin unrepentaunt herte thou tresourist to thee wraththe in the dai of wraththe, and schewing of rightwise jugement of God, that schal yelde iche man aftir hise werkis."

175 The fifte synne is envie of thi brotheris grace, as whanne thi neighbour is wise, wel governed, preisid or born up, riche, welthi, strong, faire, or vertuouse in greet habundaunce of grace. Thanne this enviouse man sclaundrith, upbreidith, reproveth, dispisith, hatith, and hyndrith, scorneth, and pursueth, to defoule and waast his brotheris goodis that ben goostli gracis as miche as he mai. As the wise

180 man seith (Prov. xiiii°): *Ambulans recto itinere et timens Deum despicitur ab eo qui infami graditur via.* "A man walking in the highe weie and dreding God is dispised of him that walkith in the wrong weye." Whanne Jesu Crist kest out a devel from a man that was doumb, as it is writen (Mat. xii°, Marc. iii°, Luc. xi°), anoon this man bigan to speke to puplische this miracle among the peple.

185 Thanne Scribis and Pharises, enviouse sectis that weren a fals privat religioun, sclaundrid that Crist wrought this miracle in Belsabub that was prince of develis. Belsabub is to seie a god of flighes or ellis a god that makith discorde. Lord, sithen thise sectis dursten seie thus to Crist, heed of mannis soule, hou miche werre schullen they moun dore seie to Hise hous-meyné? Thus prelatis and freris

190 in thise daies ben traveilid with this synne agen the Holi Goost, and schamfulli sclaundren her symple britheren that casten yvel maners from her soule or prechen the Gospel to Cristis entent, to turne the peple to vertuouse lyvyng. Thei seien this man hath eten a flighe that gyveth him lore of Goddis lawe. This is more foule to eete a flie than to be a god and chare this flighes. Thus han

169 **Whethir . . . thou,** Do you hate. 170 **longabiding,** long-suffering. 171 **ledith othir dryveth,** leads or impels; **aftir,** according to. 172 **tresourist to thee,** store up for yourself. 172–73 **in . . . wraththe,** on the day of Wrath. 173–74 **yelde . . . werkis,** yield to each man according to his works. 176 **born up,** commended; **welthi,** wealthy. 177 **habundaunce,** abundance. 177–78 **upbreidith, reproveth,** censures, chides. 179 **goostli,** spiritual. 184 **anoon,** straightway; **puplische,** publish; **peple,** people. 186 **sclaundrid,** denied; **Belsabub,** Beelzebub. 187 **flighes,** flies. 189 **werre . . . hous-meyné,** worse shall they care to say to His household. 190 **traveilid,** burdened. 192 **entent,** meaning. 194 **chare,** drive away.

195   they brought her malice aboute, to sclaundir for Lollardis that speken of God, and dryven the peple from the feith that durne not worche ne speke for sclaundir. But certis they ben not worthi Crist, that stonyen for barkyng of thise houndis; for noon is worthi to be with this Lord, that schameth His servyse in wel or in woo. And suche men schewen hem traitours to God, that with her

200   sclaundris hindren her britheren and seyn the fende mai and wil make wise hise membris that serven him in synne; but so wole not Crist Hise loved servauntis, that lyven in clennes to serve Him in vertu. O, I preie you, who hard ever a fouler blasfemye? Certis, this dispit strecchith unto the godhed to be punischid in the dai of Jugement. For Goddis lawe techith (Prov. iii°): *Noli prohibere bene-*

205   *facere qui potest si vales et ipse benefac.* "Forbede him not that mai wel do but if thou mai do wel thi silf." That a prest schulde not be lettid to preche the trouthe, ne Goddis peple to speke of her bileve, is opunli taught in the book of Numeri xi°. There it is rad that Heldad and Medad prophecied albeit that thei weren not lisensid bi Moises. Josue, the mynyster of Moises and chosen of

210   manye, grucchiden agens thise men, and mad his pleynt to Moises; and Moises seide, "Whi art thou enviouse for me, who mai werne that alle the peple prophecie, and God graunt His spirit to hem?" This is confermed in the Gospel of oure Lord Jesu Crist, bothe in Mark ix° and in Luc. ix°: *"Magister, vidimus quemdam in nomine tuo demonia eicientem qui non sequitur nos et prohibuimus eum."*

215   *Jesu autem ait: "Nolite prohibere eum."* Seint Jon evaungelist seide unto Crist: "'Maister, we han sen a man casting out develis in Thi name, that sweth not us, and we han forboden him. Forsothe Jesu seide: 'Nile ye werne him or forbeede him.'" Alas, how dorne oure bischopis, for schame, offende agens thise bothe Goddis lawes, and docke her prestis on every side, to gyve hem a charge and

220   prive hem ther office! What is to be sett biforne the bodi of Crist that prestis sacren? And sithen thei treten Cristes bodi, miche rather, seith Jerom, thei schullen preche and blesse the peple (Hec. dist. 99ᵃ). But here the enemyes of

---

195 sclaundir for, slander. **196–97 durne . . . sclaundir,** dare not act or speak for [fear of] slander. **197 that stonyen for,** who are amazed because of. **198 noon,** no one. **199 wel . . . woe,** prosperity or in adversity. **202 clennes,** purity; **hard ever,** ever heard. **206 lettid to,** prevented from. **207 bileve,** belief; **opunli,** openly. **208 Numeri,** Numbers; **rad,** read; **Heldad,** Eldad. **209 Moises,** Moses; **Josue,** Joshua, son of Nun. **210 grucchiden agens,** grumbled against; **mad his pleynt,** complained. **211 enviouse for me,** jealous on my account; **werne,** prohibit. **216 han sen,** have seen; **that . . . us,** who does not follow us. **217 forboden,** forbidden; **Nile ye werne,** Don't prevent. **218 dorne,** dare. **218–19 thise . . . lawes,** both these laws of God. **219 docke,** cut short. **220 prive hem,** deprive them. **221 sacren,** bless; **miche rather,** much sooner (i.e., it would be much better).

truthe objectun and leyn for hem Poul, where he seith (Ro. x°), *Quomodo predic-*
abunt nisi mittantur? "How schullen thei preche but if thei be sent?" With this
225   thei blynden mani folk, kutting the sentence from the wordis; for Poul meneth
that prestis schulde preche, for thei ben sent bothe of God and of the bischop
for to do that office. And the Maister of Sentence in his fourthe book and the
xxiiii. dist. seith: "It is the office of a deken to preche the Gospel; thanne bi
more strenger resoun it perteyneth to a prest." For Seint Jerom and Seint Beede
230   acorden togider and seyn: *Sicut in forma apostolorum est forma episcoporum, ita*
in septuaginta duobus discipulis est forma presbiterorum. "Right as in the apostlis
is the forme of bischopis, so in thre score and twelve disciplis is the forme of
prestis." But Crist gave charge bothe to thise bischopis and also to thise prestis,
and seide (Mat. x°): *Ecce ego mitto vos.* And Luc. x°: *Designavit Jesus alios sep-*
235   *tuaginta duos et misit illos, etc.* "Loo, I sende you as schepe among wolves." And
efte Jesu asigned threscore and twelve, and sent hem to preche. How schal thise
bischopis maynten ther constituciouns agens ther God and holi seintis? It schal
be more suffurable to Sodom and Gomor than to this peple, that disturblen
Goddis ordinaunce.
240   The sixt synne is fighting agens the truthe that a man knowith. That is, whanne
the truthe is tolde to the gilti, the whiche disposith him not to be amendid,
thanne he makith blynde ungroundid resouns with sotil argumentis and foltid
sophisticacioun, and dampneth the truthe agens his conscience with a boold
forheed that can not schame, as the prophet Jeromye seith iii°: *Frons mulieris*
245   *meretricis facta est tibi, et noluisti erubescere.* "A stroumpetis forhed is made unto
thee, and thou woldist not be aschamed." But as Poul seith (Thimo. iii°): *Quem-*
admodum Jambres et Mambres restiterunt Moisi, ita et hii resistent veritati. "Right
as Jambres and Mambres agen-stooden Moises in the sight of Pharo, so thise
agen-stonden the truthe," corruptid men in ther mynde. And if thou wilt knowe
250   what thise men ben, axe Seint Peter and he wole telle thee; for he clepith hem
bi ther name in his epistil, where seith (II. Petir ii°): *Magistri mendaces qui intro-*
ducent sectas perdicionis. Seint Petir seith: "Thise ben maistir liears that schullen
bring in among the peple sectis of perdicioun," that is, of losse and deeth.
Though ye rise with Lucifer and make youre nestis among the sterris, from thens

---

225 kutting the sentence, severing the meaning; **meneth,** means. **227 Maister of Sentence,**
Peter Lombard, author of *Sententiae.* **228 deken,** deacon. **230 acorden togider,** agree. **236**
efte, again. **228 that disturblen,** who upset. **241 gilti,** sinner. **242 ungroundid resouns,**
baseless arguments; **sotil,** subtle; **foltid,** foolish. **245 stroumpetis,** strumpet's. **248 agen-**
stooden, stood against (opposed). **250 axe,** ask; **clepith,** calls. **252 maistir liears,** master
liars.

255 ye schullen be drawen and throwen to the grounde. Whanne wole ye marke the
wordis of Crist that cursith you for youre apostasie, and for ye pullen as foxis to
her hoolis children from fadris? Crist seith to you (Mat. xxiii°): *Ve vobis scribe et
pharisei, qui circuitis terram et mare, etc.* "Woo to you, Scribis et Pharises, ypo-
critis, that cumpassen aboute the see and the lond to make you a novise, and
260 whanne ye han founden him, ye maken him helle broond double than youre-silf!"
As the unkunnyngnes of Pharoos philosophurs was made knowen, so the fals
impunyng of the truthe of thise sotil ypocritis schal hastli be made open. Alle
men take hede to thise six synnes, for thei ben cause of batailes, discencyouns,
hounger, pestelence, venjaunce, and of al maner of mischef; and at the laste thise
265 synnes ben cause whi soules ben chaff, as we seide toforne.

What is Anticrist in special with hise thre parties

Capitulum .iiii^m.

But of the greet cheef Anticrist, that passingli and in special maner bringith
forth fals lawes agens Jesu Crist and pretendith him-silf moost hooli, thus tech-
ith the Lord God bi the prophete Isaie ix°: *Longevus et venerabilis ipse est caput,
propheta docens mendacium, ipse est cauda.* "A man of greet agee and worschip-
270 ful holden to the world, he is heed and cheef Anticrist; a prophete or a prechour
techyng lesing, he is the taile of this Anticrist." Of this taile spekith Seint Petir
more pleynli and seith (II Pet. ii°): *Fictis verbis in avaricia de vobis negociabuntur.*
That is to seie: "Thise ben goostli marchauntis that schal chaffare with the peple
in feyned wordis"; and with her sweet likerouse speche thei bigilen the hertis of
275 innocentis. For Jude seith ii°: *Mirantes personas hominum questus causa.* That is
to seie: "Thei schal worschip the persoones of men bicause of wynnyng." This
taile of Anticrist schal not preche freeli. Thomas Alquin seith (li°. VII°. ca. viii°):

255 **marke,** heed. 257 **hoolis,** holes; **fadris,** fathers. 258 **Woo,** woe. 259 **see,** sea. 260 **helle**
. . . **youre-silf,** child of hell twofold more than yourselves. 261 **unkunnyngnes,** ignorance.
262 **impunyng,** slander; **sotil ypocritis,** subtle hypocrites; **hastli,** quickly. 263 **batailes,**
battles. 264 **hounger,** hunger; **pestelence,** plague. 265 **toforne,** before. 266 **cheef,** leader;
passingli, surpassingly. 269 **agee,** age. 269–70 **worschipful . . . to,** revered by. 271 **lesing,**
lying. 273 **goostli marchauntis,** merchants of spiritual things; **chaffare,** deal, trade. 274
feyned, fraudulent; **likerouse,** (falsely) pleasant; **bigilen,** seduce. 276 **bicause of wynnyng,**
for material gain. 277 **Thomas Alquin,** Thomas Aquinas.

"But for *mammona iniquitatis* — that is, for coveitise — so ferforthe crueli agen-
stooding the prechours of trouthe, that thei schul be holden in ther daies as
cursid of the peple." And Seint Jon evaungelist seith (Apoc. xiii°): *Quod nemo
emet neque vendet nisi habuerit carecterem bestie.* "Ther schal no man in that
tyme bie ne selle, be he bonde, be he free, but if he have the mark of the beest"
either in his forhed or in his right hond or ellis in noumbre; that is to seie, ther
schal no man preche Goddis word in thoo daies neither heere it but if he have
a special lettir of lisence that is clepid the mark of this beest Anticrist, or ellis
that thei maynten bi word or bi dede, or in bothe, that his lawe and his ordin-
aunce is good and trewe and worthi to be holden of the peple. But it is ferful
that folowith aftir (Apoc. xiiii°): *Si quis acceperit carecterem bestie, etc.* Seynt Jon
seith: "Who that ever worschipith this beest Anticrist, and takith this forseid
mark, he schal drink a draught of the wyn of Goddis wraththe, and he schal be
turmentid in fire and brymston in the sight of holi aungelis and in the sight of
the Lombe; and the smoke of her turmentrie schal stighe up in to the world of
worldis, that is, withouten ende."

Of this Anticrist God seith to the prophete Zachare xi°: *Sume tibi vasa pastoris
stulti.* That is to seie: "Take thou to thee the vessellis of a foltid schepard." For
loo, I schal suffre Anticrist to be rerid up in lond, the which schal not visite hem
that ben forsaken; neithir he schal seke hem that ben scatrid, neithir he schal
hele hem that ben sore. O, thou foltid schepard Anticrist! God seith thou art an
ydole havyng a bischopis habit but neithir vertu ne spirit, lijf ne dede, that
longith to a bischop. For Poul seith (Rom. viii°): *Qui non habet spiritum Christi
nec est eius.* "He that hath not the spirit of Crist, he is not His servaunt "albeit
that he have the outward tookenes; and therfore seith Seint Jon (Apoc. xvi°):
Quintus angelus effudit phiolam suam super sedem bestie, etc. "The fifthe aungel
pourid his cruet upon the seete of the beest, and his rewme is made derke; and
thei eeten her toungis togidir for sorow, and thei blasfemeden God of heven for

278 **so ferforthe,** to such an extent. 278–79 **agenstonding,** opposing. 282 **bie,** buy; **be
. . . if,** whether he is a bondsman or a free man, unless. 284 **heere,** hear. 285 **clepid,**
called. 289 **Who that ever,** Whoever. 290 **wyn,** wine. 291 **brymston,** brimstone; **aungelis,**
angels. 292 **turmentrie,** torment; **stighe,** rise. 295 **vessellis . . . schepard,** instruments of a
foolish shepherd. 296 **suffre,** permit; **rerid up,** exalted. 297 **neithir . . . scatrid,** he shall
neither seek those who have been scattered. 298 **hele . . . sore,** heal those who are injured.
299 **ydole,** idol; **bischopis habit,** bishop's clothes; **lijf ne dede,** way of life nor deed. 300
longith, pertains. 302 **tookenes,** signs. 304 **cruet,** vial; **rewme,** kingdom. 305 **eeten . . .
togidir,** eat their tongues together; **blasfemeden,** blasphemed.

her sorowis and her woundis, and thei diden no penaunce of her dedis." That is
to mene archebischopis and bischopis ben the seet of the beest Anticrist, for in
hem he sittith and regneth over othir peple in the derknes of his heresie; and in
this thei deliten hem, magnifiyng with her tungis her fals ordinaunce, the whiche
310 is sorow to men of trewe undirstonding, and thus thei putten abak Goddis holi
lawe for prechyng of Cristis Gospel, the whiche ben sorowis to hem, gendring
synnes in her sowlis that wounden hem to the deeth. And thei thus woundid
schullen never do medeful penaunce of dedis, for the whiche thei schal be
dampned. Lyncoln seith: "I quake, I drede, and ugli I am aferde; but I dare not
315 be stille leste peraventure that sentence falle on me that the prophete seith
(Isaie. vi°): *Ve mihi quia tacui.* 'Wo to me, for I have stilled.' The welle, the
bigynnyng, and the cause of al ruyn and myschef is the court of Rome." Now bi
the autorité of God and oone acordaunce of Hise holi seintis sueth an open
conclucioun, sadli groundid in trewe bileve, that in the court of Rome is the
320 heed of Anticrist and in archebischopis and bischopis is the bodi of Anticrist.
But in thise cloutid sectis, as mounkis, chanouns, and freris is the venymous taile
of Anticrist. Thise thre parties ben waried of the apostle Seint Jude, seiyng in
this forme (ca°. 1°): *Ve qui in via Caym abierunt et in errore Balaam mercede
effuci sunt et in contradiccione Chore perierunt.* That is to seie: "Woo to hem that
325 walken in the weye of Caym: thise ben fals possessioners. And woo to hem that
ben schadde out for mede in the errour of Balaam: thise ben mighti nedles
mendiners. And woo to hem that ben perischide in the agenseiyng of Chore":
thise ben proude, sturdi maynteners.

How this Anticrist schal be destroied God Him-silf techith bi the prophete
330 Daniel, and seith (ca.° viii°): *Sine manu conteretur.* That is to seie: "This Anti-
crist schal be destried withouten hand," that is, withouten power of man. For
Poul seith (II Thess. ii°): *Antichristum deus interficiet spiritu oris sui et destruet
illustracione adventus sui.* That is to seie: "Crist schal slee Anticrist with the
spirit of His mouthe, that is, with the holi word of His lawe. And the Lord schal

---

306 of her dedis, for their deeds. **306–07 That . . . mene,** That means. **309 deliten hem,**
take delight; **magnifiyng . . . tungis,** glorifying with their tongues. **311 gendring,** engender-
ing. **313 medeful,** commendable. **314 Lyncoln,** Robert Grosseteste, bishop of Lincoln; **ugli,**
terribly, sore. **315 peraventure,** perhaps. **318 autorité,** authority; **oone acordaunce,** unani-
mous agreement; **sueth,** follow. **319 sadli . . . bileve,** anchored seriously in true belief. **321
cloutid . . . chanouns,** rag-tag sects, such as monks, canons; **venymous,** poisonous. **322 thre
. . . waried,** three parts (i.e., monks, canons, and friars) are cursed. **325 Caym,** Cain. **326
schadde,** separated; **mede,** reward, bribery. **327 mendiners,** mendicants, beggars; **agen-
seiyng,** denying, gainsaying. **328 maynteners,** defenders. **329 destroied,** destroyed.

335 destrie him with schynnyng of His comyng"; that is, with turnyng of mennes
hertis bi His grace to His lawe a litil aforne His doome. But God taught more
pleynli this loore to Joob, and seide (Job xl. caº.): *Ecce spes eius frustrabitur eum
et videntibus cuntis precipitabitur.* "Loo," seith God, "that hope that Anticrist
hath in richessis and in worldli favour schal bring him to nought; and alle men
340 seing he schal be throwen doun heedlingis, so that alle the peple schal take a
weiling upon him with greet lamentacioun, wariyng him and dampnyng him with
alle hise fals ordinauncis.

What is Anticrist in special, with fyve condiciouns

Capitulum .vᵐ.

But now at the last we schullen bring to mynde and to witnesse holi Davith
the kyng, that had yovun to him the ful spirit of prophecie; and he seing the
345 comyng of Anticrist, his lyvyng and his fal, markith fyve hidouse saughtis, the
whiche he schal haunt agen the servauntis of God. Ps. foure score and ten.
The first saught of Anticrist is constitucioun, as the prophete seith: *Constitue,
domine, legis latorem super eos.* "Lord, suffre thou to ordeyne a lawemaker upon
the peple," in peyne of her synne, for thei wole not consent to the trouthe. That
350 is thus to mene: Anticrist useth fals lucratif or wynnyng lawis as ben absoluci-
ouns, indulgence, pardouns, privelegis, and alle othir hevenli tresour that is
brought in to sale for to spoile the peple of her worldli goodis; and principali
thise newe constituciouns bi whos strengthe Anticrist enterditith chirchis, soum-
neth prechours, suspendith resceyvours, and priveth hem ther bennefice, cursith
355 heerars, and takith awey the goodis of hem that fortheren the precheing of a
prest — yhe, though it were an aungel of hevene — but if that prest schewe the
mark of the beest, the whiche is turned in to a newe name and clepid a special
lettir of lisence for the more blyndyng of the lewid peple.

335–36 turnyng . . . doome, conversion of men's hearts by His grace to His law shortly
before His Judgment. **337 loore to Joob,** lesson to Job. **339–40 alle men seing,** in the
sight of all men. **340 throwen . . . heedlingis,** cast down headlong. **340–41 take . . . him,**
mourn for him. **341 wariyng,** cursing. **343 Davith,** David. **345 saughtis,** assaults. **346
haunt,** practice, use. **347 saught,** onslaught. **350 fals . . . lawis,** false lucre or laws for
material gain. **352 spoile,** despoil. **353 thise newe constituciouns,** see note; **enterditith,**
interdicts. **353–54 soumneth,** indicts. **354 resceyvours,** receivers; **priveth,** deprives. **355
heerars,** hearers; **goodis of hem,** their goods. **356 yhe,** yea.

The secounde saught of Anticrist is tribulacioun, as the prophet seith: *Despicis*
in oportunitatibus in tribulacione. That is to seie: "Anticrist vexith the peple over
might, in hunting hem on mawmentrie and doyng of ydolatrie; but ever Anticrist
maketh hem to wene that thei gon on pilgrimage and therfor he is waried of
God, that seith bi the prophete Isaye v°: *Ve qui dicitis bonum malum vel malum*
bonum, ponentes tenebras lucem et lucem tenebras, ponentes amarum in dulce et
dulce in amarum. That is to seie: "Woo to you that seyn good is yvel and yvel is
good, putting light in to derknes and derknes in to light, turnyng sweet in to
bittir and bittir in to sweet." And thus doth Anticrist whanne he transposith
vertues in to vicis, and vicis in to vertues, as pilgrimage in to outrage, and out-
rage in to pilgrimage. And for this weywarde entent God dispisith Anticrist with
alle hise blindfelt peple, and wlatith alle her mysdispendid goodis in her moost
tribulaciouns.

The thridde saught of Anticrist is Inquisiscioun. As the prophet seith: *Secun-*
dum multitudinem ire sue non queret. That is to seie: Anticrist enquerith, sechith,
and herkneth where he mai fynde ony man or womman that writith, redith,
lerneth, or studieth Goddis lawe in her modir tung, to lede her lijf aftir the
plesing wille of God; and soone he caccheth hem in hise sensuris, and aftir
smytith as he mai moost grevousli hirten hem. But he schal not make this in-
quisisioun aftir the multitude or greetnes of his wraththe, for God schal refreyne
and abregge the powere of his malice, so that he schal no more do than God
wole suffre him; that knowith the mesure of hise dedis to prove hise servauntis
bi the furneise of penaunce acceptable, and Anticrist with hise meyné, thus
hardid in malice, inexcusable.

The fourthe saught of Anticrist is persecucioun, as the prophet seith: *Insidiatur*
ut rapiat pauperem. That is to seie: Anticrist sittith and sottith in pees of this
world with riche men in her dennes, but the pore, meke, symple, and loweli, hem
he aspiseth and pursueth; hem he over-lepith and over-renneth, raveisching hem
bothe bodili and goostli. For God seid unto Job xl°: *Habet fudiciam quod influat*
Jordanis in os eius. Anticrist hath a triste and a trowing that Jordan mai flowe in

360
365
370
375
380
385

---

359 saught, assault. **361 mawmentrie,** idolatry. **362 wene,** suppose; **waried of,** cursed by.
368 outrage, excess. **370 blindfelt,** blindfolded; **wlatith,** loathes; **mysdispendid,** ill-spent.
374 herkneth, listens. **375 modir . . . aftir,** mother tongue, to lead their lives according to.
376 sensuris, censures. **377 hirten hem,** injure them. **378–79 refreyne and abregge,** curb
and restrict. **380 wole . . . knowith,** will allow him (to do); who (i.e., God) knows; **prove,**
test. **381 furneise,** furnace, crucible; **meyné,** followers. **382 hardid,** hardened. **384 sottith,**
becomes besotted. **386 aspiseth,** spies out; **over-lepith,** leaps upon. **387 goostli,** spiritually.
388 triste . . . trowing, trust and a belief.

to his mouthe, and therfor he makith his dwelling place in the herte of the see.

390 As God seith bi the prophete Ezechiel xxviii°: *In chathidera Dei sedi in corde maris cum sis homo et non deus.* Anticrist makith his boost and seith: "I have sitten in the chaier of God in the herte of the see, whane thou art but a man and not God but ever in wlank countré, fat and habunding of worldli goodis." There Anticrist with hise clerkis bilden her nestis; and if thou loke uttirli aboute thee,

395 thou schalt fynde hem among woodis and watris. As Seint Jon seith (Apoc. xvi°): *Vidi de ore draconis et de ore bestie et de ore pseudoprophete spiritus tres immundos exisse in modum ranarum.* "I saw," seith Seint Jon, "out of the mouthe of the dragoun (that is, the heed of Anticrist) and out of the mouthe of the beest (that is, the bodi of Anticrist), and out of the mouthe of the pseudo-prophete or

400 fals precheour (that is, the taile of Anticrist) thre unclene spiritis to have passid out in the maner of froggis. Froggis sitting in hoolis bi the watir-brink purchassen of the ground aboven hem and on either sighde hem; but that that is undirnethen hem thei wole not her thankis neither leesen it ne loosen it. So thise thre spiritis croking in coveitis, glotenie, and leccherie bitokenen Anticrist in hise

405 thre partise. For thei purchassen of lordis that ben aboven hem miche parte of her good with the tung of flatering and feyned ypocrisie; and of the comunes abouten hem, thei whighlen in to her handis miche parte of her catel. But that that thei han wonnen thei holden fast agen the autorité of bothe Goddis lawes; and with thise richessis thei nurischen wilde, sturdi, and laweles highnen that

410 pursuen hem that wollen ought seie agens this cursid synne. But God in this persecucioun thorugh his prophete counfortith hise servauntis and seith (Ps. xlv): *Deus noster refugium et virtus adiutor in tribulacionibus que invenerunt nos nimis propterea non timebimus dum turbabitur terra, et transferentur montes in cor maris.* That is to seie: "Oure God is refute and vertu; oure God is help in tribu-

415 laciouns, the whiche hath founden us passingli. Wherefore we schal not drede whilis that men lyvyng aftir this world schullen be troublid, and hillis schullen be born over in to the hert of the see"; that is, trewe men schal not be abaschid

---

393 wlank, flourishing; **habunding of,** abounding in. **394 bilden her nestis,** build their nests. **401–02 hoolis . . . purchassen of,** holes by the water's edge control. **402 either sighde hem,** either side of them. **403 her thankis . . . it,** voluntarily either destroy it or surrender it. **405 partise,** parts. **407 whighlen . . . catel,** wheedle for themselves much of their goods. **408 wonnen,** acquired. **409–10 thise richessis . . . synne,** these riches they abet unruly, bold, and lawless knaves who go after those who say anything against this cursed sin. **414 refute and vertu,** refuge and power. **414–15 tribulaciouns . . . passingli,** troubles, which have found us exceedingly. **416 whilis,** whilst. **417 born over,** transported; **abaschid,** dismayed.

though proud fleischeli men be confedrid to Anticrist and helpe him in his
persecucioun.

420   The fifte saught of Anticrist is execucioun; as the prophete seith: *rapere paup-
erem dum atrahit eum.* That is to seie: Whanne Anticrist seth that he availith not
in thise forseid turmentis, thanne he executith his malice agens Cristis chosen.
To this acordith Seint Jon in his Apoc. xiii°: *Faciat ut quicunque non adoraverint
ymagynem bestie occidantur.* That is to seie: The beest of the erthe schal gyve
425   power to the beest of the see, for in this tyme of execucioun the viciouse parte
of the laité, fro the highest unto the lowest, schullen consent to execute the
wickidnes of this viciouse parte of the clergie. Thanne schal this prophecie be
fulfillid (Ps. lxxviii): *Effuderunt sanguinem eorum tanquam aquam et non erat qui
sepeliret posuerunt morticina servorum tuorum escas volatilibus celi carnes sanc-*
430   *torum tuorum bestijs terre.* "Thei schal sheed out innocent blood, and ther schal
no man dore birie ther bodies, for thei schal cast ther fleische to foulis of the
heire and her careynes to beestis of the erthe." Thanne seith the prophete: *Cadet
cum dominatus fuerit pauperum.* That is to seie, as seynt Austin declarith, whanne
Anticrist weneth that he hath lordschip overe alle the servauntis of God, rering
435   upon hem diverse gynnes of turmentrie, thanne schal he falle to open reprofe for
evermore.

        The ful tyme of Anticrist durith thre yeer and an half, but that the Gospel
maketh remyssioun and elles schulde not alle fleische be saaf. This tyme was
figurid under Helie the prophete and kyng Acab, that wickid man. There tellith
440   the stori that reyn was stoppid (III. Reg. xvii°) thre yeere and sixe monethes; that
no drope fel on the erthe. Seint Jame berith witnes of this thing in his epistil
canonysid. The fleeyng of David from Kyng Saule markith this thing, who-so
takith hede (I. Reg. xviii°) and rede that book to the last ende. Also the bise-
cheing of Jerusalem maketh knowen this tyme, as Josophus tellith. Daniel taught
445   this noumbre also, in tyme and tymes and half a tyme (Dan. vii°) — and this is
thre yeere and an half, as Seint Jerom declarith in his book of seyntis. The
mighti Machabeies undir this noumbre made clene her temple; wherfore seint
Jon in his Apocalyps feele sithis rehersith this noumbre whanne he spekith of

---

418 confedrid to, allied with. **426 execute,** carry out. **430 sheed out,** shed. **431 dore birie,**
dare bury. **431–32 fleische . . . beestis,** flesh to birds of the air and their carcasses to
beasts. **434 lordschip,** dominion. **434–35 rering . . . gynnes,** mounting against them divers
instruments. **435 reprofe,** repudiation. **438 and elles,** or else; **saaf,** saved. **439 Helic . . .
Acab,** Elijah (Vulg. Elias); Ahab (Vulg. Achab). **440 reyn,** rain. **441 this thing,** see note.
443–44 bisecheing, siege. **444 Josophus,** Josephus. **447 Machabeics,** Machabees. **448
feele sithis,** many times.

Anticrist. And Crist kept this noumbre for tyme of his precheing, outake that
450 leest bi vertu of His passioun. Seint Jon Crisostum upon Mat. (Om. lvii°) seith
thus: *In tribus annis et sex mensibus hoc sacrificium christianorum tollendum est
ab antichristo fugientibus christianis per loca deserta non erit qui aut in ecclesiam
intret aut oblacionem offerat Deo.* That is to seie: "Bi thre yeere and sixe
monethis the sacrifice of Goddis preising that schulde be in mannes mouthe, the
455 sacrifice of rightwisenesse that schulde be in mannes werkis, and the sacrifice of
pees that schulde be in treting of Cristis bodi, schal be taken awey from all
feithful thorugh strong woodnes of Anticrist; thanne schalle alle trewe Cristen
flee the face of Anticrist, so that noon schullen mowen entre in to the Chirche
to do dewe servyce to her God." Aftir this, peple schal turne hem with al her
460 herte, bothe Cristen and Jewis, to the keping of Goddis lawe and doing of verry
penaunce; as Poul seith (Ro. xi°): *Cecitas ex parte contigit in Israel donec pleni-
tudo gencium intraret, et sic omnis Israel salvus fieret.* That is to seie: "Blyndnes
fel partie in Israel until the tyme that plenté of hethen men schulde entre in to
Cristendom, and thanne in the ende of the world (that is, after the distruccioun
465 of Anticrist) al Israel schulde be mad saaf." No man loke aftir Ennok and Hely
in persoone, for thanne he mai lightli be bigilid; but in spirit and in vertu now
thei ben comen to make mennes hertis redi aforn Cristis doome. To whom be
glori now and evere. Amen.

449 **outake,** except. 456 **pees,** peace. 457 **woodnes,** madness. 458 **schullen mowen,** shall
be able to. 459 **dewe,** due. 460 **verry,** true. 462–63 **Blyndnes . . . partie,** Blindness struck
partly. 465 **Ennok and Hely,** Enoch and Elijah.

Lo, He That Can Be Cristes Clerc

[Defend Us from All Lollardry]

(British Library MS Cotton Vespasian B.xvi fols. 2*v*–3*r*)

    Lo, he that can be Cristes clerc,

    And knowe the knottes of his Crede,   *(see note)*

    Now may se a wonder werke,   *see; wondrous*

    Of harde happes to take goud heede.   *misfortunes; good*

5   The dome of dethe is hevy drede   *judgment of death is a sober fear*

        For hym that wol not mercy crie.

        Than is my rede, for mucke ne mede,[1]

        That no man melle of Lollardrye.   *meddle in*

    I sey for meself, yut wist I never   *speak for myself, yet knew*

10   But now late what hit shuld be;   *recently; [Lollardy]*

    And by my trouth I have wel lever   *would rather*

    No more kyn than my a, b, c.   *know about it than*

        To lolle so hie in suyche degré,   *mumble (see note)*

        Hit is no perfit profecie;

15   Sauf seker sample to the and me   *A safe, sure example to you and me*

        To be war of Lollardie.

    The game is noght to lolle so hie,   *preach so pretentiously*

    Ther fete failen fondement;   *Where feet lack foundation*

    And yut is a moch folie   *yet; great folly*

20   For fals beleve to ben brent.

        Ther the Bibell is al myswent   *erroneous (gone astray)*

        To jangle of Job or Jeremye,   *talk about*

---

[1] *Then my advice is, neither for lucre nor reward*

That construen hit after her entent [1]
For lewde lust of Lollardie.   *ignorant wishes (desire)*

25   Hit is unkyndly for a knight,   *unnatural*
      That shuld a kynges castel kepe,   *protect*
      To bable the Bibel day and night   *spout*
      · In restyng tyme when he shuld slepe;
        And carefoly awey to crepe,   *sneakily*
30   For alle the chief of chivalrie: *Despite; authority*
        Wel aught hym to waile and wepe,   *Indeed he ought*
           That suyche lust hath in Lollardie.   *such craving*

      An old castel, and not repaired,
      With wast walles and wowes wide,   *ruined; walls*
35   The wages ben ful yvel wared   *spent*
      With suich a capitayn to abide,   *such*
        That rereth riot for to ride   *Who raised*
           Agayns the kynge and his clergie,
        With privé payne and pore pride.   *secret*
40   Ther is a poynt of Lollardie.   *That's what Lollardy leads to*

      For many a man withyn a while
      Shal aby his gult ful sore;   *pay for; sins*
      So fele gostes to begile   *many spirits*
      Hym aught to rue evermore.   *He should*
45   For his sorowe shal he never restore
        That he venemed with envye;   *What; poisoned*
        But ban the burthe that he was of bore,   *curse the day that he was born*
           Or ever had lust in Lollardie.   *Before he*

      Every shepe that shuld be fed in felde,   *sheep; field*
50   And kepte fro wolfes in her folde,   *protected from*
      Hem nedeth nether spere ne shulde, [2]
      Ne in no castel to be withholde.   *detained*
        For ther the pasture is ful colde

---

[1] *[They] interpret it according to their own lights*

[2] *To them neither spear nor shield are necessary*

	In somer seson when hit is drie;	
55	And namely when the soyle is solde,	*especially; polluted*
	For lewde lust of Lollardie.	

	An old castel draw al don,	*drags everything down*
	Hit is ful hard to rere hit newe,	
	With suyche a congregacion	*such*
60	That cast hem to be untrewe.	*requires them*
	When beggers mow nether bake ne brewe,	
	Ne have wherwith to borrow ne bie,	*buy*
	Than mot riot robbe or reve,	*steal*
	Under the colour of Lollardie.	*disguise*

65	That castel is not for a kynge	
	Ther the walles ben overthrowe;	*overthrown*
	And yut wel wors abidynge	*yet; is in store*
	Whan the captayn away is flowe,	
	And forsake spere and bowe,	*spear*
70	To crepe fro knighthode into clergie,	
	Ther is a bitter blast yblowe,	
	To be bawde of Lollardie.	*a pimp*

	I trowe ther be no knight alyve	
	That wold have don so open a shame,	
75	For that crafte to studi or strive:	
	Hit is no gentel mannes game.	*nobleman's*
	But if hym lust to have a name	
	Of pelour under ipocrasie,	*robber; hypocrisy*
	And that wer a foule defame	
80	To have suyche lose of Lollardie.	*loss because of*

	And, pardé, lolle thei never so longe,	*sermonize*
	Yut wol lawe make hem lowte.	*bow (humble them)*
	God wol not suffre hem be so stronge	
	To bryng her purpos so abowte,	
85	With *saunz faile* and *saunz doute*,	
	To rere riot and robberie.	

By reson thei shul not long route,   *wander about*
  While the taile is docked of Lollardie.

Of the hede hit is las charge,   *less serious*
90 Whan Grace wol not be his gide;   *its guide*
  Ne suffre hym for to lepe at large,   *Nor allow him to roam around at liberty*
  But hevely his hede to hide.
    Where shuld he other route or ride   *walk*
    Agayns the chief of chivalrie,
95   Not hardi in no place to abide,   *bold; remain*
    For alle the sekte of Lollardie.   *sect*

A God! what unkyndly gost   *unnatural spirit*
  Shuld greve that God grucched nought. [1]
  Thes Lollardes that lothen ymages most   *idols*
100 With mannes handes made and wrought,
    And pilgrimages to be sought,
    Thei seien hit is but mawmentrie.   *idolatry*
  He that this lose first up brought,   *evil report*
    Had gret lust in Lollardie.

105 Ho wor ful lewde that wolde byleve   *They would be utterly stupid who*
  In figure maad of stok or ston;   *wood*
  Yut fourme shuld we none repreve,   *Yet the idea of the image; censure*
  Nether of Marie ne of Jon,
    Petre, Poule, ne other none
110   Canonised by clergie;
    Than the seyntes everychon   *Nonetheless; everyone*
    Be litel holde to Lollardie.   *beholden*

And namly James among hem alle   *especially*
  For he twyes had turnement;   *torment*
115 Moch mischaunse mot him befalle   *Great misfortune might befall him*
  That last beheded hym in Kent,
    And alle that were of that assent.   *persuasion*
    To Crist of heven I clepe and crie,   *call*

---

[1] *Should lament for what God never complained about*

Send hem the same jugement,
120 And alle the sekte of Lollardie.

For that vengans agayns kynde   *nature*
Was a poynt of cowardyse;   *evidence*
And namly suych on to bete or bynde   *beat*
That might not stand, set, ne rise.
125 What dome wolde ye hym devyse   *judgment*
  By lawe of armes or gentrie,
But serve hym in the same wise,
  And alle the sekte of Lollardie.

When falsnes faileth frele folie,   *frail folly*
130 Pride wol preseyn sone amonge;   *press in*
Than willerdome with old envy   *willfulness*
Can none other way but wronge.
  For synne and shame with sorowe strong,
  So overset with avutrie,   *adultery*
135 That fals beleve is fayn to fonge   *glad to seize upon*
  The lewde lust of Lollardie.

And under colour of suiche lollynge,   *proclaiming*
To shape sodeyn surreccion   *sudden insurrection*
Agaynst oure liege lord kynge,
140 With fals ymaginacion.
  And for that corsed conclusion,
   By dome of knighthode and clergie,
  Now turneth to confusion
   The sory sekte of Lollardie.

145 For Holy Writ berith witnes,   *bears*
He that fals is to his kyng,
That shamful deth and hard distres
Shal be his dome at his endynge.
  Than double deth for suyche lollynge
150 Is hevy, when we shul hennes hye. *leave earth*
  Now, Lord, that madest of nought all thinge,
   Defende us all fro Lollardie.

Notes

Preste, Ne Monke, Ne Yit Chanoun

4   *As done.* The opening lines are ironic encomium. The author praises friars for the very qualities that are attacked in antifraternal literature: their alleged tepid devotion to religion (but their worship of money and food); their hypocrisy; and their avarice and self-indulgence. He drops the ironic pose in line 17 only to resume it sporadically (e.g., 21–22). RHR says: "The light tone of irony of the first six st. describing the contrast between precept and practice (compare lines 162–63) gives way to direct abuse, and the effectiveness of the poem is perhaps lessened by the sledgehammer blows against the friars' lechery and greed" (p. 334). In the manuscript lines 4 and 8 are offset and joined together with a line-rhyme indicator; and lines 9–10 and 11–12 of each stanza are executed as long lines. A large X is drawn over folio 63*v* and a partial X over fols. 64*r* and 64*v*.

18   *neres.* "Not kidneys, but the form with unhistoric -n used with *the* instead of *a*. Cf. No. 52, l. 38 (narse)" (RHR).

22   *puttes ham doun.* "So reduced by penance" (RHR citing Wr). The idea, ironically expressed, is that friars are weakened and humbled by their austerities.

24   *trusse of toun.* See *OED* s.v. *Truss*, signification 4: "To take oneself off, be off, go away, depart," citing *Piers Plowman* A 2.194 (as quoted in Kane's A-text): "[Liar] was nowhere welcome for his many talis, / Oueral yhuntid & yhote trusse" (lines 179–80 in Kane's numbering). Or, perhaps, with puns suggesting "when he shall bind up (truss) the paunch (the tun, i.e., his fat belly as he mounts the horse)."

27   *two and two.* Friars usually travelled in pairs, as does the friar of the *Summoner's Tale*, according to Christ's instructions to his disciples in Luke 10:1: "and he sent them two and two before his face into every city and place whither he himself was to come." The original intent of travelling in pairs was for purposes of institutional discipline, but in antifraternal literature the additional friar is depicted as an accomplice in crime.

97

35   *marcerye.* "Textiles and small wares" (RHR). The author represents the friars as vagabond peddlars, hawking their wares rather than ministering to the needy. Wandering clerics — *scholares vagi* or *vagantes* of the alleged *ordo vagorum* — were frequent objects of attack in statute and poetry. See Helen Waddell, *The Wandering Scholars*, 7th ed. (New York: Holt, 1934), Appendix E.

37   *purses, pynnes, and knyves.* Chaucer's pilgrim Friar carries "knyves / And pynnes, for to yeven faire wyves" (I 233–34). The coincidence of language is striking. In the present lyric friars make husbands anxious, since mendicants "haunt" (line 40) their doorsteps.

38   *wenches and wyves.* Although the chief satiric thrust of this lyric is antifraternal, much of it, starting with this line but especially lines 77–84, is also antifeminist: against philandering wives. The social picture that emerges in the poem is that idle housewives abet vagabond friars in committing fornication while "the gode man is fro hame." See also *Freers, Freers* 23–25; Scattergood's discussion of the fifteenth-century "indecent fable" *Lyarde* (Lincoln Cathedral MS 91), in *Politics*, p. 245; and the fifteenth-century macaronic carol entitled *The Friar and the Nun* ("Ther was a frier of order gray"; *Supplement* § 3443.5), where the "wench" is a nun, and which concludes:

> Thus the fryer lyke a pretty man,
> > *Inducas,*
> Ofte rokkyd the nunnys quoniam
> > *In temptacionibus.*

From *The Oxford Book of Late Medieval Verse and Prose*, ed. Douglas Gray (Oxford: Oxford University Press, 1988), p. 172.

40   *till.* Wr, Cook, and Krochalis and Peters read *tille* (and *wille* in line 44). I do not record further instances of final *e* readings.

45   *If.* So MS and RHR; Wr, Cook, and Krochalis and Peters ʒif.

51   *To reverce.* "To turn back or trim (a garment) with some other material" (RHR).

52   *ere.* Cook glosses "plow (?)." The meaning may be "They err by following that (fashion)."

53-54   *vaire . . . gryse . . . bugee . . . byse.* Different kinds of fur: respectively, grey, squirrel fur; another grey fur; lamb's skin (budge); a dark fur, perhaps brown. A fifteenth-century Franciscan rule states: "Also the bretherne as well as the susters shall haue no furres but of lame skynnes and purses of lether and gerdillis w^toute eny silke & none other, All other vayne araye of the worlde layde aparte after the holsome councell of the prince of the apostels." *The Thirde Order of Seynt Franceys for the Brethren and Susters of the Order of Penitentis*, in *A Fifteenth-Century Courtesy Book and Two Fifteenth-Century Franciscan Rules*, ed. R. W. Chambers and Walter W. Seton, EETS o.s. 148 (London: Oxford University Press, 1914), p. 49.

56   *bagges.* The friar of Chaucer's *Summoner's Tale* travels with another friar and a "sturdy harlot" who carries "a sak" for winnings (III 1754–55). The "bagges" of the present lyric and the "sak" of the *Summoner's Tale* symbolize the proverbial avarice of the mendicants. Chapter 6 of the Franciscan Rule begins: *Fratres nihil sibi approprient, nec domum, nec locum, nec aliquam rem* (Brothers shall own nothing of their own, not a house, not a place, nor anything else.)

61   *Trantes.* Trentals: thirty masses for the dead in purgatory, sung for a fee. RHR reads *many iape* for MS *many a iape* (Wr and Krochalis and Peters *many a jape*).

68   *Then.* So MS; Cook emends to *As.*

73   *Ich.* So MS and RHR; Wr, Cook, and Krochalis and Peters *Iche.*

76   *Nauther loude ne still.* "A poetic cliché" (RHR). But here it has the special meaning of neither open nor private confession; that is, one should never reveal secrets to friars, whether in casual conversation or in secret confessionals. In the MS *for drede of makyng wo* was lined out and the above line inserted.

81   *lymitour.* A fraternal limiter was a friar licensed to beg within a designated jurisdiction. Friar Huberd of Chaucer's General Prologue was a "lymytour" (I.209). Limiters were often singled out as the most dangerous clerics since they were alleged to prey upon the unwary.

83   *maystries.* The primary signification of this word is "sexual conquests" (masteries), but there is also a quibble on *maistrye*, domination or upper hand. RHR glosses *maystries* as "trick[s]." The word is ironic in this context since the friars were

criticized for wanting to be called "masters" (according to the antifraternal reading of Matt. 23:7). In the present lyric friars are all too "masterful." Krochalis and Peters read *hour* for *bour* (= error in transcription).

92   *two at ones*. The sexual capacities and potency of vagabond clerics were legendary. See Harry Bailly's admiration for the pilgrim Monk, an outrider.

96–97   In the manuscript there is a gap of three centimeters between lines 96 and 97.

108   *ordre*. So MS and RHR; Wr and Krochalis and Peters *order*.

110   *frere Carmes come of a k*. The best-known section of this poem concerns the cryptogram, which spells out the name KAIM, or Cain, if arranged in the poem's order: K (Carmelites), A (Austins or Augustinians), I (Jacobins or Dominicans), M (Minorites or Franciscans). The ideology harks back to the story of Cain's separation from the fellowship of Adam and to the lineage from Cain, the "bad seed" (see Gen. 4). Antifraternal writers connected Cain's exile and vagabond life in the land of Nod with the friars' mendicant existence. For other examples of Cain in antifraternal verse, see *PPC* 486 and 559; *JU* 70; *FDR* 105; Scattergood, *Politics*, p. 238 (on *Mum and the Sothsegger* lines 501–04). Margaret Aston has emphasized Wyclif's influence in the promulgation of CAIM as an explanation of fraternal origins. See "'Caim's Castles': Poverty, Politics, and Disendowment," *The Church, Politics and Patronage in the Fifteenth Century*, ed. Barrie Dobson (New York: St. Martin's Press, 1984), pp. 45–81.

120   *such throng*. For another vision of a plenitude of friars, see *The Summoner's Prologue* III.1691–98. The friars have a special "nest" in "the develes ers."

126   *shal*. So MS, Wr, and Krochalis and Peters. RHR *shall*.

127   *Templers*. RHR: "The Templars had been disbanded and their properties sequestered by Edward II, on orders of the Papacy, starting in 1309." The poem's author links the fraternal order of Knights Templar with the mendicant orders, suggesting they will experience a similar fate.

133–41   *dredful thing . . . annuels*. Alludes to the practice of hiring others to perform anniversary masses (*annuels*) for which one is responsible. See also *PPC* 414, and *FDR* 505 and note.

143   *possessioners* were beneficed or endowed clergy who were allowed to have possessions. Fraternal rules prohibited the owning of property. See Alford, *Glossary*, s.v. *Possessioner, Possession.*

145   *Tham felle.* Impersonal construction: it fell to them, it was their task.

151   *service.* "Particular ritual services paid for by the recipient, the offertories going to the administering priest." FitzRalph bitterly censured the incursion of friars into priestly offices such as this in *Defensio curatorum.*

152   *And that.* So MS (*&that*); Wr, RHR, Krochalis and Peters *That.* The ampersand is partly obscured by the rhyme-link line.

155   *frers shall annuel prestes bycome.* Friars could and did stand in for secular priests as *annuelers*, those who sang anniversary masses for a fee. Chaucer describes the pilgrim Parson, a parish priest, as "nat a mercenarye"; and he will not run off to London to seek a *chaunterie* or a job singing anniversary masses for the dead.

171   *Of twelve monethes.* Because the customary period of the novitiate lasted a year, and because he left the order before his novitiate was completed — before he was "professed" in the order (see 174) — the narrator claims not to be an apostate. The issue of apostasy was important in the bitter debates between secular and regular clergy. See *JU* 97–102, and Alford, *Glossary*, s.v. *Apostata.* The narrator of *Prestes, Ne Monkes* avers that he did not steal away from the order but that he went his way openly and "in syght of many men" (line 176).

Of Thes Frer Mynours

1   RHR thinks this poem alludes to Franciscan wall paintings rather than to "pageants and theatrical shows."

2   *hauteyn, that.* The manuscript features medial punctuation (caesura, indicated by a period stop) in many lines.

5   *With an O and an I.* The significance of these letters has not been adequately explained, but several suggestions have appeared (including the notion that the letters are a debased form of "Ho there! Hi!"). R. H. Robbins notes that there are fourteen other poems with a similar refrain (the so-called "O and I"

poems), but Robbins did not know about the secular "love" lyric with this refrain formula. See D. C. Cox, "A New O-and-I Lyric and Its Provenance," *Medium Ævum* 54 (1985), 33–46. See also the several poems — concerning Jesus's birth and Crucifixion — printed by Heuser in *Anglia,* 27 (1904), 285–89. There are Middle English lyrics with other refrains marked by letters, including "When adam delf & eue span, spir, if þou wil spede" (*Index* § 3921 printed in *RL XIV*, pp. 96–97), which features an "E & I" refrain. The presence of "E & I" refrains tends to call into question the "Ho there! Hi!" explanation of the "O and I" refrain. *Preste, Ne Monke, Ne Yit Chanoun* adduces the letters C, A, I, and M (anagram for Abel's brother Cain) to attack the friars. Richard L. Greene explains the "o" and "i" as "with two strokes of the pen," that is, "very quickly and surely," after line 100 of Dante's *Inferno* 24 ("A Middle English Love Poem and the 'O-and-I' Refrain Phrase," *Medium Ævum,* 30 [1961], 170–75); and Joseph E. Grennen argues that "o" and "i" are "grammatological" — referring to the eschatological phrase *in ictu oculi* — rather than "purely idiophonic" ("The 'O and I' Refrain in Middle English Poems: A Grammatology of Judgment Day," *Neophilologus* 71 [1987], 614–25).

6   *seyn.* So MS, RHR, and Grennen; Wr, Heuser, Cook, and Krochalis and Peters *seyn[t]*; Davies *Seint.*

8   *him.* The pronoun in this line and in the next stanza refers to contemporary depictions of Saint Francis, who was compared with Christ. The author attacks what he regards as the idolatry of Francis along with the rise of friars to power and prominence.

12   *thai.* So MS, Wr, Heuser, Krochalis and Peters (*þai*); Davies *thay.* Cook, RHR, and Grennen emend to *þat.*

14   *on him.* So MS, Cook, and Heuser; Wr *on hym.* RHR, Davies, Grennen *in him.* For an illustration of St. Francis receiving the stigmata while Christ hovers above on the Cross (and as if on wings), see the reproduction from the Beaufort Hours (British Library MS Royal 2.A XVIII fol. 9*v*, fifteenth century) in Edward A. Armstrong, *Saint Francis: Nature Mystic* (Berkeley: University of California Press, 1973), pl. 6.

17   *still.* So MS, RHR, Davies, and Grennen. Wr, Cook, Krochalis and Peters *stille*; Heuser *stylle.*

18   *Armachan.* Richard FitzRalph (d. 1360), archbishop of Armagh, who denounced mendicancy and fraternal poverty in *De pauperie Salvatoris* (On the Savior's poverty, 1356) and in *Defensio curatorum* (Defense of priests, 1357).

19   *grey goun.* Franciscan friars wore grey habits. See also line 32. As in line 8 the reference here is to Saint Francis himself.

26–27   *a frere blede . . . woundes wyde.* Saint Francis was said to have received the stigmata, and this was often represented in paintings and frescoes, notably by Giotto in the Bardi Chapel fresco, Santa Croce, Florence. (See also above, note to line 14.) RHR and Grennen read *bled* in line 26; Davies omits this stanza.

28   *the pope mot abyde.* A criticism often made against the friars was that they answered only to their Provincial and then the pope; hence they bypassed the ecclesiastical hierarchy observed by other religious institutions.

31–33   *A cart . . . be brent.* Condemned criminals stood in carts when they went off to hanging or burning. The poem's author applauds the vision of a greyfriar in a fiery cart since he wants nothing more than to see friars at the stake. These lines also allude — satirically and derisively — to the friars' claim to be the heirs of Elijah, whom God collected at the end of his life in a chariot of fire (2 Kings 2:11). Elijah, who appeared at the Transfiguration (Matt. 17), was expected to convert the Jews just before the Second Coming. For this other perspective on Elijah and the friars, see *The Lanterne of Light* 433 and note.

39   *Wyde . . . wroght.* For a satirical description of a spacious friary, see *PPC* lines 157–218.

Thou That Sellest the Worde of God

1   For the title *The Layman's Complaint*, see the Introduction. This poem and *Allas! What Schul We Freris Do* (which follows it in the manuscript) are executed in the same scribal hand.

2   *berfot.* An issue of the *usus pauper* (the controversy about the right observance of poverty) was whether friars should wear shoes, as in *PPC*: "Fraunces bad his bretheren barfote to wenden. / Nou han thei bucled schon for blenynge of her heles, / And hosen in harde weder, yhamled by the ancle" (lines 298–300). The

whole line "Be thou berfot, be thou schod" seems to echo the Invocation to Book 1 of Chaucer's *House of Fame*. Asking that his poem not be misinterpreted through malice, the narrator includes both mendicants and lay people: "dreme he barefot, dreme he shod" (line 98).

3   *nomore*. So MS and Utley; RHR and Person *nevere*.

4   *In principio*. John 1:1. The friars' pompous phrase, which they used as something like an incantation before entering homes, is turned against them. The lyric author warns mendicant simoniacs to stay away, according to the formula *In principio erat Verbum*. Chaucer says of Friar Huberd: "For thogh a wydwe hadde noght a sho, / So plesaunt was his '*In principio*,' / Yet wolde he have a ferthyng, er he wente" (I.253–55). See also *Jack Upland*: "ye winnen more with *In principio* than Crist and Hise apostlis and alle the seintes of hevene" (lines 194–95). In the MS this phrase is written *Inprincipio*. "The words are consistently joined in the MS. Possibly the poet intended to convey that they were uttered as jargon" (Utley, p. 143).

5   *all*. So Utley, RHR; Person *alle*.

14–15   *mennes howsis . . . berith wittnes*. Paul writes to Timothy that in the last days many will profess godliness but will be dedicated to worldly things: "For of these sort are they who creep into houses, and lead captive silly women laden with sins, who are led away with divers desires" (2 Tim. 3:6). Langland represents the friars through the figure of Sire *Penetrans Domos* (B passus 20); and Chaucer's Summoner portrays the friar of his tale as infiltrating hearth and home: "In every hous he gan to poure and prye" (III 1738).

14   *persen*. So Utley, RHR. Person *presen* (= error in transcription; rhymes with *reuerson*). "Utley sees in this line evidence of the poet's Lollard sympathies, for the Second Version of the Lollard Bible translates II Tim. 3:1–6 . . . 'Of these thei ben that persen housis'" (RHR).

16   *mydday develis*. Psalm 90:6: "[Thou shalt not be afraid] of the noonday devil." Utley comments: "One is reminded of the religious *incubi* of Chaucer's Wife of Bath's Tale III. 857–81. Professor La Piana has kindly called my attention to the liturgical 'a demonio meridiano libera nos Domine.' No doubt Chaucer and our poet refer to a current jest identifying the demon of the litany with the friars."

17   *for money lowlé ye lowte.* Antifraternal writers represent the friars as falsely humble and zealous in pursuit of money. Chaucer's Friar Huberd expects silver rather than weeping or prayers (I.231–32); and the friar of the *Summoner's Tale* is accompanied by a servant who carries "a sak" for the friar's winnings.

Allas, What Schul We Freris Do

1   *"The fryers Compleynt"* appears in the margin "in later hand" (Utley; see also Person). Utley and RHR entitle this poem *The Friar's Answer*, regarding it as a response to *Thou That Sellest* ("*The Layman's Complaint*").

2   *lewed men kun Holy Writ.* Two charges against Lollards, reflected in this poem, were that they made Scripture available to laymen and women and that they translated the Bible into English (see lines 9–10). A late fourteenth-century defense of translating the Bible into English, perhaps by John Purvey, begins with mention of friars: "Heere the freris with ther fautours [abettors] seyn that it is heresye to write thus Goddis lawe in English and make it knowun to lewid men" (taken from *Middle English Literature*, ed. Charles W. Dunn and Edward T. Byrnes [New York: Harcourt, 1973], p. 488). The whole defense was inserted into a translation into English of Wyclif's complaint against friars from *De Officio Pastorali*, but there is no equivalent passage in Wyclif's Latin. The chronicler Henry Knighton accused Wyclif of translating "the Gospel from Latin into English so that it was more open to laymen and ignorant people, including 'women who know how to read,' whereas previously it had been the preserve of well-read clerks of good understanding." See Margaret Aston, *Lollards and Reformers* (London: Hambledon Press, 1984), p. 206. Archbishop Arundel enjoined unauthorized Bible translations in 1409.

11   *For.* MS, RHR, Person *ffor*; Utley *Ffor*. So also at line 18.

12   *neyther fleche ne fishe.* This phrase has the look of a (later) proverb, as Heywood's "She is nother fishe nor fleshe, nor good red hearyng [herring]" or Shakespeare's "Why? she's neither fish nor fleshe; a man knows not where to have her" (*1 Henry VI* III.iii). As quoted in *The Oxford Dictionary of English Proverbs*, comp. William George Smith, s.v. *Fish nor flesh (nor good red herring), neither.* The narrator alleges that Lollards and other lay clerics produce a translation that is neither proper Latin nor good vernacular, with the further

implication that they should abstain altogether from writing the Gospel (as one would fast in Lent).

14   *In principio.* John 1:1: "In the beginning [was the Word]." See *Thou That Sellest*, line 4 and note. In the MS *for to* appears as *forto* and *In principio* as *inprincipio.*

15   *poppe.* So MS, RHR, Person. "Although not so rec. *O.E.D.*, poppe here seems to mean any priest . . . . Utley reads *coppe*" (RHR).

16   *worche and win.* Friars received frequent criticism for begging rather than working. See especially *UR* 330–53 and note.

17   *saie.* Utley's emendation of MS *sae* (= the reading of RHR and Person).

20   *Seint Polle did soo.* Acts 18:3: "And because [Paul] was of the same trade, he remained with them, and wrought; (now they were tentmakers by trade)."

23   *russet, blakk, or white.* That is, a Franciscan (grey), Dominican (black), or Carmelite (white) gown.

24   *oure werynge clothes.* Clothes we wear. MS, RHR, Person: *oure*; Utley *ouper.*

25   *I, not for me.* The speaker defends himself by saying something like "Hey, I don't beg for myself," or perhaps "Eh! not as far as I'm concerned!" Utley inserts "[aske]" before "not for me."

32   *hey.* So RHR; Person *heyfast.* Utley reads *y* as *þ* and emends to *heþ[er]*, commenting: "The MS *heþ* has probably been copied from an original *heþer* with the *er* curl ignored. Some may prefer to read *hey* "hie, hasten" or even "high"; but our scribe is consistent in preserving the distinction between *þ* and *y* by dotting his *y*'s, and there is no dot over the last letter in this word." In fact, the scribe fails to dot the *y* of *werynge* (line 24), *saye* (line 25), *disseytis* (line 29), *abyde* (line 31), *myche gyle* (line 34), *fynde* (line 35).

Freers, Freers, Wo Ye Be

1   *Freers.* MS *ffreers.* Here and elsewhere in this poem I substitute *F* for initial *ff.* The manuscript lines are written as long lines, with the Latin ending each line.

In these notes I do not record Wr's normalizations of the text in *PPS*, which include *a* for *o* in *folnes* and *floure*, final *e* on some words, *doughtour* for *doughtor*, etc. Wr reprints his *PPS* version in *Reliquiae Antiquae*.

5   *Whan seyntes.* There is a direct lineal descent from the fallen angels (here called *seyntes*) to the satanic friars.

7   *synnus seven.* The author alleges that the fallen angels transmitted the seven deadly sins (pride, envy, anger, sloth, avarice, gluttony, lust) directly to the friars. Wr, *PPS*, reads *the* for *tho* (MS *þo*).

9   *ffloure.* Wr, *PPS*, spells *fflauré*.

10   *quem.* Wr, *RA* and *PPS*, reads *quae*.

18   *fruges.* A reference to the first fruits of Romans 8:23 ("And not only it, but ourselves also, who have the first fruits of the Spirit"). See also *PPC* lines 728–29: "Right so fareth freres with folke opon erthe; / They freten up the furste-froyt and falsliche lybbeth."

23–25   *Odur thi wyff . . . or thi sun.* In antifraternal literature friars were alleged to be lecherous and untrustworthy, especially when they could enter homes. For a parallel see *Preste, Ne Monke, Ne Yit Chanoun,* lines 73–96.

29   *Jacke and Gylle.* Proverbial for every male and female. See Whiting, *Proverbs,* J2 and J7.

The Wycliffite Bible: From the Prologue

1–2   *iiij. undirstondingis . . . anagogik.* The familiar medieval four-fold interpretation of Scripture developed by exegetical thinkers such as Augustine, Bede, and Rabanus Maurus. The "literal," also called the "historical," interpretation concerns the historical events (what happened, what the Bible says); the other three senses are allegorical or "goostli," involving "deeper meanings" and including the "allegorical" or "typological" understanding (people, places, and things of the Old Testament prefigure Christ and the New Testament); the "moral" understanding (pertaining to good and evil, virtues and vices); and "anagogical" (which concerns the state of souls after death and God's ultimate dispensation). *The True Copye of a Prolog* (R. Crowley, 1550) presents the "understandings" in a slightly different order: "Literal, Moral, Aligorike, & Anagogike." Henceforth I will record only very significant variants in *The True Copye* (TC), whose orthography reflects sixteenth-century rather than fifteenth-century conventions.

4   *Pistle to Vincent.* Vincentius, once a student with Augustine in Carthage, was in the early fifth century the leader of a Donatist sect, the sect of Rogatus, and was stationed at Cartennae (Ténès) in northwest Africa. He wrote to Augustine on the subject of coercion, accusing him of straying too far into polemics and controversies and away from disciplined study. Augustine replied to Vincentius and talked about scriptural interpretation. See Augustine's *Epistle* 93.

21   *Agar.* The barren Sarah gave Hagar, her Egyptian slave, to her husband Abraham; Abraham conceived Ishmael by Hagar (Gen. 16). Hagar allegorically symbolizes the Old Testament, which must yield place to the New (= Sarah, matriarch of the chosen people). For the interpretation of Sarah, see the present text lines 18–20 (citing Galatians 4). See especially verses 21–31. For a standard interpretation of Sarah and Hagar, see Augustine, *De Civitate Dei* 15.34.

26   *Of Cristen Teching. De Doctrina Christiana* (*On Christian Doctrine*). See 3.5.

29   *the lettre sleeth.* 2 Cor. 3:6; see also Augustine's discussion in *De doctrina Christiana* 3.5.

34–35 *onesté of vertues.* TC *honestie and vertuis.*

35–37 *Onestee of vertues . . . no but charité.* TC *Honesti of vertuis perteinith to the loue of God and our neyghbours. Truth of feyth perteynith to knowe God and thy neighboure. Holy scripture cōmaūdith nothyng but charitie.*

38–39 *enfoormeth the vertues . . . condiscouns of men.* TC *enformith the good vertus either þe good conditiōs of men.*

43   *Jeremye.* Jer. 1:10.

54   *and forbeedith wickidnesse.* TC *And if it forbyd wickidnes.*

57–58 *If ye eten not . . . lijf in you.* John 6:54.

62–63   *If thin enemy . . . to hym.* Proverbs 25:21; Rom. 12:20.

63–64   *Thou schalt gadere . . . heed.* Proverbs 25:22: "For thou shalt heap hot coals upon his head, and the Lord will reward thee"; Romans 12:20: "For, doing this [feeding the enemy], thou shalt heap coals of fire upon his head." In the B text of *Piers Plowman*, Patience counsels love and understanding of one's enemies: "Cast coles on his heed of alle kynde speche; / Both with werk and with word fonde his loue to wynne" (13:144-45).

67   *enemy of a man.* TC *enemie of that man.*

68–70   *Also the same word . . . singnefieth the devyl.* Interpretation *in bono* (in a good sense), signifying Christ, and *in malo* (in an evil sense), signifying the devil. The lion, king of beasts and destroyer, is the classic example. See *De doctrina Christiana* 3.25.

71–72   *Be ye war . . . ypocrisie.* Matt. 16:6.

73   *The rewme . . . sour dough.* Matt. 13:33.

88   *The fulnesse of lawe is charité.* See 1 Cor. 13:13.

89–91   *The ende of lawe . . . feith not feyned.* 1 Tim. 1:5.

91–93   *Thou schalt love . . . lawe and prophetis.* See Matt. 22:37–40.

97   *moldewerpis.* Moles (*Talpa europaea*), but in this context of flesh versus spirit the word reveals its etymology: *molde* (mould, ground, earth) + *warp* (from OE *weorpan*, throw, cast). In the Middle Ages the mole was proverbial for blindness, avariciousness, and heresy. See Beryl Rowland, *Animals with Human Faces: A Guide to Animal Symbolism* (Knoxville: University of Tennessee Press, 1973), p. 126.

111–12   *trewe men.* This phrase could mean Lollards, men and women of the true faith, as opposed to "prelates," or false ecclesiastics. Compare "symple men" at line 149 and the phrase "preche treuly and freely" at line 153. See *Addresses of the Commons* line 15 and note, and *Chaucer's Plowman* line 3 and note.

114 *fourme.* A *forme* was "A fixed or prescribed course of study." See *MED* s.v. *forme* 9. First *MED* citation = *Wycliffite Bible.*

115-17 *This wolde be ix. yeer either ten . . . aftir his gramer.* The courses of study at medieval Oxford and Cambridge were exceedingly rigorous. Speaking of John Wyclif's career, K. B. McFarlane has written: "An undergraduate who had started at fifteen would be at least thirty-three before he had completed his training — unless, like some well-born lawyers, he succeeded in obtaining a dispensation to telescope parts of the course. Wycliffe was forty or over, having allowed his studies to be interrupted by administrative and other duties; although already a bachelor of arts in 1356, he did not take his D.D. [Doctor of Divinity degree] apparently until 1372. Not a few others were similarly long" (*John Wycliffe and the Beginnings of English Nonconformity* [New York: Macmillan, 1953], p. 21). For a helpful account of courses at Paris and Oxford, see Gordon Leff, *Paris and Oxford Universities in the Thirteenth and Fourteenth Centuries: An Institutional and Intellectual History* (New York: Wiley, 1968), and William J. Courtenay, *Schools and Scholars in Fourteenth-Century England* (Princeton: Princeton University Press, 1987).

120 *Amos . . . Damask.* See Amos 1:3. Amos begins with a denunciation of Damascus but gets around to censuring Judah and even Israel. The Prologue author's point seems to be that Oxford University is implicated in larger illicit social trends, especially in debarring "trewe men" from the study of Scripture.

124 *birling.* Pouring out (for drinking); from OE *byrelian,* from *byrle, byrele,* butler, cup-bearer.

131 *arsistris. Arcisters* or *arceters* were masters of arts who had progressed to the study of philosophy. See *MED* s.v. *arcister.*

178 *Lyre.* Nicholas of Lyra (c. 1270–c. 1349), also spelled *Lire* by the Prologue author: Franciscan exegete, who wrote the highly influential *Postilla litteralis super totam Bibliam,* a running commentary on the Old and New Testaments of the Bible. The authors of *The Wycliffite Bible* and of its General Prologue frequently advert to Lyra's glosses (along with those of the *Glossa ordinaria*) because Lyra's "commentaries often note differences between Hebrew readings in the Old Testament and readings in the Vulgate Latin" (Hudson, *The Premature Reformation,* p. 244). See also below, lines 221–25.

216–18 *as Jerom seith . . . knowe it.* Jerome's commentary on Psalm 87:6 (Hudson, *Selections from English Wycliffite Writings*, p. 174).

226 *we ben . . . stonis.* "For the identification of the stones allegorically as the gentiles, see Bede's comment on Luke 19.40, PL. 92.570" (Hudson, *Selections*, p. 174).

229–30 *lewide men . . . foundement.* Matt. 21:42–44; Acts 4:10–11. The stone = Christ has a venerable history in exegesis, notably in commentary on Nebuchadnezzar's dream of the great image, which is destroyed by the stone cut out of the mountain without hands (Daniel 2:44–45). The Smiting Stone was interpreted as Christ, whose kingdom will on the last day smash world empires.

236 *this symple creature.* A plain man. The author sometimes, as here, refers to himself in the third person. He opposes himself to pretentious or arrogant clerics, and he seems to ally himself with "trewe men" or perhaps even "pore prestis." Wyclif sometimes referred to himself as *"quidam fidelis,"* a faithful man; and Margery Kempe would call herself "this creature." See A. Hudson, "A Lollard Sect Vocabulary?" in *Lollards and Their Books*, pp. 165–80. This pose of the plain man should be compared with the persona of Jack Upland (in *JU* and *UR*) or with Piers Plowman.

237 *manie elde Biblis.* The author might refer to the Vulgate, with Jerome's commentary, and perhaps with interlinear glosses by others; the Vulgate with the ordinary gloss (*Glossa Ordinaria*); certain translations of Scripture into Old English (including the Gospels); Peter Comestor's *Historia Scholastica* (a retelling of the Bible with Comestor's comments); Richard Rolle's translation of the Psalms into English; and perhaps other translations of Scripture which have not survived. See Deanesly, *The Lollard Bible*, chap. 5 and below lines 335–40.

251 *ablatif . . . absolute.* Ablative is the fifth case in Latin, a case with adverbial function indicative of place (*where, whence, wherewith*) or *in what measure, manner* or *quality*. Ablative absolute is ablative combined with a participle to modify as a self-contained phrase the verbal predicate of a sentence. It may be translated into English by the so-called nominative absolute, often by shifting from passive to active voice, as the author of the prologue explains.

257 *same tens.* TC *same tyme.*

270   *I resolve it openli. Thus, where this reesoun.* TC punctuates: *I resolue openly thus. Where thys reason.*

284-85 *I dide . . . the Sauter.* There were two versions of the Latin Psalms, *iuxta Hebraicum* (according to the Hebrew) and *iuxta LXX* (according to the Septuagint: see below, note to line 287). The Hebrew version was in regular use until the time of Alcuin, who substituted the Latin translation of the LXX version; after Alcuin, the *iuxta LXX* or "Gallican" version was standard in medieval Vulgates. The GP authors knew and followed the Hebrew version, with Jerome's comments.

288-90 *in ful fewe . . . gloside.* "The writer is referring to the discrepancy between the wording of scriptural passages quoted in Jerome's extensive biblical commentaries (PL 23-26), and that of extant medieval bibles, a discrepancy which would reveal the hazards of textual transmission. As the writer acutely observes, the commentaries, which sometimes involve grammatical analysis, will often provide a check on the accuracy of the Vulgate itself" (Hudson, *Selections*, p. 176).

305-06 *replicacioun . . . colourable.* See *MED* s.v. *replicacioun* ("Answering, an answer, a verbal response, rejoinder; an argument . . ., etc.") and *colourable* (1. "Of arguments, superficially attractive, persuasive, plausible"; 2. "Concealing the real purpose, intended to conceal or deceive").

307-08 *LXX. translatouris.* The translators of the Greek Septuagint Bible, third century B.C., which by tradition was said to have been translated by seventy or seventy-two people in seventy-two days (hence, under divine inspiration).

332   *foure greete doctouris.* St. Ambrose of Milan (d. 397), who wrote significant allegorical commentaries on Scripture and who taught St. Augustine; St. Augustine of Hippo (354–430), the great theologian and author of *Confessions*, *De Trinitate*, *De Doctrina Christiana*, *The City of God*, and influential commentaries on Scripture; St. Jerome (d. 420), who translated the Bible into Latin (the Vulgate version); and St. Gregory the Great (d. 604), who wrote *Moralia in Job* and other major works of exegesis.

360-61 *King Alvred . . . Oxenford.* A fourteenth-century legend claimed that King Alfred of Wessex founded University College, Oxford. Forged documents supported this allegation. See, for example, Stow's *Annales* (London: T. Adams, 1615), p.

956; C. F. Bühler, "A Lollard Tract," *Medium Ævum* 7 (1938), lines 146–47 (p. 174), citing Higden's *Polychronicon* 6.1.

361–62   *Sauter into Saxon.* King Alfred translated the first fifty psalms into English prose — the first third of the *Paris Psalter*, a manuscript of the mid-eleventh century. See Janet Bately, "Lexical Evidence for the Authorship of the Prose Psalms in the Paris Psalter," *Anglo-Saxon England* 10 (1982), 69–95.

362   *Beemers.* "Czech versions [of Scripture] did exist before the Hussite period" (Hudson, *Selections*, p. 176).

The Lanterne of Light

3   *daies of greet tribulacioun.* A frequent refrain in Wycliffite and anticlerical literature, but here there may be topical specificity as well, as suggested in lines 4–5 ("losse of worldli goodis and bodili peyne"). In 1409 Archbishop Thomas Arundel promulgated his Constitutions, which prohibited unlicensed preaching in English (statutes aimed at the Lollards). In a section of the *Lanterne* (*LL*) not printed in this volume, the author complains:

> Agen this comaundement ["Thou shalt not kill"], the fende in his membris settith wacche and bisie spie where that he may fynde ony peple that wole rede, privé or apert, Goddis lawe in Englische, that is oure modir tunge. Anoon he schal be sumned to come aforne his juggis to answere what is seide to him, and bring his book with him; and eithir he must forsake his book and reding of Englische and algatis he schal forswere to speke of Holi Writ. (*LL*, ed. Swinburn, p. 100 [spelling normalized, punctuation altered])

6–8   *Quoniam . . . charité of many.* Matt. 24:12; in the Wycliffite translation: "And for wickidness schal be plenteous, the charite of manye schal wexe cold." A *locus classicus* for medieval discussions of the world grown old and the end of the world.

17   *Inimicus . . . zizania.* Perhaps a conflation of Matt. 13:25 ("Inimicus eius super-seminavit zizania") with 28 ("Inimicus homo hoc fecit"). See Swinburn's Appendix to the EETS edition of *LL*, p. 141.

69–70   *Anticrist is every man . . . agen Crist.* The standard definition of "Antichrist in general" as opposed to the specific individual, the Antichrist, who will lead the forces of evil in the world's latemost days. On these definitions of Antichrist, see Richard K. Emmerson, *Antichrist in the Middle Ages* (Seattle: University of Washington Press, 1981), pp. 62–73.

71   *Forsothe, now ben many anticristis.* 1 John 2:18, the *locus classicus* for medieval discussions of sin, Antichrist, and contemporary conditions. The passage was useful to those who would denounce rival Christian organizations, such as friars, or sects, such as the Lollards. The antichrists of 1 John were regularly explained as the hypocrites of Matt. 23 and the false prophets of Matt. 24. See Emmerson, *Antichrist*, p. 63.

75   *Forsothe the chaff . . . quenchid.* Matt. 3:12.

79–81   *Every proud soule . . . fire.* Isaiah 9:5.

82   In margin: *Nota bene.*

127–28   *Seint Bernard . . . Lincoln.* St. Bernard of Clairvaux (1090–1153) and Robert Grosseteste, bishop of Lincoln (c. 1168–1253). There is a problem in these references since Bernard anachronistically quotes Grosseteste. Ironically, Grosseteste served as regent of the Franciscan school at Oxford (1229–35) and thus fostered the friars whom the author of *LL* deplores as one of the three "parties" of Antichrist. Grosseteste appears often in Lollard tracts because he opposed the power of the Roman church. Of him Ranulph Higden says, in John Trevisa's translation: "He sente to þe ferþe pope Innocencius a pistel scharp inow þat bygynneþ in þis manere: 'Oure lord Jesus Crist.' [He] sente þat pistel for þe pope greved þe chirches of Engelond wiþ taxes and wiþ paimentis undewe and uncustemable" (*Polychronicon* 7.37; Rolls Series 41 8:241).

193   *eten a flighe.* "Evidently a taunt brought against the Lollards by their enemies. They are looked upon as followers of Beelzebub, the god of flies, through whose agency they obtain their knowledge of God's law. To have 'eten a fliȝe' is probably equivalent to being possessed by a devil. 'Fly' is used later by B. Jonson for a 'familiar demon' (1610)" (Swinburn).

208   *Heldad and Medad.* Numbers 11:26–29.

227   *Maister of Sentence.* Peter Lombard, author of *Sentences* (1152), an authoritative and systematic exposition of theology and doctrine which became standard in the schools.

231   *discipulis* in the margin; also, *est forma presbiterorum* not underlined in the manuscript.

245   *A stroumpetis forhed.* In margin: *no*[ta].

247   *restiterunt.* So the MS; Swinburn *resistiterunt.* In Wordsworth and White's edition of the New Testament Vulgate, the passage reads: "Quemadmodum autem Iamnes et Mambres restiterunt Mosi, ita et hi resistunt ueritati" (*Novum Testamentum Latine secundum editionem Sanctii Hieronymi* [Oxford: Clarendon, 1920]). In the Stuttgart Vulgate the passage reads: "quemadmodum autem Iannes et Mambres restiterunt Mosi ita et hii resistunt veritati" (*Biblia Sacra iuxta Vulgatam versionem,* ed. R. Weber [Stuttgart: Württembergische Bibelanstalt, 1969], vol. 2).

247–49 *Right as Jambres and Mambres . . . truthe.* 2 Tim. 3:8. Iamnes and Mambres (or Jannes and Jambres) were rabbinical names for Pharoah's magicians who opposed Moses and performed magic tricks (Exod. 7). William of St. Amour glossed these Old Testament magicians as types of the friars (Szittya, *The Antifraternal Tradition in Medieval Literature,* p. 218). See the antifraternal *Upland's Rejoinder,* lines 211–12: "Yee, Jamnes and Mambres japid not so the kyng, / As thou with thi cursid secte the kyng and the puple."

260   *whanne . . . youre-silf.* For a similar argument see *UR,* lines 257–63.

353   *thise newe constituciouns.* A reference to new statutes of 1409 formulated by Thomas Arundel, Archbishop of Canterbury (chief architect of *De haeretico comburendo* of 1401).

388–89 *Anticrist . . . mouthe.* Job 40:18: "and he [Behemoth, which the Wycliffite author interprets as Antichrist] trusteth that the Jordan may run into his mouth."

390   *chathidera.* So MS; Swinburn emends to *cathedra.*

420–21 *rapere . . . eum.* Psalm 10 [Hebrew]:9: "to catch the poor, whilst he draweth him to him."

423–24   *Faciat . . . occidantur.* Apoc. 13:15: " . . . and should cause, that whosoever will not adore the image of the beast, should be slain."

441   *this thing.* That is, the three and a half year reign of Antichrist, figured in other scriptural occurrences.

444   *Josophus.* Flavius Josephus (A.D. 37?–100?), author of *Antiquities of the Jews* and *Wars of the Jews.*

465   *Ennok and Hely.* A scriptural tradition (based on Malachi 4:5) and a persistent medieval tradition was that Enoch and Elijah would return to convert the Jews just before "the great and dreadful day of the Lord." Both were considered godly men who, instead of dying, were taken up by God. See Emmerson, *Antichrist,* pp. 95–101.

Lo, He That Can Be Cristes Clerc

2   *knottes of his Crede.* Students learned the Apostles' Creed by memorizing words on knots on rosary beads. For the Apostles' Creed, see *Piers the Plowman's Creed.*

11   *trouth.* So RHR; Wr *trouthe.* I make no attempt here to record Wr's further interpretation of flourishes as final *e*'s.

13   *lolle.* To speak in a mumble or in muffled tones; or to preach like a Lollard. RHR observes that in Latin poems the Lollards are compared with weeds (*lolium*). The Lollards were also known as "Lolleres," as in Chaucer's Man of Law's Epilogue: "'I smelle a Lollere in the wynd,' quod he" (II 1173). The word *lollard* may derive from the Dutch *lollaert* ("mumbler") and was perhaps deliberately confused with the English word *lollere* ("a lazy vagabond, fraudulent beggar" [*MED* s.v. *lollere*]), though Chaucer's line seems to have scatalogical connotations.

20   *For fals . . . brent.* A reference to the statute of 1401 (*De haeretico comburendo*) that authorized the burning of heretics for their beliefs.

24   *lewede lust.* Also lines 56 and 136. "Ignorant wishes" is perhaps too mild a gloss. "Stupid lechery" or "lecherous craving" might be more appropriate.

25–30   The implication is that Lollard knights slip away at night for secret Bible meetings when they should be sleeping or keeping military watch over the castle.

33   *old castel.* A reference to Sir John Oldcastle, Lord Cobham, with whom the Lollard insurrection of 1414 was chiefly associated.

57   *don.* So RHR; MS print unclear in this line. Wr, *PPS, doun.*

64   *Under.* Wr *Unde[r]*; RHR *Under*; MS *Vnde.*

85   *saunz faile . . . saunz doute.* Pretentious French phrases meaning, respectively, "without fail" and "without doubt."

105   *He wor.* So MS. Wr *He wer*; RHR *Ho wor.*

106   *maad.* So RHR; Wr *mad.* MS print unclear at this point.

116   *That last . . . Kent.* The Lollards went out of their way to critique the worship of images as blasphemous and idolatrous. They called these icons "dead images," as in the General Prologue to the Lollard Bible (probably of 1396):

> Now men kneel, and pray, and offer fast to dead images, that have neither hunger nor cold; and despise, beat, and slay Christian men, made to the image and likeness of the Holy Trinity. What honour of God is this to kneel and offer to an image, made of sinful man's hands, and to despise and rob the image made of God's hands, that is, a Christian man, or a Christian woman? When men give not alms to poor needy men, but to dead images, or rich clerks, they rob poor men of their due portion, and needful sustenance assigned to them of God himself; and when such offerings to dead images rob poor men, they rob Jesus Christ.

As quoted in Margaret Aston, *Lollards and Reformers*, pp. 159–60. The specific reference here to a statue of St. James beheaded again and again in Kent has not been identified. In another place Aston writes, of image-worship: "It seems fairly safe to regard this as the commonest facet of one of the commonest (if not *the* commonest) of Lollard beliefs, and the view that it was idolatry to serve saints' images with pilgrimage or other acts of devotion secured wide support." See *England's Iconoclasts*, vol. 1: *Laws Against Images* (Oxford: Clarendon, 1988), p. 105.

Thomas Hoccleve also was concerned that Lollard types should believe that ordinary Christians would worship the images themselves rather than Christ. See Scattergood, *Politics*, p. 255.

Literature of Richard II's Reign and the Peasants' Revolt

Introduction

The Peasants' Revolt of June and July 1381 was a milestone of medieval English politics and of Richard II's young reign. Polemical chroniclers — Thomas Walsingham, monk of St. Albans (*Historia Anglicana, Chronicon Angliae*); Henry Knighton, Augustinian canon of St. Mary-of-the-Meadows, Leicester (*Chronicon*); the Benedictine author of *Anonimalle Chronicle* (from St. Mary's, York); a chronicler of Westminster (*Chronicon Westmonasteriense*); and Sir Jean Froissart in his *Chronicles* — recount the stages of the rebellion in detail; and they represent the events as dangerously revolutionary and damaging to the body politic. These chroniclers are notoriously unreliable as reporters of fact, especially as regards the alleged "peasants" of the rising; and they often present contradictory, partisan testimony concerning the events.[1] Still, the major outlines of the revolt are clear. We know and can infer more about the 1381 rising than about similar incidents in France, in Italy, or in England later on. Some of the more important incidents in the revolt — such as Richard's confrontation with the rebels at Mile End and the death of Wat Tyler — were recorded in well-executed fifteenth-century illustrations.

The rallying-point for the rebellion was the poll tax of 1380–81, a tax that, as an anonymous poet phrased it, "has tenet [harmed] us alle." Worse, this was the third such poll tax, and it was enforced by much-hated commissions of inquiry, which investigated whether all persons were complying with the tax. The unpopular levy of 1377 was followed by the graduated tax of 1379, the latter a failure that resulted in the replacement of the Chancellor, Richard Scrope. In 1380, Parliament allowed the king, through his new Chancellor, Simon Sudbury, Archbishop of Canterbury, to assess a tax of three groats (one shilling) on every man and woman over the age of fifteen. The early 1380s were generally a time of economic hardship, when a miller "hath ygrounde smal, smal, smal" (*Ball's Letter*); and many elements of society, especially the artisan class, bitterly resented the regressive poll tax, which ruthless collectors

---

[1] On these issues, see most recently Paul Strohm, *Hochon's Arrow* (Princeton: Princeton University Press, 1992), pp. 33–56.

extracted and then — so it was alleged — diverted to their own coffers: "The kyng therof had smalle."

Grievances came to a head first in Essex, where the commons attacked tax commissioners, and then in Kent. Events quickly moved beyond tax grievances to include looting, arson, and murder. The leader in Kent was Wat (or Water or Walter) Tyler, who was not a peasant; in fact, many of the commons who took part in the rising were financially comfortable but had grievances against local officials and scores to settle. The commons were urged on by three clerics: Jack Straw, about whom little is known; John Wrawe, a former vicar who led the peasants of Essex; and John Ball, a lapsed priest whom Sudbury had imprisoned three times. On 7 June Tyler and his followers took possession of Canterbury, opened Maidstone prison, and marched toward London, attracting followers along the way. The Essex peasants also converged on London; and on Thursday, 13 June, the rebels gained entrance into the city, streaming through Aldgate (where Chaucer lived in his apartments). They burned John of Gaunt's London palace, the Savoy, along with Fleet Prison and the Hospital of St. John. King Richard, who was only fourteen, rode to Mile End on Friday, 14 June, to hear the rebels' demands, which included provisions for free labor contracts (doubtless a reference to the Statute of Laborers) and the right to rent land at fourpence an acre. Richard promised them justice, with the result that many Essex commons returned home; but other peasants broke into the Tower and executed, among others, Archbishop Sudbury and Robert Hales, Royal Treasurer and Prior of the Hospital of St. John's, who provided something like a flashpoint for the mob's fury. At Smithfield on Saturday Tyler presented the king a list of six points, two of which were "That there should be no seignory except that of the King" and "That there should be no serf in England."[2] These points resemble the doctrines said to have been preached by the renegade priest John Ball, who urged on the peasants with the notion that men and women were created equal, in Eden, according to the formula "When Adam dug and Eve span, / who was then a noble man?" During this conference with the king and after heated words with William Walworth, mayor of London, Tyler was killed by the king's valet.

The rising centered in London was the best-known of 1381; but similar, related revolts occurred at St. Albans (beginning 14 June), Bury St. Edmunds (14 June), Norfolk (14 June), and Cambridgeshire and Huntingdonshire (15–17 June). On 15 June the townsfolk of Cambridge rioted against the University, particularly attacking Corpus Christi College, which was under the patronage of the Dukes of Lancaster. The leader of the rebels at St. Albans was William Grindcob; at Bury, John Wrawe;

---

[2] D. W. Robertson, Jr., *Chaucer's London* (New York: Wiley, 1968), p. 148.

at Norfolk, Geoffrey Litster, hailed as "King of the Commons." Jack Straw, Grindcob, Ball, and Wrawe were all executed. According to one account, Straw confessed before his death that the commons, if their rising had been successful, would have killed all the magnates and high churchmen[3] — a statement which coincides with what Oldcastle acknowledged as the goals of the Lollard rebellion of 1414. Bishop Henry Despenser, who led a bloody "crusade" in Flanders, captured Litster at North Walsham, and quickly confessed and then hanged him.

Richard II won widespread support among the estates in 1395 and 1396 after military successes in Ireland; but as early as 1397 his popular consensus began to unravel. The following events would contribute to Richard's deposition in 1399: his marriage to Isabella, princess of France, who was seven years old; his reluctance to resume the war with France; his elevation of certain lesser aristocracy to ministerial positions (notably Sir John Bushy, Sir Henry Green, and Sir William Bagot); his retaining of household troops bearing his badge of the white hart; the impeachments of Thomas Beauchamp, Earl of Warwick, Thomas Arundel, Archbishop of Canterbury, and Thomas of Woodstock, Duke of Gloucester, and his likely complicity in the death of Gloucester at Calais, 1397; his banishment of the Earl of Nottingham for life, and his transmutation of the sentence on Henry of Derby, Duke of Hereford, from ten years to life, confiscating much of his father's estate after Gaunt's death (3 February 1399); his attempts to force seventeen counties which had supported his enemies in 1386–88 to pay a special charge of £10,000 each to regain the *plesaunce* or royal favor (1398); his thinly-veiled desires to repeal checks on the crown established during the Wonderful Parliament of 1388; his increasingly lavish style of living; his growing wariness and suspiciousness together with his reliance on his household retainers to protect him when he ventured out of the royal residences; and his attempts to emulate his earlier success in Ireland with an ill-timed second expedition. Because of a quarrel between royal officers and London citizens in 1392, Richard suspended the city's liberties and replaced the mayor and sheriffs, with the result that he had lost the confidence and support of England's chief city. Seventeen of twenty-four aldermen present at Parliament in 1392 were among the welcoming committee for Henry of Lancaster.[4] The last two or three years of Richard's troubled reign, as

---

[3] R. B. Dobson, *The Peasants' Revolt of 1381*, 2nd ed. (London: Macmillan, 1983), pp. 365–66. The secondary literature on the Rising is extensive. For a good start, see Dobson's Bibliography, pp. 405–19.

[4] Ruth Bird, *The Turbulent London of Richard II* (London: Longmans, 1949), p. 110. Richard also enraged Londoners by restoring the privileges of the free fishmongers (9 May 1399), with the result that the prices of fish rose (pp. 112–13).

well as the early years of Lancastrian rule, occasioned a number of poems on Richard's ministers and on statecraft generally. Of these the best known are *Richard the Redeless* (1399–1400), a narrative poem in passus attacking Richard's inexperienced advisors; *Mum and the Sothsegger* (1403–06), a poem related to *Richard the Redeless*, urging the king to heed truth-tellers; and John Gower's *Cronica Tripertita*, a poem in Latin elegiac couplets condemning Richard's arrogant "young ministers." Printed in this volume are a poem attacking Richard's ministers, especially Bushy, Bagot, and Green ("Ther Is a Busche That Is Forgrowe") and another advising King Henry V on the wisdom of listening to counsel ("For Drede Ofte My Lippes I Steke").

The first poem included here, "Man Be War and Be No Fool" (*Index* § 3306), in two couplets, exists in a unique manuscript: Cambridge University MS Dd. 14. 2 fol. 312*r*. The couplet of lines 3–4 appears in St. John's Coll. Oxford MS 209 fol. 38*r*, but this version locates the time, purposefully perhaps, as "the xiiij yere of kyng Richarde," or 1391, rather than the "iiij yere," or 1381. This short lyric helps establish the scene of the Peasants' Revolt, the sense of oppression in the realm. The text of the present edition is based on a paper print from microfilm of the Cambridge manuscript and is checked against the editions of RHR, Sisam, and Wright.

The Letter of John Ball follows, in two versions: British Library, Royal MS 13. E. ix (*Index* § 1796), and another text from Stow's *Chronicles of England*, better known as *Annales* (1580; *Index* § 1791). A third version appears in the so-called *Addresses of the Commons* (see below). The Royal MS, which includes the famous letter on fol. 287*r*, consists of geographical and chronicle material, including the work known as *Chronicon Angliae*. This *Chronicon* forms the basis for Thomas Walsingham's *Historia Anglicana*, which contains a slightly different version of Ball's Letter. In his letter — which Walsingham claims was discovered in the pocket of a man who was to be hanged — Ball cryptically and apocalyptically encourages the commons while trying to keep order in the ranks, urging them to stand "togidre in Godes name," to permit Piers Plowman to do his work, to "chastise wel Hobbe the Robbere," and to observe one leader only rather than going their own ways. He refers to himself and his fellow conspirators in code. He is "Johon Schep"; others include "Johan Nameles," "Johan the Mullere," "Johon Cartere," and "Johan Trewman."[5] A Latin poem on the death of Archbishop Sudbury (not printed in this volume) concludes with a list of nick-

---

[5] This name (and the other names or pseudonyms) should be compared with the nickname for the French peasants in the rising of 1358: *Jacques Bonhomme* ("James Goodman" = peasant, friend, Hodge). The French peasants collectively were called the "Jacquerie." See Justice, pp. 222–24.

names for the rebels: "Jak Chep [= John Ball; *Chep = schep*], Tronche, Jon Wrau,[6] Thom Myllere, Tyler [= Wat Tyler], Jak Strawe, / Erle of the Plo, Rak to, Deer, et Hob Carter, Rakstrawe [Jack Straw?]; / Isti ductores in plebe fuere priores" (these were the foremost leaders among the people).[7] Although the allusion to Piers Plowman in the *Addresses of the Commons* has a suspiciously literary quality to it, especially in proximity to Hobbe the Robber, Piers seems to have enjoyed an existence independent of Langland's poem. The anonymous composer of the *Dieulacres Abbey Chronicle*, for example, states that the rebel leaders were "Iohannis B" (presumably Ball), Iak Straw, and "Per Plowman."[8]

John Ball's *Letters* should be compared with the political prophecies in the first section of this volume and with the *Addresses of the Commons*. The *Letters*, including those in the *Addresses*, combine elements from "Abuses of the Age" lyrics with proverbial sentiments and preaching material, as George Kane, Siegfried Wenzel, and Richard Green have demonstrated.[9] This could mean that Ball, a sometime priest, turned naturally to complaint *topoi* for his epistolary material. Or perhaps the chroniclers represented his writings as containing proverbial and sententious material. Concurring evidence from several sources militates for the former; lack of reliable, firm evidence should urge caution. The text of Ball's *Letter* (Royal MS) is edited from

---

[6] John Wrawe, leader of a rising at Bury St. Edmunds on Friday, June 14, who administered a mock trial to the prior, John of Cambridge. At Bury St. Edmunds the rebels also killed chief justice Sir John Cavendish and John Lakenheath, the monk who collected the manorial dues and fines.

[7] See Wr *PPS* 1: 230. For another accounting of names, see *Nomina ductorum communium* in Walsingham's *Historia Anglicana*, ed. H. T. Riley, Rolls Series 28.1, 2 (London: Longman, Green, 1864): 11.

[8] As printed in M. V. Clarke and V. H. Galbraith, "The Deposition of Richard II," *Bulletin of the John Rylands Library*, 14 (1930), 125–81 at 164. Clarke and Galbraith transcribe the *Dieulacres Abbey Chronicle* from Gray's Inn MS No. 9 on pp. 164–81. For a brief discussion of "Per Plowman" in this chronicle, see Anne Hudson, "Epilogue: The Legacy of *Piers Plowman*," in *Companion to Piers Plowman*, ed. John A. Alford (Berkeley: University of California Press, 1988), p. 252. Hudson, citing Kane, mentions that a scribe includes a line in a manuscript of the A version of *PP*: "Preyit for pers þe plowmans soule." See also Susan Crane, "The Writing Lesson of 1381," in *Chaucer's England*, ed. B. Hanawalt (Minneapolis: University of Minnesota Press, 1992), p. 211.

[9] Kane, "Some Fourteenth-Century 'Political' Poems," in *Medieval English Religious and Ethical Literature: Essays in Honour of G. H. Russell*, ed. Gregory Kratzmann and James Simpson (Cambridge: Cambridge University Press, 1986), pp. 82–91; Wenzel, *Preachers, Poets, and the Early English Lyric* (Princeton: Princeton University Press, 1986), pp. 197–98 (in the larger context of Type B complaint lyrics); Green, "John Ball's Letters: Literary History and Historical Literature," in *Chaucer's England*, ed. Hanawalt, pp. 176–200.

a paper print of the manuscript and is checked against the editions of Thompson and Riley for the Rolls Series, against RHR's edition, and against Green's transcription in the Appendix to his article on "John Ball's Letters," p. 195. The text of Ball's *Letter* (Stow version) is taken from *The Chronicles of England* (London: R. Newberie, 1580), p. 485 (STC 23333), and is checked against the 1611 T. Adams edition of Stow's *Annales* (p. 470; STC 23337); Stow's *A Summarie of Englyshe Chronicles* (H. Binneman, 1574; STC 23324), p. 235; and RHR's edition. RHR prints from the edition of Edmund Howe (1615). In Stow's editions the *Letter* appears as prose.

Related documents include the *Addresses of the Commons* from *Chronicon Henrici Knighton*. Henry Knighton was an Augustinian canon of St. Mary of the Meadows, Leicester (died 1396). His *Chronicon* provides the most complete witness to the Great Plague of 1348–49; and Knighton also demonstrates considerable antipathy to the Lollards, perhaps because Leicester was a center of Lollard activity. His *Addresses of the Commons* include alleged statements by commons like those mentioned in Ball's *Letter* or in the Latin poem on Sudbury — namely, Jakke Mylner (John the Miller), Jak Carter, Jakke Trewman, and John Ball (two more letters). These *Addresses* seem to constitute variants of John Ball's *Letter* dispersed among several voices, for the same themes and personalities appear here: the commons are oppressed, the nation's morals have declined; people are exhorted to work "with skile" (reason), to be careful, to adhere to the values of Piers Plowman (righteousness), and to restrain urges for vengeance and thievery ("Hobbe Robbyoure").[10] These sentiments draw upon themes prominent in "Abuses of the Age" lyrics. The text of the present edition is based on Lumby's recension for the Rolls Series and is checked against R. F. Green's transcriptions in the Appendix to his article on John Ball's *Letters*. Green based his text on British Library, MS Cotton Tiberius C. VII. fols. 174r–174v, which he compared with British Library, MS Cotton Claudius E. III, fol. 269v.

To help complete the story of the Great Rising, I print John Ball's sermon theme as recorded in Walsingham's *Historia Anglicana*. This theme interrogates the notion that class distinctions inhere in the nature of things or that God ordained class when he created Adam and Eve. The couplet could be said to uphold the dignity of work (digging, spinning); and it harmonizes not only with the moral-political elements of Ball's *Letter* and the *Addresses of the Commons* but also with an important four-

---

[10] Green, citing Dobson, suggests that the *Addresses* are not speeches of commons but additional letters by Ball under his various pseudonyms ("John Ball's Letters," p. 182). He also documents the common phrasing between and among the letters: "Now is time" (pp. 186–87), the grinding small, mention of Piers Plowman, Hobbe the Robber, and the pseudonyms of the commons (p. 181); Ball's pseudonym, the guile motif, and the beware theme (p. 196, note 29). Also see Justice on insurgent literacy, pp. 13–66.

teenth-century literary theme: *gentilesse*. Dante and Chaucer both distinguish between hereditary gentility ("old riches") and true gentility based on virtuous actions (wealth of the spirit). Ball's reported sermon theme is proverbial as well as moral; and its political content has been doubted.[11] Yet its quasi-literary content agrees with other themes associated with Ball and the Rising.

An important witness to contemporary attitudes toward Richard and his court is *On the Times*, a 236-line rhymed macaronic complaint lyric in English and Latin beginning "Syng I wolde, butt, alas!" (*Index* § 3113). *On the Times* is preserved complete in three mid-fifteenth-century manuscripts: British Library, MS Harley 536, fols. 34*r*-35*v* (A-Text); British Library, MS Harley 941, fols. 21*v*-23*v* (B-Text); and Trinity College Dublin, MS 516, fols. 108*r*-110*r* (C-Text). The poem was first edited by Thomas Wright for *Political Poems and Songs* (1857). Wright gave the poem its title because of its attacks on contemporary mores and on fashions in clothing, and he dated the poem to 1388 on the basis of references to the retreat of "Jak" and "Jak nobil," whom he identified as Robert de Vere, Duke of Dublin, and Michael de la Pole, Earl of Suffolk. He believed that lines 109-12 refer to the flight of de Vere and the Earl of Suffolk to the continent, an allusion that Janet Coleman has accepted in her reading of *On the Times*. Wright printed the C-Text of *On the Times*; but Richard Firth Green has commented on the deficiencies of C and suggests that the B-Text would be preferable as a base-text, certainly to C but also to the A-Text as well. Green argues that the date of the poem is more likely ca. 1380, just prior to the Peasants' Revolt, and that "Jak" refers to Jack Philipot, while "John," he believes, alludes to John of Gaunt. The A-Text has been edited by Jeanne Krochalis and Edward Peters. Following Green's suggestions on preference of manuscript, this edition of the poem is based on B (MS Harley 941). B is written in long lines with the English line as the first half and the Latin as the second. The English half-lines rhyme with the next English half-line, and the Latin with the Latin, in couplets.

Next is a reflection on Straw's rebellion that begins: "Tax has tenet us alle" (*Index* § 3260), a macaronic lyric (English/Latin) in eight-line stanzas and in two versions: Corpus Christi College Cambridge MS 369 fol. 46*v* (in 48 lines), and Oxford University MS Digby 196 fols. 20*v* -21*r* (in 64 lines). The Cambridge version was printed by Wr *PPS* 1: 224–26 and again by Dobson in *The Peasants' Revolt of 1381*, the latter including English translations of the Latin verses; the Oxford version was printed by RHR and by Krochalis and Peters. In the present text, I follow the Cambridge MS but, like Wr and Dobson, I supplement from the Oxford text in lines 41–60.

---

[11] For example, Kane has argued that the theme attacks "the parasitism of what Langland called *wastours*, drones" ("Some Fourteenth-Century 'Political' Poems," p. 83). But Ball, according to Walsingham, explicated the proverb as an argument against traditional estates concepts.

Richard II's Reign and the Peasants' Revolt

The penultimate poem of this section, which begins "Ther is a busche that is forgrowe" (*Index* § 3529), is a political allegory on Richard II's ministers, including Sir John Bushy, speaker of the Commons in 1394 and 1397; Sir Henry Green; and Sir William Bagot. This occasional lyric addresses political events of Richard's last three years as sovereign, and specifically the struggle for power surrounding the death of Thomas of Woodstock, Duke of Gloucester, while at Calais in the custody of Thomas Mowbray, Earl of Nottingham (September, 1397). Gloucester (the swan in the poem's animal allegory),[12] Thomas Beauchamp, Earl of Warwick (the bearward), and Richard Fitzalan, Earl of Arundel (the steed), had made an oath to stand against the king, but Nottingham betrayed them to the king, who had them arrested. In the parliament near Westminster, Bushy impeached the three conspirators. Arundel was beheaded on Tower Hill, and Warwick confessed to treason, with the result that Richard banished him for life to the Isle of Man. At the Shrewsbury parliament (1398) Henry of Derby, Duke of Hereford (the heron), alleged that Mowbray (now Duke of Norfolk) informed him Richard was going to proceed against him as he had against Gloucester, Arundel, and Warwick; and he challenged Norfolk to deny it. Richard called for a judicial battle but suspended it when the time came (September, 1398), banishing Hereford for ten years and Norfolk for life. When the Duke of Lancaster died (3 February 1399) Richard confiscated much of the Lancastrian inheritance and extended Hereford's banishment from ten years to life, actions which precipitated Henry's combative return from France just as Richard was leaving England for a second campaign against the rebel Irish. Henry caught up with and executed Bushy and Green at Bristol; Bagot was executed in Cheshire. The poem, in fifteen tail-rhyme stanzas which dates to about 1400, exists in a unique manuscript formerly designated Deritend House, and printed by William Hamper (who at one time owned the manuscript) in *Archaeologia* and by Wr *PPS* 1: 363–66. The manuscript's current whereabouts is a mystery. Hamper transcribed the poem and sent it to the Society of Antiquaries in a letter dated "Deritend House, Birmingham, Dec. 5, 1823," and he provided the somewhat cumbersome title, "Sarcastic Verses, Written by an Adherent to the House of Lancaster, in the last year of the reign of Richard the Second, A.D. 1399." Hamper's letter to Henry Ellis, Secretary of the Society of Antiquaries, reads: "The attention of the Society of Antiquaries having been lately drawn to the circumstances connected with the latter days of King Richard the Second, I conceive that

---

[12] John Gower, in *Cronica Tripertita* (about 1400), uses similar animal ciphers for his political allegory: Gloucester is the swan, Warwick the bear, and Arundel the horse. Part 1 of Gower's *Cronica* focuses on the political events of 1387–88; part 2, on 1397; and part 3, on 1399. See John H. Fisher, *John Gower: Moral Philosopher and Friend of Chaucer* (New York: New York University Press, 1964), pp. 109–11.

the enclosed Verses, from a coeval manuscript in my possession, may be acceptable to them; and shall therefore beg you to introduce them at your leisure." The text of this edition is based on Hamper's and is compared with Wright's version. I have given special consideration to the readings of Hamper's edition, since Wright clearly based his text on Hamper's and not on the manuscript, which he did not have the opportunity to consult.

The final poem included here begins "For drede ofte my lippes I steke" but has been entitled *Treuth, Reste, and Pes* by Kail (EETS) and *What Profits a Kingdom (1401)* by RHR (*Index* § 817). The poem warns the king — Henry IV — against paying heed to tale-tellers ("false reportours"; "tale-tellere"); and it is couched in the language and conventions of wisdom literature. According to Kail (and repeated by RHR), the poem alludes to certain statutes proclaimed in 1401. On 25 January the Commons asked the king not to listen to those who might report on their deliberations before they had come to a definite conclusion. The Commons also urged the king not to listen to French slander against certain loyal lords. There are other parts of the poem which might be occasional as well (see Kail's Introduction, pp. xi–xii). This is a refrain poem with each stanza concluding with the word "pes." It exists in a single manuscript — Bodleian Library Oxford MS Digby 102 fols. 100*r*–101*v* — and is 167 lines in length (twenty-one stanzas of eight lines each, missing a line, and rhyming *abab bcbc*), executed as prose (but with stanzas marked with ¶), in a crowded hand. The present text is based on an (imperfect) electrostatic copy of the manuscript folios and is checked against the editions of Kail and RHR.

Select Bibliography

Manuscripts

Cambridge University MS Dd. 14. 2 fol. 312*r* (1432)

British Library, Royal MS 13. E. ix fol. 287*r* (c. 1400)

British Library, MS Harley 941 fols. 21*v*–23*v*

Corpus Christi College Cambridge MS 369 fol. 46*v* (1385–1400)

Olim Deritend House, Birmingham (c. 1400)

Bodleian Library Oxford MS Digby 102 fols. 100*r*–101*v* (1400–25)

Richard II's Reign and the Peasants' Revolt

Previous Editions

Man Be Ware and Be No Fool (Cambridge University MS)

Robbins, Rossell Hope, ed. *Historical Poems of the XIVth and XVth Centuries.* New York: Columbia University Press, 1959. ["On the Evil State of England (1381)," p. 54.]

Sisam, Kenneth, ed. *XIVth-Century Verse and Prose.* Oxford: Clarendon, 1921, 1922. [Sisam prints the St. John's College Oxford MS 209 fol. 57r. See p. 161.]

Wright, Thomas, ed. *Political Poems and Songs Relating to English History.* 2 vols. Rolls Series 14. London: Longman, Green, 1859, 1861. [Wright prints the St. John's College Oxford MS. See I, 278.]

The Letter of John Ball (Royal MS)

Green, Richard Firth. "John Ball's Letters: Literary History and Historical Literature." *Chaucer's England: Literature in Historical Context.* Ed. Barbara Hanawalt. Medieval Studies at Minnesota 4. Minneapolis: University of Minnesota Press, 1992. [Transcribes Ball's *Letter* in his Appendix, p. 195.]

RHR, p. 55.

Rickert, Edith, comp. *Chaucer's World.* Ed. Clair C. Olson and Martin M. Crow. New York: Columbia University Press, 1948. [Modern English translation of the letter and some of Walsingham's history of the Peasants' Revolt, pp. 360–62. Includes selected testimony from other writings on the Revolt.]

Thompson, E. M., ed. *Chronicon Angliae 1328–1388.* Rolls Series 64. London: Longman, Green, 1874.

Walsingham, Thomas. *Thomae Walsingham, quondam monachi S. Albani, Historia Anglicana.* Ed. H. T. Riley. Rolls Series 28. 2 vols. London: Longman, Green, 1863–64. [Version of Ball's *Letter* in II, 33–34.]

The Letter of John Ball (Stow)

RHR, p. 54.

Stow, John. *The Chronicles of England, from Brute unto this present yeare 1580*. London: R. Newberie, 1580. [*Letter* appears on p. 495. STC 23333; UMI Reel S1/1010.]

——. *A Summarye of the Chronicles of England*. London: T. Marshe, 1570. [Ball's *Letter* appears on fol. 235. STC 23322; UMI Reel S1/356.]

Addresses of the Commons (Knighton)

Green, Richard Firth. "John Ball's Letters: Literary History and Historical Literature." [See above under *The Letter of John Ball* (Royal MS). Transcribes the *Addresses*, pp. 193–94.]

Lumby, J. R., ed. *Chronicon Henrici Knighton*. Rolls Series 92. 2 vols. London: Eyre and Spottiswoode, 1889–95. [The *Addresses* appear in II, 138–40.]

John Ball's Sermon Theme (Walsingham)

Walsingham, Thomas. *Thomae Walsingham, quondam monachi S. Albani, Historia Anglicana*. Ed. H. T. Riley. Rolls Series 28. 2 vols. London: Longman, Green, 1863–64. [The sermon theme appears in II, 32.]

On the Times (British Library, MS Harley 941)

Wright, Thomas, ed. *Political Poems and Songs Relating to English History*. 2 vols. Rolls Series 14. London: Longman, Green, 1859, 1861. [Prints the C-Text in Vol. 1, pp. 270–78.]

Krochalis, Jeanne, and Edward Peters, eds. *The World of Piers Plowman*. Philadelphia: University of Pennsylvania Press, 1975. [Prints the A-Text, pp. 87–95.]

Tax Has Tenet Us Alle (Corpus Christi College MS)

Dobson, R. B. *The Peasants' Revolt of 1381*. 2nd ed. London: Macmillan, 1983. [Pp. 358–62.]

Krochalis, Jeanne, and Edward Peters, eds. *The World of Piers Plowman*. Philadelphia: University of Pennsylvania Press, 1975. [Pp. 95–97 but based on the Digby MS rather than the CCC MS.]

RHR, pp. 55–57. [Prints Digby version.]

Wright, Thomas, and J. O. Halliwell, eds. *Reliquiae Antiquae*. 2 vols. London: Pickering, 1841, 1843. [*Tax Has Tenet* in II, 283–84.]

Ther Is a Busch That is Forgrowe (Deritend House MS)

Hamper, William, ed. "Sarcastic Verses, Written by an Adherent to the House of Lancaster, in the last year of the reign of Richard the Second, A.D. 1399." *Archaeologia* 21 (1827), 88–91.

Wright, Thomas, ed. *Political Poems and Songs Relating to English History*. Rolls Series 41.1. 2 vols. London: 1859, 1861. [Text of *Ther is a busch* in I, 363–66.]

Truthe, Reste, and Pes (Digby MS)

Kail, J., ed. *Twenty-Six Political and Other Pieces*. Part 1. EETS o.s. 124. London: Kegan Paul, 1904. ["Treuth, reste and pes" on pp. 9–14.]

RHR, pp. 39–44.

Historical Sources and Studies

Bird, Ruth. *The Turbulent London of Richard II*. London: Longmans, 1949. [Valuable history of Richard's reign from the perspective of London. Includes helpful explanations of the primary sources, a detailed chronology of events, and a map of London.]

Clarke, M. V., and V. H. Galbraith. "The Deposition of Richard II," *Bulletin of the John Rylands Library* 14 (1930), 125–81. [Print the *Chronicle of Dieulacres Abbey, 1381–1403* on pp. 164–81. Good discussion of sources and personalities involved in the Rising.]

Dobson, R. B. *The Peasants' Revolt of 1381*. 2nd ed. London: Macmillan, 1983. [The best source of history, with Dobson's comments, and documents in English translation. Aids for the student include "The Chronology of the Revolt" (pp. 36–44); map: "London in 1381" on p. 152; and a full Index.]

Hilton, Rodney. *Bond Men Made Free: Medieval Peasant Movements and the English Rising of 1381*. London: Temple Smith, 1973. [Sets 1381 Rising in context of other historical movements.]

Hilton, R. H., and T. H. Aston, eds. *The English Rising of 1381*. Cambridge: Cambridge University Press, 1984. [A valuable collection of essays.]

Justice, Steven. *Writing and Rebellion: England in 1381*. Berkeley: University of California Press, 1994. [Views the rebellion as a contest over literacy and control of the written word. Places the "peasantry" within a larger context of public discourse.]

McKisack, May. *The Fourteenth Century 1307–1399*. Oxford: Clarendon, 1959. [Still one of the best general histories of this period. Helpful explanations of the primary sources in the Bibliography.]

Robertson, D. W., Jr. *Chaucer's London*. New York: Wiley, 1968. [Lively retelling of the 1381 Rising from a literary and historical perspective. See chapter 4, "A Brief Chronicle," pp. 127–78.]

Taylor, John. *English Historical Literature in the Fourteenth Century*. Oxford: Clarendon, 1987. [A patient and valuable exposition of the chronicles and their sources, with a good bibliography. See also chapter 12, "Political Poems and Ballads," and Appendix V, "Chronicle Accounts of the Peasants' Revolt."]

Thomson, John A. F. *The Transformation of Medieval England, 1370–1529*. London: Longman, 1983. [A helpful introduction to England in the later Middle Ages. The aids for students include a "Framework of Events" before major sections, a "Compendium of Information," maps, and a bibliography.]

General Studies

Baldwin, Anna P. "The Historical Context." *A Companion to Piers Plowman*. Ed. John A. Alford. Berkeley: University of California Press, 1988. Pp. 67–86.

Bowers, John M. "Piers Plowman and the Police: Notes Toward a History of the Wycliffite Legend." *Yearbook of Langland Studies* 6 (1992), 1–50. [Documents the affiliations between *Piers Plowman* and texts identified as "Wycliffite." Bowers includes an analysis of John Ball's letters.]

Cohn, Norman. *The Pursuit of the Millennium: Revolutionary Millenarians and Mystical Anarchists of the Middle Ages*. Rev. ed. New York: Oxford University Press, 1970. [Attempts to place John Ball and the Peasants' Rising in a context of what he terms "the egalitarian millennium." See especially pp. 198–200.]

Coleman, Janet. *Medieval Readers and Writers 1350–1400*. New York: Columbia University Press, 1981. [Good literary and historical introduction to the later fourteenth century. See chapter 3, "The Literature of Social Unrest," pp. 58–156.]

Embree, Dan. "The King's Ignorance: A Topos for Evil Times." *Medium Ævum* 54 (1985), 121–26. [Advances the idea that the king's ignorance and helplessness in the face of abuses and official corruption is a topos of complaint literature. His discussion includes *The Simonie* and *Truthe, Reste, and Pes* ("For drede ofte my lippes I steke").]

Green, Richard Firth. "Jack Philipot, John of Gaunt, and a Poem of 1380." *Speculum* 66 (1991), 330-41. [Argues that the contemporary allusions in *On the Times* accord better with events of about 1380 than of 1388.]

_____. "John Ball's Letters: Literary History and Historical Literature." *Chaucer's England: Literature in Historical Context*. Ed. Barbara Hanawalt. Medieval Studies at Minnesota 4. Minneapolis: University of Minnesota Press, 1992. [Sets Ball's Letters in a convincing social and literary context of preaching material, and demonstrates the conventional nature of much of Ball's rhetoric. Transcribes Ball's *Letter* in his Appendix, p. 195, and the *Addresses of the Commons,* pp. 193–95.]

Kane, George. "Some Fourteenth-Century 'Political' Poems." *Medieval English Religious and Ethical Literature: Essays in Honour of G. H. Russell*. Ed. Gregory Kratzmann and James Simpson. Cambridge: D. S. Brewer, 1986. Pp. 82–91. [Polemical argument against reading *Song of the Husbandman*, *The Simony*, or the poems and documents concerning John Ball as poems of "protest" or "dissent." These are better seen as complaint literature in the tradition of estates satire.]

Kinney, Thomas L. "The Temper of Fourteenth-Century Verse of Complaint." *Annuale Mediaevale* 7 (1966), 74–89. [Brief discussion of "Ther Is a Busch," p. 85.]

Introduction

Maddicott, J. R. "Poems of Social Protest in Early Fourteenth-Century England." *England in the Fourteenth Century: Proceedings of the 1985 Harlaxton Symposium*. Ed. W. M. Ormrod. Woodbridge, Suffolk: Boydell Press, 1986. Pp. 130–44. [Contrasts the specificity of later verses of complaint — specifically, the literature of 1381 — with earlier fourteenth-century complaints and satires, which Maddicott regards as closer to traditional laments and venality satire. Includes discussion of *The Simonie* and *The Song of the Husbandman*.]

Pearsall, Derek. "Interpretative Models for the Peasants' Revolt." *Hermeneutics and Medieval Culture*. Ed. Patrick J. Gallacher and Helen Damico. Albany: State University of New York Press, 1989. Pp. 63–70. [Illustrates differences between contemporary interpretations of the 1381 Rising and later understandings of it.]

Peck, Russell. A. "Social Conscience and the Poets." In *Social Unrest in the Late Middle Ages*. Ed. Francis X. Newman. Binghamton: Medieval and Renaissance Texts and Studies, 1986. Pp. 113–48. [Discusses John Ball's *Letters* and the blending of Piers Plowman conventions with Chaucerian in protest literature of the early fifteenth century.]

Robbins, Rossell Hope. "Dissent in Middle English Literature: The Spirit of (Thirteen) Seventy-Six." *Medievalia et Humanistica*, 9 (1979), 25–51.

Scattergood, V. J. *Politics and Poetry in the Fifteenth Century*. London: Blandford, 1971. [See chapter 10, "English Society III: Verses of Protest and Revolt." Discusses John Ball on pp. 354–56; "Ther Is a Busch" on pp. 110–12.]

Strohm, Paul. *Hochon's Arrow: The Social Imagination of Fourteenth-Century Texts*. Princeton: Princeton University Press, 1992. [Interrogates archival records, chronicles, and literary texts for their truth claims; reads the 1381 rising as an aspect of the carnivalesque. See especially Introduction: "False Fables and Historical Truth" (pp. 3–10), and chapter 2, "'A Revelle': Chronicle Evidence and the Rebel Voice" (pp. 33–56).]

Bibliography

Robbins, Rossell Hope. "XIII. Poems Dealing with Contemporary Conditions." *A Manual of the Writings in Middle English 1050–1500*. Vol. 5. Gen. ed. Albert E. Hartung. New Haven: The Connecticut Academy of Arts and Sciences, 1975. Pp.

1385–1536, 1631–1725. [Discusses *Man Be Ware* (§ 253) on pp. 1510–11, bibliography pp. 1709–10; *The Letters of John Ball* and *Addresses of the Commons* (§ 256) on pp. 1511–12, bibliography pp. 1710–11; *John Ball's Sermon Theme* (§ 255) on p. 1511, bibliography pp. 1710; *Tax Has Tenet Us Alle* (§ 257) on pp. 1512–13, bibliography p. 1712; *There Is a Busch That Is Forgrowe* (§ 87) on p. 1440, bibliography p. 1670; *Truthe, Reste, and Pes* (§ 58) on p. 1419, bibliography p. 1661.]

Man Be Ware and Be No Fool

(Cambridge Univ. MS Dd.14.2 fol. 312*r*)

Man be ware and be no fool:
Thenke apon the ax, and of the stool.   *executioner's block*
The stool was hard, the ax was scharp,
The iiij yere of kyng Richard.

The Letter of John Ball (Royal MS)

(British Library, Royal MS 13.E.ix fol. 287*r*)

Littera Johannis Balle missa communibus Essexiae

Johon Schep, som tyme Seynte Marie prest of York, and now of Colchestre,
greteth wel Johan Nameles, and Johan the Mullere, and Johon Cartere, and
biddeth hem that thei bee war of gyle in borugh, and stondeth togidre in Godes
name, and biddeth Peres Ploughman go to his werk, and chastise wel Hobbe the
5   Robbere, and taketh with yow Johan Trewman and alle hiis felawes, and no mo,
and loke schappe you to on heved, and no mo.

Johan the Mullere hath ygrounde smal, smal, smal;
The Kynges sone of hevene schal paye for al. [1]
Be war or ye be wo;   *Be wary before; sorry*
10   Knoweth your freend fro your foo.   *foe*
Haveth ynow, and seith "Hoo!"   *Be content; Stop*
And do wel and bettre, and fleth synne,   *avoid sin*
And seketh pees, and hold you therinne.   *stick to it*
And so biddeth Johan Trewman and alle his felawes.

---

[1] *The Son of heaven's King shall redeem everything*

135

The Letter of John Ball (Stow)

(From Stow, *Annales*)

John Bal Saint Marie priest, greeteth wel all maner of men, and biddeth them in the name of the Trinitie, Father, Son, and Holy Ghost, stand manlike together in truth, and helpe truth, and truth shal helpe you:

	Now raigneth pride in price,	*reigns; much valued*
5	Covetise is holden wise,	*Greed is held to be*
	Leacherie without shame,	
	Gluttonye without blame:	
	Envie raigneth with treason,	*Envy rules*
	And slouth is taken in greate season;	*sloth*
10	God doe bote, for now is time.	*God provide the remedy*
	Amen.	

Addresses of the Commons

(From *Chronicon Henrici Knighton*)

Jakke Mylner

Jakke Mylner alloquitur socios sic: Jakke Mylner asket help to turne hys mylne aright. He hath grounden smal, smal; the Kings sone of heven he schal pay for alle. Loke thi mylne go aright, with the foure sayles, and the post stande in steddefastnesse.

5	With ryght and with myght,	
	With skyl and with wylle,	*intellect; will*
	Lat myght helpe ryght,	
	And skyl go before wille	
	And ryght before myght,	
10	Than goth oure mylne aryght.	
	And if myght go before ryght,	
	And wylle before skylle	
	Than is oure mylne mys-adyght.	*improperly adjusted*

Jak Carter

Jakke Carter prayes yowe alle that ye make a gode ende of that ye have
15   begunnen, and doth wele and ay bettur and bettur, for at the evyn men heryth the
day. For if the ende be wele, than is alle wele. Lat Peres the Plowman my brother
duelle at home and dyght us corne, and I will go with yowe and helpe that I may

1 **Mylner . . . mylne,** Miller . . . mill; **alloquitur socios sic,** speaks to his comrades in this
way; **asket,** requires. **3 Loke . . . aright,** Make sure your mill works properly. **14–15 make
. . . begunnen,** do a good job of finishing what you have begun. **15 doth wele . . . heryth,**
do well, and always better and better, for in the evening men praise. **17 dyght us corne,**
harvest wheat for us.

to dyghte youre mete and youre drynke, that ye none fayle. Lokke that Hobbe
Robbyoure be wele chastysed for lesyng of youre grace; for ye have gret nede to
20   take God with yowe in alle youre dedes. For nowe is tyme to be ware.

Jakke Trewman

Jakke Trewman doth you to understande that falsnes and gyle have regned to
long, and trewthe hat bene sette under a lokke, and falsnes regneth in every
flokke. No man may come trewthe to, bot he syng *si dedero*. Speke, spende and
spede, quoth Jon of Banthon, and therefore synne fareth as wilde flode, trew love
25   is away, that was so gode, and clerkus for welthe worche hem wo. God do bote,
for nowghe is tyme.

Exemplar epistolae Johannis Balle

Jon Balle gretyth yow wele alle and doth yowe to understande, he hath rungen
youre belle.
    Nowe ryght and myght,
30   Wylle and skylle,
    God spede everydele.
Nowe is tyme Lady helpe to Jhesu thi sone, and thi Sone to His Fadur, to make
a gode ende, in the name of the Trinité of that is begunne amen, amen, pur
charité, amen.

18 to dyghte . . . fayle, fetch your food and drink, so that none of you falter; **Lokke that**,
Beware lest. **18–19 Hobbe Robbyoure**, Hob the Robber. **19 lesyng**, losing. **21 Jakke
. . . doth**, Jack Trewman gives. **21–22 falsnes . . . long**, deceit and fraud have reigned too
long. **22 trewthe . . . lokke**, truth (troth) has been locked up. **23 flokke**, flock (congrega-
tion); **trewthe . . . *dedero***, come to truth unless he can sing "If I should give." **23–24 Speke
. . . quoth**, Speak, spend and prosper, says. **24 fareth . . . flode**, behaves like a wild river.
25 clerkus . . . wo, clerks for riches cause them grief; **do bote**, provide the remedy. **27
Exemplar . . . Balle**, Model for John Ball's letter; **gretyth**, greets; **doth . . . understande**,
lets you know. **31 everydele**, in everything. **32 helpe to**, to aid. **33–34 pur charité**, by
charity.

Prima epistola Johannis Balle

35   John Balle seynte Marie prist gretes wele alle maner men and byddes hem in the name of the Trinité, Fadur, and Sone and Holy Gost stonde manlyche togedyr in trewthe, and helpez trewthe, and trewthe schal helpe yowe.

Now regneth pride in pris,	*supremely*
And covetys is hold wys,	*[to be] wisdom*
And leccherye withouten shame	*[is] shameless*
And glotonye withouten blame.	
Envye regnith with tresone,	
And slouthe is take in grete sesone.	
God do bote, for nowe is tyme. Amen.	*bestow [fitting] reward*

35 Prima . . . Balle, John Ball's first letter; **seynte . . . hem**, Saint Mary's priest greets favorably all manner of men and asks them. **36 stonde . . . togedyr**, stand together in a manly way. **37 helpez**, aid.

John Ball's Sermon Theme

(Walsingham, Historia Anglicana)

Whan Adam dalf, and Eve span,	*dug; spun*
Wo was thanne a gentilman?	*Who; nobleman*

On the Times

Syng I wolde, butt, alas!	*but*
decendunt prospera grata.	*good times are fading away*
Ynglond sum tyme was	*once*
regnorum gemma vocata,	*called the jewel of realms/nations*
5 Of manhod the flowre,	
ibi quondam floruit omnis;	*where once all flourished*
Now gone ys that oure —	*hour (time)*
traduntur talia sompnis.	*such things are fading into dreams*
Lechery, slewthe and pryde —	*sloth*
10 *hec sunt quibus Anglia paret.*	*these are the things which England obeys*
Sethyn trewth was set asyde,	*Since truth*
dic qualiter Anglia staret.	*tell how England stands*
Wheche oure fryndes were	*Those who; friends*
nostri fiunt inimici,	*now have become our enemies*
15 With bow, schyld and spere:	
poterunt — eu! — talia dici.	*Alas! that such things could be said*
Oft tymes we have herd	*heard*
mala nobis esse futura,	*that there would be evils for us*
But ever we have deferred	*put off*
20 *a nobis commoda plura.*	*more favorable opportunities for ourselves*
Loo! withyn oure lond	
insurgunt undeque guerre.	*wars rise up everywhere*

But God put to his hond,   *Unless; intervene*
   fiet destructio terre.   *there will be a destruction of the land*

25   On water and on lond,
   que quondam nos timuerunt,   *[powers] which once feared us*
   Now many a thowsand,
   nos per rus per mare querunt.   *seek us out through countryside and by the sea*
   The dred of God ys went,   *fear; has vanished*

30   *humanus sed timor astat.*   *but fear of people remains*
   Whoo sayth the trewthe ys schent;   *Whoever speaks; ruined*
   regnum violentia vastat;   *violence lays waste to the realm*
   Rowners and flatereres,   *Whisperers*
   hi sunt regno nocituri;   *these will injure the realm*

35   Wold God suche klaterers   *gossips*
   subdant sua colla securi.   *might submit their necks to the axe*
   Ynglond, awake now —
   consurgunt jugiter hostes,   *[our] enemies jointly arise*
   And goode hede take thu:

40   *fac ostia, dirige postes.*   *bar the gates, batten the doors*
   The ryche maketh myry,   *merry*
   sed vulgus collacrematur;   *but the common people weep*
   The pepulle ys wery,   *Humankind*
   quia ferme depopulatur.   *since (the land) is nearly laid waste*

45   The chyrche ys greved   *aggrieved*
   quia spirituales cedunt.   *because the spiritual leaders withdraw*
   And some bene myschevyd;   *Some are brought to disaster*
   plus dampni crescere credunt.   *they believe more harm is coming*
   Ynglond goose to noght   *goes; ruin*

50   *plus facit homo viciosus;*   *and the sinful creature is more esteemed*
   To lust mon ys broght,   *mankind*
   nimis est homo deliciosus.   *Mankind is too given to delights*
   Godys dere halydays   *God's precious holy days*
   non observantur honeste.   *aren't observed honorably*

55   For unthryfty playes   *Since profligate diversion*
   in eis regnant manifeste;   *openly rules these days*
   Unthryft and wombes joyse   *Profligate; bodily*
   steriles et luxuriosi,   *sterile and lustful*
   Gentyles, gromes, and boyse,   *Nobility, grooms; churls (youth)*

60   *socii sunt atque gulosi.*   *are gluttons all alike*
   Sugget and suffrayn   *Subject; sovereign*
   uno quasi fune trahuntur.   *are drawn as if with a single line*

141

	Putt thay bene to payne	*torture*
	ad eos quicunque locuntur.	*whoever speaks against them*
65	At Wesmynster halle	
	leges sunt valde scientes;	*there are men most learned in law*
	Noght ellys before thayme alle,	*Nevertheless*
	ibi vincuntur jura potentes.	*there the powerful laws are chained*
	That never herd the case,	*One who never heard the case*
70	*juramento mediabit,*	*will arrange things with an oath*
	The mater wylle he face	*He will outface (face down) the evidence*
	et justum dampnificabit,	*and will condemn the just*
	And an obligacion	*legal contract (surety)*
	de jure satis valitura	*that would be valid enough in law*
75	Throgh a fals cavelacoun,	*legal quibble*
	erit effectu caritura.	*will be emptied of its force*
	His own cause mony mon	
	nunc judicat et moderatur.	*now judges and oversees*
	Law helpis nott then,	
80	*ergo lex evacuatur.*	*for alas! the law is eviserated*
	Monslaghter and theft	
	crucis ad votum redimuntur.	*are exonerated when cash speaks up for them*
	Be warre of ylle sponon weft;	*Beware of ill-spun wool*
	quia pravi prave locuntur.	*since corruption haunts the corrupt*
85	Jurrers with payntyt sleves,	*Jurors; sleeves*
	inopes famuli dominorum,	*retainers of noblemen*
	Theys hurtes and greves,	*These; oppress*
	nobis Deus ipse deorum.	*God of gods Himself knows*
	Grete hurt to this lond	*Great harm*
90	*est usurpata potestas;*	*is power falsely claimed*
	Therefore putt to his hond	
	regis metuendi majestas.	*the majesty of the fearsome king*
	For harmes that wil falle,	*Against; may*
	nonnulla statuta parantur;	*no statutes are drafted*
95	The kyng knows nott alle,	
	non sunt qui vere loquuntur.	*there are none who speak the truth*
	He and he says welle,	*This one and that one*
	sed sermo placere videtur;	*and the speech seems to please*
	The kattys nek to the bel	*cat's neck*
100	*hic et ille ligare veretur.*	*he fears to tie (the string) here and there*
	What ys the cause of this?	
	vere violentia legis.	*the violence against the law*

	Amend that ys amysse	*what*
	poterit clementia regis.	*the mercy of the king will be able to*
105	Now without a jak	*jack (quilted jerkin/coin)*
	paucos timuit remanere;	*few fear to remain*
	Sum have hym on his bak,	*him (the jerkin/coin)*
	sed bursa mallet habere.	*but would prefer to have him in their purses*
	Goode Jak, where is John?	*(see note)*
110	*ubi gratia nunc requiescit?*	*Where does his grace now lie at rest*
	Jak, now grace ys gone;	
	ad regna remota recessit.	*he has gone off to distant realms*
	Jak nobil with hym ys;	*noble (a coin)*
	iter simul accipuerunt.	*they've gone on a journey together*
115	Of bothe ys grete mys;	*Both (the duke & his money) are greatly missed*
	illos multi modo querunt.	*many now seek them*
	Galauntes, Purs Penyles —	
	per vicos ecce vagantur.	*behold, they wander through the countryside*
	Yf yt be as I gesse,	
120	*male solvunt quod mutuantur.*	*they repay badly what they borrow*
	On with another anone	*One; soon*
	satagit committere guerram.	*is busy to commit war*
	Now ys he here, now is he gone,	
	destruxit ut advena terram.	*he ravages the earth like a stranger*
125	Freshest of the new towche,	*fashion*
	incedunt ridiculose,	*they strut ridiculously*
	Lytel or noght in the powche,	*purse*
	pascuntur deliciose.	*they dine deliciously*
	Brodder then ever God made	
130	*humeris sunt arte tumentes;*	*they puff out (their) shoulders artificially*
	Narow thay bene, thay seme brod,	*[Though] narrow; broad*
	nova sunt haec respice gentes	*they are a "new fashion" of gents*
	They bere a newe facoun,	*fashion*
	humeris in pectore tergo;	*with shoulders in the back of the chest*
135	Goddes plasmacoun	*shaping of them*
	non illis complacet ergo.	*therefore is not pleasing to them*
	With wyde koleres and hye,	*collars; high*
	gladio sunt colla parata,	*their necks are prepared for the sword*
	War ye the profycy;	*Beware of the prophecy*
140	*contra tales recitata.*	*tales are told against such men*
	Longe spores on the hele,	*spurs; heel*
	et rostra fovent ocrearum.	*they cherish the pointed toes of their slippers*

	They thynk it dose wele,	
	si non sit regula Sarum.	*even if it may be not the rule of Sarum*
145	A strayt bend have the hose,	
	laqueantur ad corpora crura.	*the shins are adorned to the crotch*
	They may nott, I suppose,	
	curvare genu sine cura:	*to bend the knee without care*
	When other men kneles	*kneel*
150	*pia Christo vota ferentes,*	*saying pious vows to Christ*
	Thay stondyn at here helys,	*their heels*
	se non curvare valentes;	*unable themselves to bend their [knees]*
	For hurtyng of herre hose	*For fear of damaging their hose*
	non inclinare laborant	*they take pains not to bend*
155	I trow, for herre long toose	*believe; their; toes*
	dum stant ferialiter orant.	*while they pray standing up in a workaday manner*
	Mony a mon they lett	*hinder*
	et turbant ad sacra stando;	*by standing they cause confusion in the service*
	Crystys curse they get,	
160	*nisi desistant aliquando.*	*unless they desist somewhat*
	Womon, lo! with wantoun brestes	*(see note)*
	procendunt arte prophana;	*behave with a profane art*
	Prechers ne pristes	*Neither preacher nor priest*
	possunt hec pellere vana.	*are able to warn [them] off these vanities*
165	With poyntys ful stronge	*enormous*
	caligas de more sigillant	*they decorate [their] boots fashionably*
	Now schort and now longe,	
	ventus velud ecce vacillant.	*behold, just as the wind they vary*
	Theyer knokuld elbows	
170	*manice laqueant lacerate* [1]	
	In frost and in snows,	
	ut aves spectant laqueate.	*like snared birds they look*
	When frost awakes,	
	et stringunt frigore gentes,	*and people huddle together for cold*
175	Theyer teth then quakes,	*Their; chatter*
	sese quasi concientes.	*as if clattering on their own*
	Ful oftymes ywys	*truly*
	gelido fervent in amore,	*they burn in icy love*
	There specyall when thay kysse	*Their sweetheart; kiss*

---

[1] *Their cut sleeves adorn (expose) their knuckled elbows*

180 *distillat nasus in ore.*	*the nose drips in the mouth*
Huffe o galant ther a towche,	*(see note)*
unguentum stillat amoris.	*she drips the balm of love*
I wolde fulle were there powche	*I wish their pouch (vagina?) were filled*
tanti dulcedine roris!	*with the sweetness of such great dew*
185 Lo! this fore a grete nede,	
sua miscent ora libenter.	*they freely mix their mouths*
Whoo so ever takes hede	
manat liquor irreverenter.	*liquid (saliva?) irreverently flows*
"Vye velabel!" they kry,	*Long live beauty; cry*
190 *fragrantia vina bibentes,*	*drinking fragrant wines*
They drynke tyl thay be dry,	
lingua sensuque carentes.	*lacking tongue and sense*
They kry, "Ful the bolles!"	*Fill the bowls*
"Bonus est liquor, hic maneamus!	*The liquor is good; let's stay here*
195 Fore alle Crystyn soles,	*Christian souls*
dum durant vasa, bibamus!"	*while the bottles last, let's drink*
Qwen men rest takes,	*When*
noctis sompno recreati,	*renewed by a night's sleep*
Seche felows awakes	
200 *ad dampna patranda parati*	*having been prepared [by drink] for wreaking havoc*
"Armes, sydes, and blode!"	
horum quidam recitauit;	*one of them swears*
Yit when he ys most wode,	*crazed*
tunc blandus sermo domauit.	*then the flattering word will prevail*
205 Peraventure at an owre	*By chance, after an hour*
poscunt hi tempore plausus	*They demand [performance] time for clapping*
A countur-tenore,	
cantabit carcere clausus.	*shut up in a prison will sing*
Of the cherche that I wryte,	
210 *non forte placet sibi psalmus;*	*[to sing] a psalm perhaps pleases him (the tenor)*
Noght say I for despyte,	*shameful behavior*
sic me Deus adjuvet almus.	*so help me sweet God*
Alas and waylaway!	
decus ecclesie tenebrascit.	*the glory of the Church grows dark*
215 Lyght wylle fayl, darre y say	
Sanctus nunc Spiritus assit.	*now let the Holy Spirit be here*
Symon, that fals man	
decus nocet ecclesiarum;	*harms the Churches' dignity*
Myche sorow he began,	

220	*virus diffudit amarum.*	*poured forth a bitter poison*
	And than fals avaryce	*Thereafter*
	satis ecclesiam laqueasti;	*you have ensnared the Church enough*
	With mony other vice	*many a vice*
	Christi sponsam violasti.	*you have ravished the bride of Christ*
225	Here mekyl more myght I say,	*On this matter a great deal more*
	tamen ordo vetat feriarum;	*yet festive propriety prohibits*
	Of seche more se ye may	*such; you may behold*
	in libris ecclesiarum.	*in the books of the Church*
	The lanterne of lyght	
230	*non fulget luce serena;*	*does not shine with a steady light*
	Yt ys nott alle oryght:	
	populus bibit ecce venena.	*Behold, the people drink poisons*
	Owre kynge and his lond	
	servet, regat et tueatur,	*may He keep, rule, and protect*
235	God that with Hys hond	
	celum, terram moderatur,	*judges heaven [and] earth*
	In age as he grows	*As he [the king] grows older*
	sua crescat gratia fructu;	*May his grace flourish in fruit [children?]*
	Fulle lytelle he knowes	
240	*quanto dolet Anglia luctu.*	*with how much sorrow England suffers*

Hec quicumque legat / non dampnet metra que pegi
Anglica lingua negat / semet subdere legi. [1]

O rex, si rex es, rege te, et eris sine re rex
Nomen habes sine re, te nisi recte regas. [2]

Explicit autem scriptum. Nunc finem feci, da mihi quod merui.

[This work is finished. Now I have made an end. Grant me what I deserve.]

---

[1] *Whoever may read these things / let him not condemn the meters I have fashioned; / The English language refuses / to submit itself to any law.*

[2] *O king, if you are a king, rule yourself, and you will be a king though you have nothing. / You have the name without the thing, unless you, king, rightly rule yourself.*

Richard II's Reign and the Peasants' Revolt

Tax Has Tenet Us Alle

(Corpus Christi Coll. Cambridge MS 369 fol. 46v)

	Tax has tenet us alle,	*ruined*
	probat hoc mors tot validorum;	*death of so many worthy folk proves it*
	The kyng therof hade smalle,	*received little of it*
	ffuit in manibus cupidorum.	*it was in the hands of greedy persons*
5	Hit hade harde honsalle,	*fortune*
	dans causam fine dolorum.	*providing cause in the end for grief*
	Revrawnce nede most falle,	*needs must*
	propter peccata malorum.	*because of the sins of the wicked*
	In Kent this kare began,	*unhappiness*
10	*mox infestando potentes,*	*soon disturbing the powerful*
	In rowte the rybawdus ran,	*In a mob the robbers ran*
	sua pompis arma ferentes;	*bearing arms in display*
	Folus dred no mon,	*Fools; fear*
	regni regem neque gentes.	*Neither the king's rule nor the people*
15	Churles were hor chevetan,	*Scoundrels; chieftains*
	vulgo pure dominantes.	*wholly dominating the people*
	Thus hor wayes thay wente,	*their*
	pravis pravos aemulantes.	*the wicked emulating the wicked*
	To London fro Kent	
20	*sunt predia depopulantes.*	*emptying estates as they go*
	Ther was an uvel covent,	*evil*
	australi parte vagantes;	*wandering through the south*
	Sythenne they sone were schent,	*Afterwards; destroyed*
	qui tunc fuerant superantes.	*who were once the conquerors*
25	Bondus they blwun bost,	*Bondsmen boast*
	nolentes lege domari;	*unwilling to yield to the law*
	Nede they fre be most,	*must needs be free*

147

	vel nollent pacificari.	*or they would not be peaceful*
	Charters were endorst,	
30	*hos libertate morari;*	*allowing them to be free*
	Ther hor fredam thay lost,	*their freedom*
	digni pro caede negari.	*denied because of their murders*
	Laddus loude thay loghte,	*Churls loudly laughed*
	clamantes voce sonora;	*crying with loud voices*
35	The bischop wen thay sloghte,	*when; slew*
	et corpora plura decora.	*and many more excellent people*
	Maners down thay drowghte,	*Manors; pulled*
	in regno non meliora;	*none better in the realm*
	Harme thay dud inoghe,	*Injury; did enough*
40	*habuerunt libera lora.*	*they had free rein*
	Jak Strawe made yt stowte	*swaggered*
	in profusa comitiva;	*with his vast following*
	And seyd al schuld hem lowte,	*bow to them*
	Anglorum corpora viva.	*all living Englishmen*
45	Sadly can they schowte,	*Powerfully; shout*
	pulsant pietatis oliva,	*they beat down the olive of piety*
	The wycche were wont to lowte,	*Those who; defer*
	aratrum traducere stiva.	*drawing the plow in the furrow*
	Hales, that dowghty knyght,	*(see note)*
50	*quo splenduit Anglia tota,*	*in whom all England shone*
	Dolefully he was dyght,	*Grievously; dealt with*
	cum stultis pace remota.	*when fools banished peace*
	There he myght not fyght,	
	nec Christo solvere vota.	*nor reconcile his vows to Christ*
55	Savoy semely sette,	
	heu! funditus igne cadebat.	*alas! it fell completely through fire*
	Arcan don there they bett,	
	et eos virtute premebat.	*And he through his virtue conquered them*
	Deth was ther dewe dett,	*their due debt*
60	*qui captum quisque ferebat.*	*whoever made them captive*

Richard II's Reign and the Peasants' Revolt

Owre kyng hadde no rest,
   alii latuere caverna;   *others lay hidden in caves*
To ride he was ful prest,
   recolendo gesta paterna.   *recalling the deeds of his father*
65   Jak Straw down he kest
   Smethefeld virtute superna.   *At Smithfield through heavenly grace*
Lord, as thou may best,
   regem defende, guberna.   *defend, rule the king*

There Is a Busch That Is Forgrowe

[On King Richard's Ministers]

(*Olim* Deritend House, Birmingham)

	Ther is a busch that is forgrowe;	*overgrown*
	Crop hit welle, and hold hit lowe,	*keep it*
	Or elles hit wolle be wilde.	*else; will*
	The long gras that is so grene,	*green*
5	Hit most be mowe, and raked clene —	*mowed*
	For-growen hit hath the fellde.	*It has overgrown the field*
	The grete bagge, that is so mykille,	*i.e., Bagot (see note): mighty*
	Hit schal be kettord and maked litelle;	*quartered?*
	The bothom is ny ought.	*The bottom [of the bag] is almost gone*
10	Hit is so roton on ych a side,	*rotten; each side*
	Ther nul no stych with odur abyde,	*No stitch will remain with another*
	To set theron a clout.	*rag*
	Thorw the busch a swan was sclayn;	*(see note)*
	Of that sclawtur fewe wer fayne.	*slaughter; happy*
15	Alas that hit be-tydde!	*occurred*
	Hit was a eyrer good and able,	*brooding falcon*
	To his lord ryght profitable;	
	Hit was a gentel bryde.	*noble bird*
	The grene gras that was so long,	
20	Hit hath sclayn a stede strong	*slain; (see note)*
	That worthy was and wyth.	*strong*
	Wat kyng had that stede on holde,	*Whatever*
	To juste on hym he myght be bold,	*joust against*
	Als schulde he go to fyth.	*Whenever he should; fight*
25	A bereward fond a rag;	*bear keeper*

150

Of the rag he made a bag;
   He dude in gode entent.   *did it*
Thorwe the bag the bereward is taken;
Alle his beres han hym forsaken —
30   Thus is the berewarde schent.   *destroyed*

The swan is ded, his make is woo,   *mate; sorrowful*
Her eldest bryd is taken her fro   *(see note)*
   In to an uncod place.   *uncouth*
The stedes colt is ronnon a-way,
35   An eron hath taken hym to his praye: *heron*
   Hit is a wondur casse.   *situation*

The berewardes sone is tendur of age;
He is put to mariage,
   Askyng wille yowe telle.
40   Yut he hoputh, thorw myth and grace,   *hopes; force*
With the beres to make solas,
   And led hem at his wille.   *lead them*

A eron is up and toke his flyt;   *heron; flight*
In the north contré he is light   *has landed*
45   (Thus here ye alle men saye).   *hear*
The stede colt with hym he brynges;   *i.e., Thomas*
These buth wonder and y thinges   *are; in*
   To se hem thus to playe.

The gees han mad a parlement,
50   Toward the eron are they went,   *have they gone*
   Mo then I con telle.   *More than; can*
The pecokes that buth so fayr in syght,   *are*
To hym ben comen with alle hur myght,   *their*
   They thenke with hym to dwelle.

55   Upon the busch the eron wolle reste,   *heron (i.e., Henry)*
Of alle places it liketh hym beste,
   To loke aftur his pray.   *prey*
He wolle falle upon the grene;
There he falleth hit wille be sene,   *Where*

151

60   They wille not welle away.

        The bag is ful of roton corne,   *wheat*
        So long ykep, hit is forlorne;   *kept; ruined*
            Hit wille stonde no stalle.
        The pecokes and the ges all so,   *also*
65   And odor fowles mony on mo,   *many other birds*
            Schuld be fed withalle.

        The busch is bare and waxus sere,   *becomes dried up*
        Hit may no lengur leves bere;   *longer bear leaves*
            Now stont hit in no styde.   *Now it stands in no place*
70   Ywys I con no nodur bote,   *Truly I know no other remedy*
        But hewe hit downe, crop and rote,   *top; root*
            And to the toun hit lede.   *bring*

        The longe gras that semeth grene,
        Hit is roton alle bydene: *all through*
75   Hit is non best mete.   *food for an animal*
        Til the roton be dynged ought,   *flailed out*
        Our lene bestes schul not rought,   *lean; sleep*
            Hur liflode to gete.   *livelihood*

        The grete bage is so ytoron,   *i.e., Bagot; torn*
80   Hit nyl holde neyther mele ne corne;
            Hong hit up to drye!
        Wen hit is drye, then schalt thou se   *When*
        Yif hit wil amended be,
            A beger for to bye.   *beggar; buy*

85   Now God that mykelle is of myght,
        Grant us grace to se that syght,
            Yif hit be thy wille.
        Our lene bestes to have reste
        In place that hem lyketh beste,   *best pleases them*
90   That were in point to spylle.   *about to die*

Truthe, Reste, and Pes

[What Profits a Kingdom (1401)]

(Bodleian Library Oxford MS Digby 102 fols. 100r–101v)

	For drede ofte my lippes I steke,	*keep shut*
	For false reportours that trouhte mys-famed.[1]	
	Yut Charitee chargeth me to speke	*requires*
	Though trouthe be dred, he nys not ashamed.	*fearful; is not*
5	Trouthe secheth non hernes ther los is lamed;[2]	
	Trouthe is worschiped at every des.	*dais*
	In that kyngdom ther trouthe is blamed,	
	God sendes vengeaunce to make trouthe have pes.	
	Trouthe is messager to ryght,	
10	And ryght is counseille to Justice;	
	Justice in Goddis stede is dyght.[3]	
	Do evene lawe to fooll and wyse.	*equal justice*
	Set mesure in evene assise,	
	The righte weye as lawe ges.	*goes*
15	And lawe be kept, folk nyl not ryse.	*If; will not rebel*
	That kyngdom shal have reste and pes.	
	Yif suche a tale-tellere were,	
	To a kyng apayre a mannys name,	*harm; man's*
	The kyng shulde bothe partyes here,	*hear*
20	And punysche the fals for defame.	

---

[1] *On account of false witnesses, who misreport [the] truth*

[2] *Truth does not seek out corners where reputation is crippled*

[3] *Justice is appointed as God's representative*

Than fals men wolde ases for blame;   *cease*
For falshed, body and soule it sles.   *slays*
Falshed endes ay in shame,   *always*
And trouthe, in worschipe and in pes.

25   Whanne lawe is put fro right assise,   *When law is deprived of true justice*
     And domes man made by mede,   *judgments; bribery*
     For fawte of lawe yif comouns rise,   *lack*
     Than is a kyngdom most in drede.
     For whanne vengeaunce a comouns lede,   *governs*
30   Thei do gret harm er they asses.   *before; cease*
     There no man other doth mysbede,   *injure*
     That kyngdom shal have reste and pes.

     Whan craft riseth agens craft
     In burgh, toun, or citée,
35   They go to lordes whan lawe is laft,   *abandoned*
     Whoche party may strengere be.   *Which; stronger*
     But wyse men the sonere se   *more quickly see*
     By witles wille they gedre pres,   *gather [a] crowd*
     Or lordis medle in foly degré,   *crime*
40   Let lawe have cours in reste and pes.   *take [its]*

     Yit there is the thridde distaunce   *third dissension*
     Bryngeth a kyngdom in moche noyghe: *great distress*
     Ofte chaunge of governaunce
     Of all degré, lowe and hyghe.
45   A kyng may not al aspie,   *observe*
     Summe telle hym soth, summe telle hym les.   *lies*
     The whete fro the chaff ye tryghe,   *wheat; sift*
     So mowe ye leve in reste and pes.   *may; live*

     I speke not in specyale   *specially*
50   Of oo kyngdom the lawe to telle;   *a single*
     I speke hool in generale   *wholly*
     In eche kyngdom the lawe to telle.
     Also is writen in the Gospelle
     A word that God Hym-selven ches: *chose*

55	Rathere than fighte, a man go selle	
	On of his clothes, and bighe hym pes.	*purchase*
	A worthi knyght wol worchip wynne;	*gain honor*
	He wil not yelde hym though me thret,	*yield; someone threaten*
	But rathere as Malice doth begynne,	
60	Quenche hit at the firste het.	*Stop; blow*
	For, and ye lete it growe gret,	*if*
	Hit brenneth breme as fyre in gres.	*It burns as fiercely as fire in grease*
	Laweles novellerye loke ye lete,	*innovation see that you prevent*
	So mowe ye lyve in reste and pes.	
65	Old speche is spoken yore:	
	What is a kyngdom tresory?	*kingdom's*
	Bestayle, corn stuffed in store,	*Cattle; wheat; reserve*
	Riche comouns, and wyse clergy;	
	Marchaundes, squyers, chivalry	*Merchants, squires*
70	That wol be redy at a res,	*attack*
	And chevalrous kyng in wittes hyghe,	*with keen wits*
	To lede in were and governe in pes.	*war*
	Among philosofres wyse	
	In here bokes men writen fynde	*find written*
75	That synne is cause of cowardyse;	
	Wel lyvyng man, hardy of kynde;	
	Wikked lyvere, graceles, blynde,	
	He dredeth deth, the laste mes.	*mass (extreme unction)*
	The good lyvere hath God in mynde,	
80	That mannys counseil maketh pes.	*man's*
	What kyng that wol have good name,	
	He wol be lad by wys counsayle	*led*
	That love worschip and dreden shame,	*honor*
	And boldely dar fende and assayle.	*ward off*
85	There wit is, corage may not fayle,	
	For wysdom nevere worschip les.	*lost*
	Corage in querell doth batayle,	*quarrel*
	And ende of batayle bygynneth pes.	

	Defaute of wit maketh long counsayle;	*Lack*
90	For witteles wordes in ydel spoken.	*in vain*
	The more cost, the lesse avayle;	
	For fawte of wyt, purpos broken.	*lack*
	In evyl soule no grace is stoken,	*put*
	For wikked soule is graceles.	*without grace*
95	In good lyvere Goddis wille is loken,	*behavior; locked up*
	That mannys counsell maketh pes.	

	To wete yif parlement be wys,	*know whether*
	The comoun profit wel it preves.	
	A kyngdom in comouns lys,	*lies*
100	Alle profytes, and alle myscheves.	*misfortuntes*
	Lordis wet nevere what comouns greves	*know; oppresses*
	Til here rentis bigynne to ses.	*Until their incomes; cease*
	There lordis ere, pore comons releves,	*show mercy*
	And mayntene hem in werre and pes.	

105	Make God youre ful frend;	
	Do the comaundement that He bede.	*bade*
	Though all the world agen yow wend,	*turn against you*
	Be God youre frend, ye thar not drede:	*If God is; need not fear*
	For there as God His frendis lede,	*when; leads*
110	He saveth hem bothe on lond and sees.	*seas*
	Who-so fighteth, God doth the dede,	
	For God is victorie and pes.	

	What kyngdom werreth hym-self with-ynne	*wars with itself*
	Distroyeth hym-self, and no mo.	*itself; no other*
115	With-oute here enemys bygynne	
	On eche a syde assayle hem so.	*each side*
	The comouns, they wil robbe and slo,	*kill*
	Make fyere, and kyndel stres.	*fires; ignite straws*
	Whan ryches and manhode is wastede and go,	*gone*
120	Than drede dryveth to trete pes.	*fear impels*

	The world is like a fals lemman:	*sweetheart*
	Fayre semblaunt and moche gyle.	*appearance; guile*
	Withouten heire dyeth no man,	*heir dies*

	God is chief Lord of toun and pyle.	*stronghold*
125	God maketh mony heire in a whyle,	*many heirs*
	For God ressayveth eche reles;	*receives; release*
	God kan breke hegge and style,	*hedge; stile*
	And make an hey wey to pes.	*highway*

	God made lordis governoures	
130	To governe puple in unyté.	*people*
	The puple, ne ryches, nys not youres:	*Neither people nor riches are*
	Al is Goddis, and so be ye.	
	Eche day ye may youre myrrour se:	*mirror see*
	Eche man after other deses.	*dies*
135	Youre auncetres arn gon, after shal ye,	*ancestors are*
	To endeles werre or endeless pes.	

	Eche kyng is sworn to governaunce	
	To governe Goddis puple in right.	
	Eche kyng bereth swerd of Goddis vengeaunce	*bears [a] sword*
140	To felle Goddis foon in fight.	*slay; foes*
	And so doth everons honest knyght	*always*
	That bereth the ordre as it wes;	*upholds; was*
	The plough, the chirche, to mayntene ryght	*I.e., the commons*
	Are Goddis champyons to kepe the pes.	

145	The world is like a chery fayre,	
	Ofte chaungeth all his thynges.	*its*
	Riche, pore, foul, and fayre,	
	Popes, prelates, and lordynges,	
	Alle are dedly, and so ben kynges.	*mortal*
150	Or deth lede yow in his les,	*Before; untruth*
	Arraye by tyme youre rekenynges,	*quickly; accounts*
	And trete with God to gete yow pes.	*deal*

	What bryngeth a kyngdom al above?	*i.e., into peace*
	Wys counseil and good governaunce.	
155	Eche lord wil other love,	
	And rule wel labourers sustynaunce.	
	God maketh for His frendis no destaunce,	*dissension*
	For God kan skatre the grete pres.	*scatter; mob*

157

God for His frendis math ordynaunce,   *makes [an] ordinance*
160   And governeth hem in werre and pes.

Good lyf is cause of good name;
Good name is worthi to have reveraunce.
. . . .
Synne is cause of grevaunce.
165   Eche kyngdom hongeth in Goddis balaunce;   *hangs*
With hym that holdeth, with hym that fles.   *runs away*
Ye have fre wille, chese youre chaunce   *fortune*
To have with God werre or pes.

Notes

Man Be Ware and Be No Fool

1   *Man be ware.* The sentiment has proverbial values. See R. Green, "John Ball's Letters," in *Chaucer's England*, ed. B. Hanawalt, p. 196, note 29; *The Letter of John Ball* (Royal MS), line 9; and *Addresses of the Commons*, line 20.

4   *iiij yere of kyng Richard.* So the Cambridge MS. K. Sisam, *Fourteenth Century Verse and Prose*, prints a couplet from St. John's College, Oxford, MS 209 fol. 57v, that closely resembles lines 3–4 of the present poem: "The ax was sharpe, the stokke was harde, / In the xiiii yere of Kyng Richarde." Sisam entitles the poem "On the Year 1390–91," which was the fourteenth year of Richard II's reign. The fourth (*iiij*) year of Richard's reign was 1381. After citing the couplet from the St. John MS, RHR comments: "The year 1381 seems more appropriate for this complaint [than 1390–91, as in Sisam], in view of the repression following the Revolt, to which the quatrain may refer." In 1391 Richard was sufficiently at odds with the city of London, however, for Gower to shift his dedication of the *Confessio Amantis* from him to Henry of Lancaster.

The Letter of John Ball (Royal MS)

1   *Johon Schep*, or "John the Shepherd," is Ball's pseudonym. Because of other references to *Piers Plowman* in the letter, Ball here may allude to the opening lines of Langland's poem: "In a somer seson, whan softe was the sonne, / I shoop me into shroudes as I a *sheep* were" (Schmidt ed. of B text). Walsingham characterizes Ball as a "lapsed priest," and Ball himself may refer to his status in the phrase "som tyme Seynte Marie prest of York." *Johan Nameles* is another pseudonym but perhaps without a specific referent. "John Nameless," that is, may simply refer to others who share Ball's political sympathies. In line 2, "John the Mullere," or Miller, and "Johon Cartere," or Carter, may be types, since John is a most common name, as in the carpenter from Chaucer's Miller's Tale. The military leader of the rebellion Wat Tyler was, according to Froissart, a roof tiler by trade.

4   *Peres Ploughman*. Ball appropriates the figure of Piers as symbol of the political cause, representing the commons as industrious and faithful while characterizing their enemies, symbolized by *Hobbe the Robbere* (lines 4–5), as parasites. *Johan Trewman* (line 5) is another pseudonym, this one for a morally righteous Christian such as Chaucer's Plowman, who is "a *trewe* swynkere [worker] and a good" (I 531). John A. Alford says: "Again and again [late fourteenth-century] writers . . . extol truth as the political virtue *par excellence*" (*A Companion to Piers Plowman*, p. 33). See also Peck, pp. 113–16, on the truth trope in Ball's letters, and Alford, *Glossary*, s.v. *Treuthe*, and *Addresses* note to lines 15 and 17. Two "names" in this *Letter* also appear in the *Addresses to the Commons*: *Jakke Mylner = Johan the Mullere*; *Jakke Trewman = Johan Trewman*.

4–5   *Hobbe the Robbere*. Hobbe the Robbere also may derive from *Piers Plowman* since Langland mentions a "Roberd the Robbere" in B passus 5.463. Some have identified this "Hobbe" (a nickname of Robin/Robert [*MED* s.v. *Hobbe*]) as Robert Hales, the hated Treasurer of England just before and during the Rising, whom the mob executed on Friday, 14 June 1381.

6   *loke schappe you to on heved*. "Obey only one leader (or head)." Ball cautions his troops to observe discipline in the ranks, since there may be spies or infiltrators in their midst. He reinforces the warning in the poem (lines 9–10). Riley transcribes *schappe* as *scharpe* (*Historia Anglicana*, 2:34, and note 3 continued from p. 33); Thompson *loke ʒe shape you* (*Chronicon Angliae*, p. 322).

7   *Johan the Mullere hath ygrounde*. This cryptic line, in form so like a political prophecy, seems to refer to hard times, the cause for rebellion. Green cites a well-known Latin proverb: "Though its earliest English appearance seems to be in George Herbert's *Jacula Prudentum* (1640), this proverb was certainly known in the Middle Ages: 'Sera deum mola sed tenues molit undique partes.' Walther, *Proverbia* 4:805 (no. 28057); compare 4:815 (no. 28109) and 5:551–52 (nos. 32568a/b)" (p. 198, note 52).

9   *Be war or ye be wo*. Proverbial, according to Whiting, *Proverbs*, p. 626 (§ W45). First citation = Ball's Letter; numerous refs. including sententious poems. *ye*. So Riley and Green (*ʒe*); MS and RHR *þe*. Thompson *ʒe*. According to *Fasciculi Zizaniorum*, a collection of anti-Wycliffite and pro-mendicant tracts (probably Carmelite) compiled in the late fourteenth century but assembled in the 1430s: "there was a certain company of the sect and doctrines of Wycliffe which conspired like a secret fraternity and arranged to travel around the whole of

England preaching the beliefs taught by Wycliffe" (as quoted in Dobson, *The Peasants' Revolt of 1381*, p. 378). For information on the *Fasciculi Zizaniorum*, see James Crompton, "*Fasciculi Zizaniorum*," *Journal of Ecclesiastical History* 12 (196), 35–45, 155–66. The chroniclers stressed a connection between heresy and the Rising, but modern historians have been unable to confirm it.

10   *Knoweth your freend.* The *Anonimalle Chronicle* says that the commons had among themselves a "wache worde": "With whom haldes yow?" (i.e., whose side are you on?). The reply to this was supposed to be: "Wyth kynge Richarde and wyth the trew communes." On this watchword, see Strohm, *Hochon's Arrow*, pp. 41–42.

11   *Haveth ynow, and seith "Hoo!"* This line seems to urge restraint among the insurgents. See also the cautionary note about Hobbe the Robbere in *Ball's Letter* (line 4) and *Addresses of the Commons* (line 17). The Westminster chronicler and Walsingham both emphasize that when the rebels sacked Gaunt's Savoy palace they refrained from looting. Knighton testifies when one rebel tried to carry off a "fine piece of silver," his colleagues threw him and the silver into the fire, saying (in reported speech) that they were "zelatores veritatis et justitiae, non fures aut latrones" (lovers of truth and justice, not robbers or thieves). See *Chronicon Henrici Knighton*, p. 135; Strohm, *Hochon's Arrow*, p. 44; Derek Pearsall, *The Life of Geoffrey Chaucer* (Oxford: Blackwell, 1992), p. 144.

12   *do wel and bettre.* An allusion to *Piers Plowman*'s famous *Vita de Dowel, Dobet & Dobest.* Ball equates "do well" with seeking political justice. As in *Piers Plowman* solutions to political grievances appear to reside as much in heaven (Christ's sacrifice, line 7; fleeing sin, line 11) as in earthly deeds. Peck points out that this is the earliest specific reference to Langland's poem.

The Letter of John Ball (Stow)

In his *A Summarye of the Chronicles of Englande* (London: T. Marshe, 1570) — a forerunner or precursor of his *The Annales* or *The Chronicles* — Stow first printed Ball's *Letter*, though with significant variation from the *Annales* version. (Ball's *Letter* does not appear in the 1565 *Summarye*.) The following transcription is from a microfilm version of the T. Marshe 1570 edition in the Huntington Library (STC 23322, Reel S1/356; University Microfilms 15587), from fol. 235. I transcribe without editorial intervention:

John Ball saint mary priest, greteth well all maner of men, and biddeth them in the name of the trinitie father, sonne, and holy ghost, stand manliche together in truthe, and helpes truthe, & truth shal helpe you, now reigneth pride in price, and couetise is holde wyse, and lechery without shame, & glotony without blame, enuy reigneth with treason, and slouth is take in great season. God doe boote, for nowe is time amen.

1–3   Peck discusses the "stand manlike" trope (p. 114) and sees the line on truth as a variation on John 8:32: "You shall know the truth and the truth shall make you free" (p. 115). The address "John Bal . . . greeteth," here and elsewhere, reflects a Pauline epistolary formula (p. 114).

4   *pride.* This prophecy illustrates well the principle of making predictions in the guise of complaint. The poem mentions six of the seven deadly sins: pride, avarice, lust, gluttony, envy, sloth. Wrath is missing.

8   *treason.* So the T. Marshe 1570 (printed above) and H. Binneman 1574 editions of the *Summarie* (STC 23322, 23324, p. 235), and the R. Newberie 1580 edition of *The Chronicles* (STC 23333, p. 485). The T. Marshe 1592 edition of *The Annales* and subsequent editions I have checked emend to *reason*, which is RHR's reading. This reading should be compared with line 39 of *Addresses of the Commons* (*tresone*).

10   *for now is time.* Peck comments on the "fierce restlessness or sense of the immediacy of time's demands" as apocalyptic metaphors, both here and in other protest literature surrounding the Peasants' Revolt (p. 116).

Addresses of the Commons

1   *mylne.* The mill here seems to be a figure for the political cause, the rebellion. When the mill is working properly, with its four sails turning yarely, then all goes well. But they must proceed with circumspection and reason (*skyl*).

3   *foure sayles.* The four sails of a windmill. The *post* is the grinding axel.

5–13   *With ryght and with myght.* This lyric is a variant of a popular complaint type, cited by Wenzel (1978) as the first of four special versions of Type B complaint. He prints the following extract from "The Sayings of the Four Philosophers" in *Speculum Christiani*:

162

Notes

My3te is ry3te,
Ly3te is ny3te,
Fy3t is fly3t.

See *Preachers, Poets, and the Early English Lyric*, p. 185; *Index* § 2167. For a version even closer to the lyric type, see *Addresses*, lines 27–29.

6   *skyl.* Implies "reason," "intellect," "discretion," or "self-control," as well as "craft."

13   *mys-adyght.* MED glosses this specific usage as "improperly adjusted," though "ill-used," or "abused" are implicit as well.

14   *have.* So Green; Lumby *hane*.

16   *Peres the Plowman.* See *The Letter of John Ball* (Royal MS), line 4 and note.

18–19   *Hobbe Robbyoure.* See *The Letter of John Ball* (Royal MS), note to lines 4–5.

20   *For nowe is tyme to be ware.* The sentiments in this line appear on fourteenth-century church bells. See Susan Crane, "The Writing Lesson of 1381," in *Chaucer's England*, ed. Barbara Hanawalt (Minneapolis: University of Minnesota Press, 1992), p. 220, note 36 (citing Caroline Barron).

21–22   *falsnes and gyle have regned to long.* These lines should be compared with Wenzel's third poem of the "Type B" complaint lyrics (*Hallas! men planys of litel trwthe*). See below, note to line 23.

22   *trewthe.* Truth, with the meaning of *troth*, keeping one's word. Aston has pointed out that this word appears often in Lollard writings. Writing about Knighton's phrases *trewe prechoures* and *false prechoures*, she observes: "Knighton provides no explanation of his two examples, presumably because he expected his reader to understand their force without his aid. It is not difficult to guess their import: *trewe prechoures* are those who propound Wycliffite doctrine, *false prechoures* those who controvert this, or who preach unorthodox beliefs rejected by the Lollards" (*Lollards and Their Books*, p. 166). See also R. F. Green, "John Ball's Letters," pp. 183–84.

23 *si dedero.* A satirical Latin song, in couplets, that begins "Si dedero decus accipiam flatumque favoris: / Ni dedero, nil percipiam, spem perdo laboris." See H. Walther, *Initia carminum ac versuum medii aevi posterioris latinorum* § 17697; *Reliquiae Antiquae*, ed. T. Wright and J. O. Halliwell (New York: Pickering, 1843), 2:6:

> Si dedero, decus accipiam flatumque favoris:
> Ni dedero, nil percipiam, spem perdo laboris.
>
> Si dedero, genus accumulo famamque potentis;
> Ni dedero clauso sacculo, perit ars sapientis;
>
> Si dedero, mihi laus, lex, et jus prospera dantur:
> Ni dedero, mihi fraus, fel, faex adversa parantur;
>
> Si dedero, mereor in summa sede locari:
> Ni dedero, tenui compellor in aede morari;
>
> Si dedero, veneratus ero, vocor et gratiosus:
> Ni dedero, diffamor ego, vocor et vitiosus.

A fourteenth-century quatrain contains a reference to the Latin song: "Now goot falshed in everi flok, / And trwethe is sperd under a lok; / Now no man may comen ʒer to / But yef he singge *si dedero*" (*Reliquiae Antiquae*, ed. Wright and Halliwell, 2:121; *Index* § 2319, *Contra falsos iudices*). For other references, see *The Macro Plays*, ed. Mark Eccles, p. 190 (note to *The Castle of Perseverance* line 879); *Peter Idley's Instructions to His Son*, ed. Charlotte d'Evelyn (London: Oxford University Press, 1935), line 560 and note (p. 216); and W. K. Smart, "Some Notes on *Mankind*," *Modern Philology*, 14 (1916), 296–97, who adduces John Lydgate's "Si dedero ys now so mery a song." The phrase "Si dedero," according to Smart, "is a popular expression for bribery or buying of favors of any sort" (p. 296). See also *The Simonie*, line 24. I am indebted to Paul F. Schaffner and Siegfried Wenzel for their help with this Latin song.

24 *Jon of Banthon.* Not identified. The manuscripts record his name as *Bāthon.*

24–25 *trewe love is away.* An important motif of Middle English moral and didactic poetry is that charity — love — has grown cold in the world's last days, according to Christ's description of the end of the world in Matthew 24:12: "And because iniquity hath abounded, the charity of many shall grow cold." This scriptural passage was often interpreted to mean that when antichrists (1 John 2, Matt. 24:6), false prophets (Matt 24:11), and specifically the friars (the hypocrites and those who love to be called "master" of Matt. 23) shall effect such iniquity, then Christian charity will cool on earth as "many" will follow these false leaders. See, for example, a lyric from Merton College Oxford MS 248 fol. 166*v* entitled *De mundo* (On the world):

Hallas! men planys of litel trwthe;	*complain*
hit ys dede and tat is rwthe;	*it; dead; that; pity*
falsedam regnis and es abowe,	*falsehood; is on high*
and byrid es trwlove.	*buried is true love*

In *Religious Lyrics of the XIVth Century*, ed. C. Brown, rev. G. V. Smithers, 2nd ed. (Oxford: Clarendon, 1957), p. 54; *Index* § 2145. (I have normalized the spelling.) See also *Munus fit iudex*, line 23: "Symony is above, and awey is trwlove" (RHR, p. 144), and R. F. Green, "John Ball's Letters," p. 184. Siegfried Wenzel analyzes *Hallas! men planys* as a third popular version of Type B complaint lyrics. This lyric derives from two Latin hexameters. See *Preachers, Poets, and the Early English Lyric*, p. 191.

29–31 See above lines 5–13 and note.

31 *everydele*. So Green (adopting the reading from the Cotton Claudius MS); Lumby *every ydele* (the reading of the Cotton Tiberius MS). The Cotton Claudius reading is superior, since Ball would not ask God to bring prosperity to "idle men."

38–43 *Now regneth pride in pris*. These lines (and material in Jakke Trewman's address) are a version of Wenzel's popular verses of "Type B" complaint lyrics. He cites *Index* § 2356 (*Now pride ys yn pris*) which, like the present poem, contains not the traditional four evils but the seven deadly sins (*Preachers, Poets*, p. 197). See also *When Rome Is Removed into England*, line 5 and note; *The Letter of John Ball* (Stow version).

John Ball's Sermon Theme (Walsingham)

1 Both Walsingham's *Historia Anglicana* and the *Chronicon Angliae* claim that John Ball, priest, taught the "perverted doctrine" (*perversa dogmata*) and the "false ravings" (*insanias falsas*) of John Wyclif, whom Walsingham elsewhere

describes as "vetus hypocrita, angelus Sathanae, antichristi praeambulans" (an old hypocrite, Satan's angel, a walking antichrist) as well as a heretic with "dampnatas opiniones." See *Chronicon Angliae*, ed. E. M. Thompson (Rolls Series 64, 1874), p. 281; *Historia Anglicana*, ed. H. T. Riley (Rolls Series 28.1), 2:32. For another setting of this theme, see the moral lyric beginning "When adam delf & eue span, spir, if þou wil spede" from Cambridge Univ. MS Dd. 5. 64, III (fols. 35v–36r), as printed in *Religious Lyrics of the XIVth Century*, ed. Carleton Brown and rev. G. V. Smithers, 2nd ed. (Oxford: Clarendon, 1957), pp. 96–97; *Index* § 3921. The theme is proverbial. See Whiting, *Proverbs*, § A38.

2   *gentilman.* Walsingham and especially Froissart describe how Ball preached egalitarian doctrine.

On the Times

2   *decendunt.* A: *descendunt* with *decedunt* written above. C: *procedunt*, with *discendunt* written above it.

5   In B this line was skipped by the scribe, then written in at the top of the page, with an arrow curling downward to locate the place where it should be inserted.

7   *oure.* A: *tour.* Wr and C: *honowr.*

9   *slewthe.* A: *slouthe.* Wr and C: *lust.*

11   *Sethyn trewth was.* A: *Sith trouthe ys.* C: *Sone trowyth ys.*

     asyde. B: *o syde.*

13   *Wheche.* A: *Whiche.* C: *Where.*

14   *nostri fiunt.* A: *nostri fient.* C: *nostri sunt jam.*

15   *schyld.* A and C: *scheld.*

16   *eu.* A: *en.* C: *heu.*

17   A: *Ofte tymes have we herd.* C: *Oftyn tyme have we here.*

19   A: *But ever desired we.* C: *But ever have we desire.* B clearly reads *deferred* rather than *deserred.* Richard Green (correspondence April 5, 1995) suggests the gloss

"we have continually put off more favorable opportunities [*i.e.*, to remedy the situation] for ourselves."

20   *commoda.* C: *commercia*

26   The scribe has inserted *que* above the line with a caret.

28   *per rus.* Or perhaps B: *per ens.* A: *parvo.* C: *per rus et mare.* Green suggests by correspondence: "C's *per rus et mare* is grammatical (unlike A's *paruo per mare*) and yields a sort of sense 'through the countryside and by the sea' but is clumsy at best. Perhaps the original read *parvum per mare* [i.e., 'across the Channel'] which would explain B's *per rus per mare.*"

29   *went.* B: *want.* A and C: *went.*

31   C: *Ho seythe truth he is schent*

33   *Rowners.* C: *Robberes*

35–36   The B scribe skipped the long line, but added it at the bottom of the page, with an arrow indicating where it should be placed.

35   *klaterers.* C: *flaterars*

36   A and C: *sua subdant colla securi*

42   *collacrematur.* A and C: *collachrimatur.*

44   *depopulatur.* B: *deppulatur.* A and C: *depopulatur*

46   *spirituales cedunt.* A: *spiritualia cadunt.* C: *spiritualia cedunt.*

47   A: *Sume bethe myschevyd.* C: *And so sume be myschevyd.*

49   *goose.* The second -*o* is superscript. A: *goith.* C: *goth*

50   *plus facit homo viciosus.* A: *plus fecit homo vitiosus.* C: *et plus hoc facit ut vitiosus.*

53   A: *Goddes halydayys ar noght.* C: *Goddes dere halydayys ar noght.* See line 55, which, in B, is also shortened, thus rhyming *halydays/playes.*

55   A: *For unthrifty pley is worght.* C: *For onthryfty pley ys worght.* See note to line 53 on B's rhyme.

58   B writes *in eis regnant ma* before striking this out and writing *steriles & luxuriosi* above the crossout.

62   *fune*. A and C: *fine*.

63   C: *Put these to the peynys.*

65–88   *Wesmynster*. These lines resemble the complaints about law courts in poems such as *London Lickpenny* and *The Simonie*.

67   *Noght ellys*. A: *neuertheles*; C: *neuer þe lesse*.

68   *vincuntur*. B: *vincunt*. A and C: *vincuntur*.

71   *face*. I am indebted to Richard Green for the gloss "outface," or "face down."

82   *crucis* here seems to be a reference to a coin.

83   Green notes a similar use of the proverb in the *Towneley Second Shepherd's Play*: "Ill spon weft, iwys, ay commys foull owte"(line 587).

92   *metuendi*. A and C: *metuenda*.

95   *The kyng knows nott alle*. Topos of "the king's ignorance." See *Truthe, Reste, and Pes*, lines 45–46, and *The Simonie*, lines 313–24.

99   *The kattys nek to the bel*. This line refers to the well-known fable of belling the cat which Langland used in his political allegory, *Piers Plowman* B Prologue 146–208. There the cat is probably John of Gaunt, uncle to Richard II and his guardian. In 1376 Bishop Thomas Brinton preached a sermon that mentioned the fable of the mice and the cat. The identity of the cat in *On the Times* is less certain.

107   B inserts *hym* above the line.

109   *Goode Jak . . . John*. Wright identified the first *Jak* with Robert de Vere, Duke of Dublin, and *Jak nobil* (line 113) with Michael de la Pole, Earl of Suffolk. Green believes "Goode Jak" refers to Jack Philipot, who helped finance Thomas of Woodstock's expedition to France, thus providing the soldiers with "loricos vel tunicas, quas vulgo 'jakkes' vocant." "*John*" in Green's political explanation denotes John of Gaunt, who might have been expected to reimburse Philipot for aid to his brother (pp, 336–39). That "Jak" probably refers to a person may be seen in the word's repetition in proximity (lines 105, 109, 111, 113).

110   *gratia.* Green suggests a reference to "his grace" John of Gaunt, with a pun on "kindness" and "thanks."

112   *regna remota.* Green explains these lines as John of Gaunt's absence from England during the late 1370s and early 1380s, including the 1378 St.-Malo expedition, an expedition to Scotland in 1380, and a diplomatic mission to Scotland in 1381.

117   *Purs Penyles.* This allegorical figure appears in other late medieval writings, including *The First Shepherd's Play* from the Towneley cycle of mystery plays: "I may syng / With purs penneles...." See *MED*, s.v. *peniles* (b). A satire on contemporary fashion begins in this line with the introduction of *Galauntes* who cavort with *Purs Penyles* as if they had both wealth and leisure.

123   B: *Now ys he here gone.* A & C: *Now is he here, and now is he gon.*

125   *Freshest.* B: *Freshet.* A: *Fresshest.* C: *Fresch.*

       new towche. The phrase is reminiscent of Chaucer's Pardoner: "Hym thoughte he rood al of the newe jet" (CT General Prologue, line 682).

131   B: *Narow thay bene thay seme brod.* So too in C. Gloss based on A: *Narugh they be, thouȝ they seme brode.*

132   A: *nova sunt; factio gentis.* C: *vana sunt hoc facite, gentes.*

139   *War ye.* C's reading. B: *Where ever.* A: *Ware.*

144   A: *non sit regula Sarum.* C: *cum non sit regula Sarum.*

146   A: *laqueantur a corpore crura.* C: *laqueant ad corpora crura.* Perhaps the sense is: "the legs are laced [with points] to the body."

157   *Mony.* B *Monᵍ* (y inserted above a caret).

160   B and C: *nisi deus instat aliquando.* Emendation from A.

161   B: *Womonly brestes.* A: *Women, lo! with wantounly brestes.* C: *Women lo! with here brestes.*

162   B: *pretendunt.* The sense of B 161–62, which reads: *Womonly brestes pretendunt arte prophana,* is perhaps something like "with profane art they puff out their chests like women."

168   A: *ut ventus ecce! vacillant.* C: *ventus velut ecce vacillant.*

169   A: *Now knokelyd elbowys.* C: *Her knokelys elbowys*

175   A: *Than ther teth quakis.* C: *Here chekys than quakys.*

176   A: *sed se quasi concutientes.* C: *sese quasi concutientes.*

181   *Huffe o galant.* RHR comments on the phrase: "'Galaunt' continued in use well into the sixteenth century, and there is a considerable body of literature on these overdressed braggarts" (p. 322). RHR edits a satirical lyric against sumptuous clothing that contains the refrain, "Huff! a galawnt, vylabele! / Thus syngyth galawntys in here revelere" (no. 52, *Historical Poems of the XIVth and XVth Centuries*). "Huff" is a term associated with braggarts and bullies, as is indicated by a stage direction in the Digby mystery play: "Her xal entyr a galavnt þus seyying: Hof, hof, hof, a frysche new galavnt!" (RHR, pp. 322–23). A: *Huf a galaunt thee atowche.* C: *Of a galaunt the towch.* Krochalis and Peters gloss "Huf" as "If." Green suggests that the sense of B might be: "If a gallant alludes [OED s.v. **Touch** v. 18b] to it [*þer a = þeron?*] (with 'it' being the dripping nose)."

182   Green wonders if the line might not be an ostentatiously polite way the gallant alludes to his lady's dripping nose?

183   *powche.* Perhaps "mouth" rather than "vagina."

189   *Vye velabel.* These words are similar to the refrain term in RHR's no. 52, which he entitles "Huf! A Galaunt." See above, note to line 181. Perhaps A is the more sound reading with *Vive la bele!*

197–200   appear in C as lines 177–80. Though Krochalis and Peters normally follow A, they follow C's line order in this instance.

200   *dampna.* B dampnᵃ (*a* inserted above a caret).

201   *Armes, sydes, and blode.* Blasphemous oaths against Christ's body.

202   *recitauit.* A and C read future tense *recitabit*, which makes better sense. So too in line 204 with *domabit.*

206   *poscunt*: A's reading. B: *possunt.*

207   B and A: *A contur tenore.* C: *A cowntur-tenur at Newgat.* Krochalis and Peters emend according to C, an emendation that provides a more stable meter than that of the London MSS.

211   A: *Now sey I for this dispite.* C: *Nowt I say for despyte.*

217   *Symon.* Simon Magus (Acts 8.9–24), who gave his name to the word "simony." He offered money to the apostles so that he might pass on the power of the Holy Spirit through the laying on of hands. R. F. Green suggests a possible jibe at Simon Sudbury, Archbishop of Canterbury at the time of the Peasants' Revolt. See note to "Tax has tenet us alle," line 35, below.

227   *ye.* A and B. C: *he*

229   *lanterne of lyght.* Perhaps an allusion to John 8:12, the source for the title of the Wycliffite treatise.

232   *venena*: C's reading. B: *vena.*

233   A: *Oure kynge and oure lond.* C: *Ouer kynge and his lond.*

234   *servet*: A & C. B: *servat.*

        et tueatur. B: *et tudatur.* C: *te a tudatur.* A and Wr: *et teneatur.*

238   *fructu.* Glossed here as "fruit [children?]"; but perhaps an allusion to St. Paul on the first fruits of grace (Rom. 8:23); or to James 1:18.

Latin epilogue *O rex.* The B Prologue of *Piers Plowman* contains similar verses: "Dum rex a regere dicatur nomen habere / Nomen habet sine re nisi studet iura tenere" (140). Since the name of "king" comes from *regere*, to rule, unless a man takes care to maintain law he bears the name without the substance.

Tax Has Tenet Us Alle

1   *Tax.* The poll taxes of 1377, 1379, 1380–81, which were one of the chief causes of the rebellion of 1381. The manuscript lines are executed as long lines, with the Latin ending each line. Lines 1–4 might be considered an example of what Embree terms "the king's ignorance topos." See the note to lines 45–46 of *Truthe, Reste, and Pes,* and *On the Times,* lines 93–96.

3   *smalle.* The tax collectors diverted much of the collections to their own pockets.

9   *Kent.* "The first concentration of the peasants was at Maidstone under Wat Tyler, and the first town to endorse them was Canterbury" (RHR).

25   *blwun.* Wr, *RA*, *blwū (?).* To "blow" boasts is to boast a lot as a "blowhard" might do.

29   *endorst.* Wr, *RA*, reads *endost.*

32   *pro caede.* Wr, *RA*, reads *procede.*

35   *bischop.* Archbishop of Canterbury and Chancellor of England, Simon Sudbury, who originated the poll tax. The rebels executed him in London. R. F. Green has argued that the verses below (from *Syng y wold, butt, alas!* [*On the Times, Index* § 3113]) allude to the archbishop and suggest that the whole poem points to events of 1380 rather than 1388, as previously believed:

> Symon, þat fals man,
> *decori nocet ecclesiarum;*
> Myche sorwe he began,
> *virus diffudit amarum.*
>   (C Text)

See "Jack Philipot, John of Gaunt, and a Poem of 1380," *Speculum* 66 (1991), 330–41 at p. 340. Green concludes: "This poem [*Tax Has Tenet Us Alle*] too is macaronic, and it bears a striking metrical and stylistic resemblance to *On the Times.* It is tempting to see these two pieces as the work of a single author, who, writing on the eve and on the morrow of the Peasants' Revolt, has, as it were, bequeathed us both prologue and epilogue to that dramatic event" (p. 341).

41–60   Not in the Cambridge MS. Supplied from the Oxford text, checked against RHR and Wr.

41   *Jak Strawe.* In the literature of the Peasants' Revolt, Jack Straw is often cited as a rebel leader. Straw and Thomas Farringdon burned Robert Hales's great manor of Highbury (see note to line 49). Compare also Chaucer's Nun's Priest's Tale: "Certes, he Jakke Straw and his meynee / Ne made nevere shoutes half so shrille / Whan that they wolden any Flemyng kille, / As thilke day was maad upon the fox" (VII.3394–97).

48   *stiva.* Wr, *RA*, reads *otiva (?).*

49   *Hales.* Sir Robert Hales, Prior of the Hospital of St. John of Jerusalem and
       Royal Treasurer. When Hales, along with Archbishop Simon Sudbury and
       others, took refuge in the Tower, the rebels dragged them out to Tower Hill
       and beheaded them (Friday, 14 June 1381).

52   *stultis.* Wr, *RA*, reads *stultus.*

55   *Savoy.* The wealthy and beautiful ("semely") palace of John of Gaunt, Duke of
       Lancaster, located on the Strand near the river Thames. On Thursday, 13 June,
       the rebels burned the Savoy to the ground and turned Gaunt's coat of arms
       upside down (sign of a traitor to the realm).

57   *Arcan.* Joshua had forbidden his troops to pillage Jericho after its fall but
       Achan disobeyed and was stoned to death (Joshua 7). The leaders of the
       Peasants' Revolt also issued orders against looting, but the orders were widely
       violated. Wr, *RA*, and Krochalis and Peters, who follow the Digby MS rather
       than the Cambridge MS, read *Arcadon* for *Arcan don.*

61-64 *Owre kyng . . . paterna.* Richard was the son of Edward, the Black Prince,
       celebrated military leader and hero of the battle of Poitiers (1356), who cap-
       tured the French king John. The Black Prince led his captive through the streets
       of London in a triumphal procession. During the Peasants' Revolt, while some
       secluded themselves from the mob's fury, Richard valiantly confronted the
       rebels at Smithfield (Saturday, 15 June), parleying briefly with Walter (or Wat)
       Tyler, the rebel leader. When William Walworth, mayor of London, tried to
       arrest Tyler and when Tyler drew a dagger, a valet killed Tyler and the crowds
       eventually dispersed.

62   *alii.* Cambridge MS *alios.*

65-66 *Jak Straw . . . superna.* Jack Straw was executed but not at Smithfield. It was
       Wat Tyler who was struck down at the Smithfield conference.

65   *he kest.* So Cambridge MS; RHR *þey cast.*

Richard II's Reign and the Peasants' Revolt

Ther Is a Busch That Is Forgrowe

1   *busch.* A patent reference to Sir John Bushy, speaker of the House of Commons and one of Richard's favorites. Henry Bolingbroke, Duke of Hereford (later King Henry IV), beheaded Bushy at Bristol in 1399. The author of *Richard the Redeless* makes similar punning references to Bushy and Green in passus 2, lines 152–53: "Thus baterid this bred [bird] on *busshes* aboute / And gaderid gomes on *grene* ther as they walkyd" (ed. Skeat). In Shakespeare's *Richard II*, Bolingbroke contemptuously refers to Bushy, Green, and Bagot as the "caterpillars of the commonwealth" (II.iii.165). See also the Gardener's statements about Richard's ministers in III.iv.

4   *grene.* A reference to Sir Henry Green who, with Bushy (note to line 1), guided Richard's legislation through the House of Commons and who was also beheaded at Bristol.

6   *the.* So Wr; Hamper *th'*.

7   *bagge.* A reference to Sir William Bagot, another of Richard's ministers in the House of Commons.

8   *kettord. MED*, directing to "? Cp. *cater, katur* num" (from OF *catre*, four), cites this word only from this poem, with the notation "? Quartered."

13   *swan.* Thomas of Woodstock, duke of Gloucester, whose badge was a swan (which he had adopted from his father Edward III). Thomas Mowbray, duke of Norfolk, executed Gloucester at Calais in 1397. Some have felt that Norfolk was acting under King Richard's orders. The author of the present poem attributes Gloucester's death to Bushy. Hamper identifies the *swan* as "Hugh Earl of Stafford" and the *eldes bryd* of line 32 as "Edmund Earl of Stafford, eldest surviving son."

14   *sclawtur.* So Wr; Hamper *sclawt*ͬ.

20   *stede.* "A horse was the crest of the earl of Arundel, who was beheaded in the 21st Ric. II" (Wr). Richard Fitzalan, Earl of Arundel, was appealed by eight lords appellant of killing Simon Burley; and John of Gaunt ordered Arundel's property confiscate, condemning him to death. He was executed on Tower Hill in 1397.

25   *bereward.* "The earl of Warwick banished to Isle of Man" (Wr). His badge was a black bear. RHR glosses the political allegory of this stanza: "a bearward (the Earl of Warwick) found a rag, and made a bag through which he is undone (i.e., he aided to raise up Bagot, who became instrumental in his banishment)." *A Manual of the Writings in Middle English 1050–1500*, ed. Hartung, 5:1440.

26   *the.* So Wr; Hamper *th'.*

32   *Her eldest . . . fro.* Trans.: "Her eldest bird has been taken away from her." For this line Wr reads: "Her eldes[t] bryd his taken her fro"; Hamper: "Her eldes bryd his taken her fro." Of the *bryd* Wr glosses: "Humphrey [Plantagenet], Gloucester's only son, was, after his father's death, carried to Ireland and imprisoned in the castle of Trim."

34   *stedes colt.* "Thomas earl of Arundel, son of the earl beheaded in the 21st Ric. II" (Wr).

35   *An eron.* The heron is Henry Bolingbroke, Duke of Lancaster, whose cause Thomas Arundel has joined.

36   *wondur.* So Wr; Hamper *wond^r.*

37   *berewardes sone.* "Richard Beauchamp, under nineteen, was at this time married to Elizabeth, daughter of Thomas lord Berkeley" (Wr). *tendur,* so Wr; Hamper *tend^r.* On "berewardes" see note to line 25.

44   *contré.* So Wr; Hamper *contr'.* Hamper glosses: "Ravenspur in Yorkshire, where Henry landed."

47   *and y thinges.* So Hamper and Wr. *y* = in. The syntax seems defective.

49   *gees.* The Percy family of Northumbria. Hamper's note: "The Commons."

52   *pecokes.* The Neville family of Yorkshire. Hamper's note: "The Lords."

55   *the busch.* So Wr; Hamper *th' busch.*

57   *aftur.* So Wr; Hamper *aft^r.*

58   *the grene.* So Wr; Hamper *th' grene.*

60 Of lines 34–60 RHR explains: "the steed's colt (Thomas of Arundel) has escaped, and has joined the heron (the Duke of Lancaster); and the bearward's son (Richard Beauchamp) has been married off, but is watching to join the heron. The heron and the colt are up in the North in company with the geese and the peacocks (the Percys and the Nevilles). The heron will alight on the bush, and will fall upon the green."

64 *the ges.* So Wr; Hamper *th' ges.* *all so.* So Hamper; Wr *alleso.*

67 *sere.* So Wr; Hamper *ser'.*

68 *lengur.* So Wr; Hamper *leng*^r*.*

70 *Ywys I con no nodur bote.* So Wr; Hamper *y wys y con no nod*^r *bote.*

73 *The longe.* So Wr; Hamper *th' longe.*

77 *rought.* From OE *hrútan* to snore. See Chaucer's Reeve's Tale, said of Symkyn's family: "Men myghte hir rowtyng heere two furlong; / The wenche rowteth eek, *par compaignye*" (lines 4166–67).

83 *Yif.* Wr *ʒyf.*

87 *Yif.* Wr *ʒyf.*

89 *beste.* Wr's insertion (in brackets).

90 *were.* So Wr; Hamper *wer'.* Hamper glosses *in point to spylle*: "This expression occurs in Henry's declaratory speech on assuming the royal power. 'The rewme was *in point to be undone* for defaut of governance, and undoyng of the gude lawes.' — *Archaeologia*, vol. XX, p. 201, note p." See also *The Simonie* line 432.

Truthe, Reste, and Pes (What Profits a Kingdom)

2 *For.* MS *ffor.* I substitute capital F for ff at the beginning of lines throughout this poem. RHR, of the complaints in 1401–02, quotes the following from *English Chronicle*: "And aboute this tyme the peple of this land began to

grucche ayens kyng Harri, and beer him hevy, because he took thair good and paide not therfore; and desirid to haue ayeen king Richarde. Also lettriʒ cam to certayn frendis of Richard, as thay hadde be sent from hymself, and saide that he was alive; wherof moche peple was glad and desirid to haue him kynge ayeen." Kail and RHR base their dating of the poem (1401) on allusions like this.

45–46   *A kyng may not al aspie*. Embree has identified the content of these two lines as a topos: the "king's ignorance." See "The King's Ignorance: A Topos for Evil Times," *Medium Ævum* 54 (1985), 121–26 at 121. See also *The Simonie* lines 313–24.

52   *the lawe to telle*. This looks like dittography from line 50. Perhaps the correct reading in line 52 = *the lawe to selle* (?).

55–56   *Rathere . . . bighe hym pes*. See Luke 22:36: "But now he that hath a purse, let him take it, and likewise a scrip, and he that hath not, let him sell his coat, and buy a sword." And compare Matt. 19:21: "If thou wilt be perfect, go sell what thou hast, and give to the poor, and thou shalt have treasure in heaven." See also the note to lines 57–60.

57–60   *A worthi knyght . . . the firste het*. These lines include a rough paraphrase of a famous passage from the Sermon on the Mount: "But I say to you not to resist evil: but if one strike thee on thy right cheek, turn to him also the other: And if a man will contend with thee in judgment, and take away thy coat, let go thy cloak also unto him" (Matt. 5:39–40).

60   *at the firste het*. RHR: "at the first go."

76   *Wel lyvyng man, hardy of kynde*. The man who lives well (as opposed to the "wikked lyvere"), is by nature courageous. Living well here means living virtuously. See also line 79: "The good lyvere hath God in mynde." The syntax of lines 76–80 is difficult.

78   *mes*. Kail glosses this as "adversity," while RHR has "mass, sacrament." The idea is that death is the final rite of passage for the soul, whether for a "wel lyvyng man" or for a "wikked lyvere."

94   In the margin next to this line appears the word *nota*, "note."

98   For the concept of the "comoun profit," see Russell A. Peck, *Kingship and Common Profit in Gower's Confessio Amantis* (Carbondale: Southern Illinois University Press, 1978), and Alford, *Glossary*, s.v. *Commune Profit*.

140   *To felle Goddis foon*. "Written apparently in support of the statute *De Haeretico Comburendo* passed in 1401" (RHR). This statute authorized the burning of heretics and had a chilling effect especially on the Lollards.

145   *chery fayre*. "A frequent symbol for the transitoriness of life; compare Gower, *Conf. Amantis*, Pro. I.19: 'For al is but a chery feire / This worldes good'; Hoccleve, *De Reg. Principum*, clxxxv.47: 'Thy lyfe, my sone, is but a chery feire'" (RHR). See also Chaucer's *Troilus*: " . . . and thynketh al nys but a faire, / This world that passeth soone as floures faire" (5.1840–41).

159   *math*. Syncopated form of *maketh*.

163   The MS lacks a line here.

Poems against Simony and the Abuse of Money

Introduction

Poems and documents attacking simony and the abuse of money constitute a significant aspect of medieval anticlerical, political complaint. Simony — from Simon Magus, who offered the disciples money to acquire the power of the Holy Ghost (Acts 8) — is the buying and selling of ecclesiastical preferment. Anticlerical writers censured simony and avarice in general as part of the ecclesiastical reform movement after the Investiture Controversy; and Latin diatribes against Rome continued and extended the antisimoniac tradition.

In the twelfth century poets writing in goliardic meters (trochaic or dactylic tetrameter) attacked, often in parody, the increasing importance of money in Church affairs. Many venality satires may be found in Thomas Wright's still valuable collection for the Camden Society entitled *The Latin Poems Commonly Attributed to Walter Mapes* (1841). The author of the famous *Apocalypse of Bishop Golias*, for example, denounces the archdeacon's selling of the Church (with considerable *paranomasia* on *venal*, *vend* and *venia* [=pardon]):

> Ecclesiastica jura venalia
> facit propatulo; sed venalia
> cum venum dederit, vocat a venia,
> quam non inveniens venit ecclesia.
> > (169–72, ed. Wright)
> (He openly sells rights of the Church; but when he calls this a
> "venial" sin, as in "pardon," and finds none, he sells the Church.)

Other goliardic poems against ecclesiastical greed in Wright's volume include *Golias in Romanum Curiam* ("Utar contra vitia carmine rebelli," also entitled *Invectio contra avaritiam*), which satirizes the substitution of "money" for "spirit" (*nummus est pro numine*), the silver mark for the Gospel writer (*pro Marco marca*), and the money chest (*arca*) for the altar (*ara*); *De mundi miseria* ("Ecce mundus moritur vitio sepultus"), which ironically speaks of money's restorative properties (lines 29–32); *Contra avaritiam* ("Captivata largitas longe relegatur"); *De cruce denarii* ("Crux est denarii potens in saeculo"). The Benedictbeuern MS (thirteenth century) associated

179

with the *Carmina Burana* provides the well-known *Gospel according to the silver mark*, a scriptural parody which begins, "Initium sancti evangelii secundum Marcas argenti."[1] Wright also prints a poem on *Nummus*, coin, which will result later on in the English "Sir Penny" verses. This begins: "Manus ferens munera pium facit impium."[2]

In this section I include an example of this Latin verse, which begins *Beati qui esuriunt / Et sitiunt* (from British Library MS Harley 913 fol. 59r–59v), as edited and translated in Wr *PSE* pp. 224–30. This poem, written in the manuscript as prose but with alternating four- and three-beat lines and intricate rhyme schemes characteristic of goliardic lyrics, dates from the beginning of the fourteenth century (reign of Edward I) and is entitled by Wright "Song on the Venality of the Judges." I have checked Wright's edition against a photostat of the manuscript. I include but slightly modernize Wright's translation.

One of the chief documents in the Middle English Abuse of Money tradition is *The Simonie*, also known as "On the Evil Times of Edward II" and "Symonie and Couetise" (*Index* § 4165; *Supplement* § 1992). The anonymous author of *The Simonie*, which Wright dates to about 1321, complains that those who govern abuse their power egregiously — so much so that God has sent famines and plagues as punishments for wrongdoing. A dominant motif of the poem is that the poor man — "Godes man" — stands outside the doors of court while the rich man, bearing gifts, is welcomed inside (lines 9–30, 55–66, 121–44, 169–80). It offers traditional estates satire that begins with the court of Rome and high prelates and proceeds through the clerical ranks (including monks, parsons, and friars) to knights, squires, justices, bailiffs, sheriffs, beadles, and merchants.[3] The linking of anticlerical satire and the abuse of money anticipates *Piers Plowman*. Like *Piers Plowman*, *The Simonie* is lively and vivid, with touches of arch wit. A newly-installed parson will spend money so quickly that the corn in his barn will not be eaten by mice (lines 69–70). What kind of "penance" do monks perform? "Hii weren sockes in here shon [shoes], and felted botes above" (line 146). Those who live according to a monastic rule live a life of ease rather than

---

[1] Text, translation, and commentary in Jill Mann, "Satiric Subject and Satiric Object in Goliardic Literature," *Mittellateinisches Jahrbuch* 15 (1980), 63–86 at 75–77.

[2] In an Appendix to *The Latin Poems of Walter Mapes*, Wright includes a medley of poems on Sir Penny: *Versus de Nummo* (pp. 355–56); *De dan Denier* (French, thirteenth century: pp. 357–59); *In erth it es a litill thing* (pp. 359–61); *Peny is an hardy knyght* (p. 361); and *Rycht fane wald I my quentans mak* (Scottish, sixteenth century, p. 362).

[3] For a summary of *The Simonie's* contents, see Robbins, "Poems," p. 1437. For the most useful discussion of medieval estates satire, see Jill Mann, *Chaucer and Medieval Estates Satire* (Cambridge: Cambridge University Press, 1973), especially pp. 205–06.

easing the lives of others (lines 151–56). A false physician will "wagge his urine in a vessel of glaz," swear that the patient is sicker than he really is, and comfort the anxious wife. The author adds that such a doctor may know "no more than a gos [goose] wheither he wole live or die" (lines 211–21). On a few occasions the author includes something like dialogue, as when the false physician says to the housewife, "Dame, for faute [lack] of helpe, thin housebonde is neih [almost] slain" (line 216), or when the beggar in the street cries out, "Allas, for hungger I die / Up rihte!" (lines 400–01). There are several apocalyptic passages in the poem. The author points to recent natural disasters as evidence of divine disfavor; and in a memorable sequence he alludes to an English *gamen*, game, in which people begin cursing one another on Monday. And now, he says, God has abandoned the land, sending a great "derthe" that has caused a bushel of wheat to soar to "foure shillinges or more" (line 393). Wr regards this as a reference to the great famine of 1315 and its consequences. The poem contains colorful language, snatches of song, and proverbs. The new parson, rather than reading the Bible, "rat on the rouwe-bible" ("reads" the fiddle [line 88]); he will discharge "a prest of clene lyf" and then replace him with "a daffe" (lines 97, 99). A wanton priest will provide himself with "a gay wench of the newe jet" and, "when the candel is oute," "clateren cumpelin" ("recite compline" [lines 118–20]).

Pearsall argues that the form of *The Simonie* derives from "the loose septenary/ alexandrine long line of the thirteenth century, of mixed Anglo-Norman descent," a verse line that was "invaded," he says, "by the cadences of the native four-stress line, with or without alliteration." This poem "uses the septenary/alexandrine monorhymed quatrain with a bob and sixth line rhyming together, but is deeply infiltrated by the rhythms of the native four-stress line, with sporadic alliteration."[4] The combination of the Anglo-Norman line with the four-stress cadence makes for animated, convincing verse.

The Simonie exists in three manuscripts: National Library of Scotland, Advocates Library MS 19. 2. 1, fols. 328*r*–334*v* (the Auchinleck MS, about 1330); Cambridge University Library MS Peterhouse 104, fols. 210*r*–212*r*, of the late fourteenth century; and Oxford University, Bodleian Library MS 48 fols. 325*v*–331*r* of about 1425 (*MED*). Ross tentatively identifies the dialects of the three versions as East Midland (Auchinleck), Kentish (Peterhouse), and East Midland (Bodley). The three MS versions are quite different from one another; Embree and Urquhart have argued that the extant versions derive from a lost original but that the Auchinleck text probably preserves more authentic readings than the other two. They have urged that

---

[4] *Old English and Middle English Poetry* (London: Routledge, 1977), pp. 151, 152.

the three versions be printed in a parallel-text edition. Embree is completing such an edition, which will be especially welcome because the three versions of *The Simonie* anticipate and invite comparison with the three states of *PP*. The text of *The Simonie* in this edition is based on the facsimile edition of the Auchinleck MS and is completed by a photostatic copy of the Bodley MS (lines 477–end). These versions are checked against Wright's edition of 1839 (Wr) and the text in Brandl and Zippel's 2nd ed. of *Middle English Literature* (Br), and compared with both the Peterhouse (C) version (as printed by Brandl and Zippel) and the Bodley (B) version (as printed by Ross). Ross rearranges the MS stanzas according to his theories about the poem's logic of composition. I have not followed his rearrangements.

The next two poems of this section concern the venality satire theme of *Sir Penny* (a.k.a. *Dan Denarius*). This theme occurs in fifteenth-century English lyrics with some frequency, but these have precursors in continental literature.[5] These poems depict *Sir Penny* as all powerful in the earthly realm: he is like a king to whom all must bow; and all human "joy" — so these lyrics allege — depends on money. Poems on *Sir Penny* are related to lyrics on the power of the purse (such as those with the refrain "Gramersy myn owyn purs"). Of this latter kind the wittiest is by Geoffrey Chaucer, *The Complaint of Chaucer to His Purse*. The first poem on *Sir Penny* printed in this collection is "Above all thing thow arte a kyng" (*Index* § 113). This is a carol, a unique fifteenth-century text in 80 lines and in quatrains rhyming *abcb* (with internal rhyme in the *a* and *c* lines) from British Library MS Royal 17. B. xlvii fols. 160*v*–162*r*. The manuscript bears the title *money, money*; and the lyric emphasizes the importance of money in all spheres of human activity. The present text is based on an excellent electrostatic print from microfilm of the Royal MS and is checked against the editions of Greene and RHR. The second *Sir Penny* lyric printed here begins "In erth it es a litill thing" (*Index* § 1480), a Scots poem in 123 lines from British Library MS Cotton Galba E. ix fols. 50*v*–51*r*, which bears the heading *Incipit narracio de domino denario* (Here begins the statement of Dan Denarius).[6] There is an abbreviated version of this poem from Caius College Cambridge MS 174, which Wright and Halliwell printed in *Reliquiae Antiquae* (2:108–10). The present text is based on a fine electrostatic print from microfilm of the Cotton Galba MS and is

---

[5] See the Latin poems on *nummus* and the German lyrics on *pfennig* discussed by John A. Yunck, *The Lineage of Lady Meed: The Development of Mediaeval Venality Satire* (Notre Dame: University of Notre Dame Press, 1963). The medieval penny was a valuable silver coin worth one-twelfth of a shilling. In the time of Edward III the penny contained eighteen grains of silver.

[6] For a summary of the poem's contents, see Robbins, "Poems," p. 1467.

checked against the editions of Wr (*Walter Mapes*) and of Robbins (*Secular Lyrics of the XIVth and XVth Centuries*, who titles the poem *Sir Penny, II*).

The final poem — "In London There I Was Bent," or *London Lickpenny* (*Index* § 3759) — offers both a venality satire against the legal system and a lively social picture, including street cries of various sections in and around London. The story concerns a Kentish countryman who visits London seeking justice in the law courts. He enters crowded Westminster Hall, where his hood is stolen, and then he tries the King's Bench, which concerned itself chiefly with criminal law. The law clerks show no interest in the poor Kentishman. Next he moves to the Court of Common Pleas, also in Westminster, but the sergeant of the law with his silk hood will not even say "mum" to him; so he proceeds to the Chancery and the clerks of the Rolls. Although the Kentishman shows considerable deference to these clerks, and though they agree that he has a good legal case, it does not go forward because he lacks money. Deciding he can find no justice in Westminster Hall, he encounters a crowd of Flemish merchants just outside the doors, but he cannot purchase any of their wares, nor can he buy an early meal from cooks at Westminster gate. He wanders to the city of London and hears the street-cries of fruit-sellers and vendors of herbs. He walks through Cheapside, Candlewick street, Eastcheap, and Cornhill, where he discovers his own hood for sale — the one stolen from him in Westminster Hall. Trying to escape from his nightmare visit to London, the plowman goes to Billingsgate but cannot afford to hire a barge man to ferry him over the Thames; eventually he makes his way to Kent, vowing to "meddle" in the law no more. London is called "a lick-penny (as Paris is called by some, a *pick-purse*) because of feastings" (Skeat). This often-printed poem exists in two manuscript versions from the Harley Collection in the British Library: MS 367, in 112 lines and in rime royal stanzas, and MS 542, in 128 lines and in eight-line stanzas rhyming *ababbcbc*, the so-called *Monk's Tale* stanza, a common ballade form. Both versions are in four-stress lines. The original poem dates from the early fifteenth century and was formerly attributed to John Lydgate, who composed in both rhyme royal and in the *Monk's Tale* stanza. A headnote to the version in Harley 367 reads: "London Lyckpenny A Ballade com-pyled by Dan John Lydgate monke of Bery about [space in the manuscript for number] yeres agoo, and now newly oū'sene and amended." The manuscript version of Harley 367, which RHR prints, was executed by John Stow (died 1605), author of *The Survey of London* and *Annales*, and it evidences considerable emendation to avoid archaic or unknown words and phrases, including *qui tollis*, *woon*, and *umple*. Both recensions of the poem contain editorial intervention, but the 542 version seems earlier and less redacted than Harley 367; but neither can be said to witness the original poem. The present edition is based on a paper print from the manuscript and is checked against a paper print of Harley 367 and against the editions of Hammond

(*Anglia* 20 [1898], 542) reprinted in *English Verse between Chaucer and Surrey*, pp. 237–39, 476–78; Holthausen's composite text (*Anglia* 43); Skeat's print of Harley 367 in *Specimens of English Literature 1394–1579* (with valuable notes); and RHR's version of Harley 367.

Select Bibliography

Manuscripts

British Library MS Harley 913 fols. 59*r*–59*v* (c. 1330).

National Library of Scotland, Advocates Library MS 19. 2. 1 (Auchinleck MS), fols. 328*r*–334*v* (1330–40) [476 lines in 79 six-line stanzas].

Cambridge University Library, MS Peterhouse 104, fols. 210*r*–212*r* (1350) [468 lines].

Oxford University MS Bodley 48 fols. 325*v*–331*r* (c. 1425) [414 lines, including 114 lines not found in other versions].

British Library MS Royal 17.B.xlvii fols. 160*v*–162*r* (fifteenth century).

British Library MS Cotton Galba E. ix fols. 50*v*–51*r* (1440–50).

British Library MS Harley 367 fols. 127*r*–126*v* (c. 1600–25).

British Library MS Harley 542 fols. 102*r*–104*r* (c. 1600).

Previous Editions

Beati qui esuriunt

Wright, Thomas, ed. *The Political Songs of England from the Reign of John to that of Edward II*. London: Printed for the Camden Society by J. B. Nichols and Son, 1839. Pp. 224–30.

Introduction

The Simonie

The Auchinleck Manuscript. National Library of Scotland, Advocates' MS. 19.2.1. With an Introduction by Derek Pearsall and I. C. Cunningham. London: The Scolar Press; New York: The British Book Centre, 1977. [A folio-sized facsimile edition.]

Hardwick, Charles, ed. *A Poem on the Times of Edward II*. Percy Society 28, no. 2. London, 1849. [Peterhouse MS. Printed in seventy-eight eleven-line stanzas.]

Brandl, A., and O. Zippel, eds. *Mittelenglische Sprach- und Literaturproben*. Berlin, 1915; second ed. 1927. Rpt. under title *Middle English Literature*, New York: Chelsea, 1947, 1949, 1965. [Prints the Edinburgh Auchinleck MS and the Cambridge Peterhouse MS side by side for comparison.]

Wright, Thomas, ed. *The Political Songs of England from the Reign of John to that of Edward II*. London: Printed for the Camden Society by J. B. Nichol and Son, 1839. Pp. 323–45. [From the Auchinleck MS, Glossary at bottom of pages, and Notes at the back of the volume.]

Ross, Thomas W. "On the Evil Times of Edward II." *Anglia* 75 (1957), 173–93. [Prints the Bodley MS with considerable editorial intervention.]

Above All Thing Thow Arte a Kyng (Royal MS)

Greene, R. L., ed. *Early English Carols*. 2nd ed. rev. Oxford: Clarendon, 1977. [§ 393, pp. 231–32. Notes p. 449. Good edition, normalized (with some errors in transcription corrected by RHR). Excellent notes.]

RHR, pp. 134–37.

In Erth It Es a Litill Thing (Sir Penny)

Wright, Thomas, ed. *The Latin Poems Commonly Attributed to Walter Mapes*. Camden Society 16. London: Camden Society, 1841. [Prints the Cotton Galba version in the "Appendix of Translations and Imitations," pp. 359–61.]

Wright, Thomas, and J. O. Halliwell, eds. *Reliquiae Antiquae*. 2 vols. London: Pickering, 1841, 1843. [Volume 2, pp. 108–10. Prints version in Caius College, Cambridge.]

RHR, pp. 51–55.

London Lickpenny

Hammond, Eleanor, ed. *English Verse between Chaucer and Surrey*. Durham: Duke University Press, 1927. [Prints Harley 542 on pp. 238–39; notes on pp. 476–78.]

———. "London Lickpenny." *Anglia* 20 (1898), 404–20. [Prints Harley 542 and 367 parallel.]

Holthausen, F. "London Lickpenny." *Anglia* 43 (1919), 61–68. [Composite text of both Harley 367 and 542, in the eight-line stanza; attempts to reconstruct the poem's metre as five rather than four stress.]

RHR, pp. 130–34. [Prints Harley 367.]

Skeat, W. W., ed. *Specimens of English Literature from the Ploughmans Crede to the Shepheardes Calendar*. 2nd ed. Oxford: Clarendon, 1879. [Prints Harley 367 on pp. 24–27. Important notes on pp. 373–76.]

General Studies

Kaeuper, Richard W. *War, Justice, and Public Order: England and France in the Later Middle Ages*. Oxford: Clarendon, 1988. [See especially chapter 4, "Vox Populi," for historically-informed analyses of satires and complaints.]

Kinney, Thomas L. "The Temper of Fourteenth-Century English Verse of Complaint." *Annuale Mediaevale* 7 (1966), 74–89. [Places *The Simonie* in context of complaint and satire.]

Little, Lester K. *Religious Poverty and the Profit Economy in Medieval Europe*. Ithaca: Cornell University Press, 1978. [An excellent study of changing views of the apostolic life in the later Middle Ages.]

Maddicott, J. R. "Poems of Social Protest in Early Fourteenth-Century England." *England in the Fourteenth Century: Proceedings of the 1985 Harlaxton Symposium*. Ed. W. M. Ormrod. Woodbridge, Suffolk: Boydell Press, 1986. Pp. 130–44. [Contrasts the specificity of later verses of complaint — specifically, the literature of 1381 — with earlier fourteenth-century complaints and satires, which Maddicott regards as closer to traditional laments and venality satire. Includes discussion of *The Simonie* and *The Song of the Husbandman*.]

Scattergood, V. J. *Politics and Poetry in the Fifteenth Century.* London: Blandford, 1971. [See chapter 9: "English Society II: Some Aspects of Social Change." VJS discusses "Above All Thing" on pp. 332–33 and 339, and "In Erth It Es a Litill Thing" on p. 338.]

Yunck, John A. "Dan Denarius: the Almighty Penny and the Fifteenth Century Poets." *American Journal of Economics and Sociology* 20 (1961), 207–22. Reprinted in *Die englische Satire.* Ed. Wolfgang Weiss. Darmstadt: Wissenschaftliche Buchgesellschaft, 1982. Pp. 69–88. [Examples of poems on Sir Penny, with bibliography.]

———. *The Lineage of Lady Meed: The Development of Mediaeval Venality Satire.* Notre Dame: University of Notre Dame Press, 1963. [A valuable study of Latin, French, and English venality satires with special emphasis on *Piers Plowman* and the English fourteenth century.]

———. "Satire." *A Companion to Piers Plowman.* Ed. John A. Alford. Berkeley and Los Angeles: University of California Press, 1988. Pp. 135–54. [Keyed to *PP* but wide-ranging and valuable.]

Studies of The Simonie

Embree, Dan, and Elizabeth Urquhart. "*The Simonie*: The Case for a Parallel-Text Edition." *Manuscripts and Texts: Editorial Problems in Later Middle English Literature.* Ed. Derek Pearsall. Cambridge: Brewer, 1985. Pp. 49–59. [Pertinent information about the MSS and their production, with plausible conjecture about authorship and scribal transmission. Three extant MSS derive from a lost original.]

Finlayson, John. "*The Simonie*: Two Authors?" *Archiv für das Studium der neueren Sprachen und Literaturen* 226 (1989), 39–51. [Argues that the Peterhouse MS is "a deliberate and accomplished rewriting of the original poem represented by A (Auchinleck) and B (the Bodley text)."]

Pearsall, Derek. *Old English and Middle English Poetry*. London: Routledge, 1977. [Excellent discussion of *The Simonie* in the context of Alliterative Poetry in chapter 6.]

Salter, Elizabeth. *"Piers Plowman and The Simonie."* *Archiv für das Studium der neueren Sprachen und Literaturen* 203 (1967), 241–54. [Argues that *The Simonie* was a source for *PP*.]

Bibliography

Robbins, Rossell Hope. "XIII. Poems Dealing with Contemporary Conditions." *A Manual of the Writings in Middle English 1050–1300*. Vol. 5. Gen. ed. Albert E. Hartung. New Haven: The Connecticut Academy of Arts and Sciences, 1975. Pp. 1385–1536; 1631–1725. [Discusses *The Simonie* (§ 82) on p. 1437; bibliography on p. 1669; *In Erth It Es a Litill Thing* (§ 154) on p. 1467; bibliography on pp. 1684–85; *Above All Thing Thow Arte a Kyng* (see § 158, under *London Lickpenny*) on p. 1468; *London Lickpenny* (§ 158) on p. 1468, bibliography on pp. 1685–86.]

Beati qui esuriunt

[*Song on the Venality of the Judges*]

(British Library MS Harley 913 fols. 59*r*–59*v*)

Beati qui esuriunt
et sitiunt, et faciunt
   justiciam,
et odiunt et fugiunt
5   injuriae nequiciam;
quos nec auri copia
nec divitum encennia
   trahunt a rigore,
   nec pauperum clamore;
10 quae sunt justa judicant,
et a jure non claudicant
   divitum favore.

Sed nunc miro more
multos fallit seculum,
15 et trahit in periculum,
   mundi ob favorem,
   ut lambeant honorem.
Hoc facit pecunia,
quam omnis fere curia
20   jam duxit in uxorem.

Sunt justiciarii,
quos favor et denarii
   alliciunt a jure;
hii sunt nam bene recolo,
25 quod censum dant diabolo,
   et serviunt hii pure.
Nam jubet lex naturae,

quod judex in judicio
nec prece nec precio
30   acceptor sit personae.
Quid, Jhesu ergo bone,
fiet de judicibus,
qui prece vel muneribus
   cedunt a ratione?

35 Revera tales judices
nuncios multiplices
   habent — audi quare:
Si terram vis rogare,
accedet ad te nuncius,
40 et loquitur discretius,
   dicens, "Amice care,
   vis tu placitare?
Sum cum justitiario
qui te modo vario
45   possum adjuvare;
   si vis impetrare
per suum subsidium,
da michi dimidium,
   et te volo juvare."

50 Ad pedes sedent clerici,
qui velut famelici
   sunt, donis inhiantes;
   et pro lege dantes,
quod hii qui nichil dederint,

189

55 quamvis cito venerint,
  erunt expectantes.

  Sed si quaedam nobilis,
  pulcra vel amabilis,
    cum capite cornuto,
60   auro circum voluto,
  accedat ad judicium,
  haec expedit negotium
    ore suo muto.

  Si pauper muliercula,
65 non habens munuscula,
    formam neque genus,
    quam non pungit Venus,
  infecto negotio
  suo pergit hospitio,
70   dolendo corde tenus.

  Sunt quidam ad hanc curiam,
  qui exprimunt juditiam;
    dicuntur relatores;
    caeteris pejores.
75 Utraque manu capiunt,
  et sic eos decipiunt
    quorum sunt tutores.
    Et quid janitores?
  Qui dicunt pauperibus
80 curiam sequentibus,
    "Pauper, cur laboras?
    Cur facis hic moras?
  Nisi des pecuniam
  Cuique ad hanc curiam,
85   in vanum laboras.
    Quid, miser, ergo ploras?
  Si nichil attuleris,
    stabis omnino foras."

De vicecomitibus,
90 quam duri sunt pauperibus,
    quis potest enarrare?
    Qui nichil potest dare,
  huc et illuc trahitur,
  et in assisis ponitur,
95   et cogitur jurare,
    non ausus murmurare.
  Quod si murmuraverit,
  ni statim satisfecerit,
    est totum salsum mare.

100 Hoc idem habent vitium,
  cum subeunt hospitium
    cujusdam patriotae,
    vel abbathiae notae,
  quo potus et cibaria,
105 et cuncta necessaria,
    eis dentur devote.

  Nil prosunt sibi talia,
  nisi mox jocalia
    post prandium sequantur,
110   et cunctis largiantur,
  bedellis, garcionibus,
  et qui sunt secum omnibus.
    Nec adjuc pacantur,
    nisi transmittantur
115 robae suis uxoribus
  ex variis coloribus.

  Si non clam mittantur,
    et post sic operantur:
  quotquot habent averia
120 ad sua maneria
    cum impetu fugantur,
    et ipsi imparcantur
  quousque satisfecerint,

	ita quod duplum dederint;		incipiunt perpropere
125	tunc demum liberantur.	135	terras et domos emere,
			et redditus placentes;
	Clericos irrideo		nummosque colligentes,
	suos, quos prius video		pauperes despiciunt,
	satis indigentes,		et novas leges faciunt,
	et quasi nil habentes,	140	vicinos opprimentes;
130	quando ballivam capiunt;		fiuntque sapientes.
	qua capta mox superbiunt,		In hoc malum faciunt,
	et crescunt sibi dentes,		et patriam decipiunt,
	collaque erigentes,		nemini parcentes.

[*Blessed are they who hunger and thirst, and do justice, and hate and avoid the wickedness of injustice; whom neither abundance of gold nor the jewels of the rich draw from their inflexibility, or from the cry of the poor; they judge what is just, and do not fall off from the right for the sake of the rich. / But now the age deceives many in a wonderful manner, and draws them into danger, for love of the world, that they may lick up honors. The cause of this is money, to which almost every court has now wedded itself. / There are judges, whom partiality and bribes seduce from justice; these are they, I remember well, that pay toll to the devil and serve him alone. / For the law of nature commands that a judge in giving judgment should not be an acceptor of anybody either for prayer or money. What therefore, O good Jesus, will be done with the judges, who for prayers or gifts recede from what is just? / In fact such judges have numerous messengers — listen for what purpose: If you wish to claim land, a messenger will come to you and speak in confidence, saying, "Dear friend, do you wish to plead? I am one who can help you in various ways with the judge; if you wish to obtain anything by his aid, give me half, and I will help you." / At his feet sit clerks, who are like people half-famished, gaping for gifts; and proclaiming it as law, that those who give nothing, although they come early, will have to wait. / But if some noble lady, fair and lovely, with horns on her head, and that encircled with gold, come for judgment, such a one despatches her business without having to say a word. / If the woman be poor and has no gifts, neither beauty nor wealthy background, whom Venus does not stimulate, she goes home without effecting her business, sorrowful at heart. / There are some at this court who express judgment, whom they call relaters, worse than the others. They take with both hands and so deceive those whose defenders they are. And what shall we say to the door-keepers? who say to the poor that follow the court, "Poor man, why do you trouble yourself? Why do you wait here? Unless you give money to everybody in this court, you labor in vain. Why then, wretch, do you lament? If you have brought nothing, you will stand altogether out of doors." / Concerning the sheriffs, who can relate with sufficient fulness how hard they are to the poor?*

Simony and the Abuse of Money

He who has nothing to give is dragged hither and thither, and is placed in the assises, and is obliged to take his oath, without daring to murmur. But if he should murmur, unless he immediately make satisfaction, it is all salt sea. / The same people have this vice, when they enter the house of some countryman, or of a famous abbey, where drink and victuals, and all things necessary, are given to them devoutly. Such things are of no avail, unless by and by the jewels follow after the meal, and are distributed to all, beadles and attendant boys, and all who are with them. Nor even yet are they paid, unless robes of various colors are sent to their wives. If these are not sent privately, then they proceed as follows: whatever cattle they find are driven off violently to their own manors, and the owners themselves are put in confinement until they make satisfaction, so that they give the double; then at length they are liberated. / I laugh at their clerks, whom I see at first indigent enough, and possessing next to nothing, when they receive a bailiwick; which received, they next show themselves proud, and their teeth grow. Holding up their necks they begin very hastily to buy lands and houses, and agreeable rents; amassing money themselves, they despise the poor and make new laws, oppressing their neighbors; and they become wise men. In this they do wickedness and deceive their country, sparing no one. (Wright's translation)]

The Simonie

[Symonye and Covetise, or *On the Evil Times of Edward II]*

(Auchinleck MS fols. 328r–334v; and MS Bodley 48 fols. 325v–331r)

Whii werre and wrake in londe and manslauht is i-come, [1]
Whii hungger and derthe on eorthe the pore hath undernome,   *famine; earth; seized*
Whii bestes ben thus storve, whii corn hath ben so dere, [2]
Ye that wolen abide, listneth and ye mowen here
     The skile. [3]
I nelle liyen for no man, herkne who so wile.   *won't lie; listen whoever*

God greteth wel the clergie, and seith theih don amis,   *they do wrong*
And doth hem to understonde that litel treuthe ther is;   *fidelity*
For at the court of Rome, ther Treuthe sholde biginne,   *where; originate*
Him is forboden the paleis, dar he noht com therinne [4]
     For doute;   *fear*
And thouh the Pope clepe him in, yit shal he stonde theroute. [5]

Alle the Popes clerkes han taken hem to red,   *have decided*
If Treuthe come amonges hem, that he shal be ded.
There dar he noht shewen him for doute to be slain, [6]
Among none of the cardinaus dar he noht be sein,   *cardinals; seen*
     For feerd,   *fear*
If Symonie may mete wid him he wole shaken his berd. [7]

---

[1] *Why war and vengeance and manslaughter has come into the land*

[2] *Why animals are so starved, why wheat has become so expensive*

[3] *You who will wait, listen and you will hear / The reason*

[4] *The palace is off-limits to him, he dare not enter in*

[5] *And though the pope bid him come in, yet shall he stand outside*

[6] *He dare not show himself there for fear of being slain*

[7] *If Simony should meet with him, he will challenge him*

Simony and the Abuse of Money

    Voiz of clerk is sielde i-herd at the court of Rome;   *Voice; seldom heard*

20   Ne were he never swich a clerk, silverles if he come, [1]

    Though he were the wiseste that evere was i-born,

    But if he swete ar he go, al his weye is lorn [2]

       I-souht,

    Or he shal singe *Si dedero*, or al geineth him noht. [3]

25   For if there be in countré an horeling, a shrewe,   *fornicator; rascal*

    Lat him come to the court hise nedes for to shewe,

    And bring wid him silver and non other wed,   *pledge*

    Be he nevere so muchel a wrecche, hise nedes sholden be spede [4]

       Ful stille,   *discreetly*

30   For Coveytise and Symonie han the world to wille. [5]

    And erchebishop and bishop, that ouhte for to enquere   *archbishop*

    Off alle men of Holi Churche of what lif theih were,   *Of; they*

    Summe beth foles hemself, and leden a sory lif,   *are fools themselves; lead*

    Therfore doren hii noht speke for rising of strif   *they dare say nothing*

35   Thurw clerkes,   *Because of*

    And that everich biwreied other of here wrecchede werkes. [6]

    But certes Holi Churche is muchel i-brouht ther doune,   *indeed; much*

    Siththen Seint Thomas was slain and smiten of his croune. [7]

    He was a piler ariht to holden up Holi Churche,   *stout pillar*

40   Thise othere ben to slouwe, and feintliche kunnen worche, [8]

       I-wis,   *In truth*

    Therfore in Holi Churche hit fareth the more amis.   *it goes worse*

---

[1] *Even if he is such a clerk, if he comes without silver*

[2] *Unless he sweats before he goes, all his journey is lost*

[3] *Either he shall sing* Si dedero *[If I give], or he shall gain nothing at all*

[4] *No matter how much of a scoundrel he is, his needs shall be taken care of*

[5] *For Avarice and Simony have the world as their own*

[6] *And because every clerk revealed the foul deeds of the other*

[7] *Since Saint Thomas à Becket was slain and bereft of his crown*

[8] *These other [churchmen] are too torpid, and feebly know how to operate*

Simony and the Abuse of Money

But everi man may wel i-wite, who so take yeme,   *know; takes heed*
That no man may wel serve tweie lordes to queme.   *the pleasure of two lords*
45   Summe beth in ofice wid the king, and gaderen tresor to hepe,[1]
And the fraunchise of Holi Churche hii laten ligge slepe[2]
    Ful stille;   *Very dormantly*
Al to manye ther beth swiche, if hit were Godes wille.[3]

And thise ersedeknes that ben set to visite Holi Churche,   *archdeacons*
50   Everich foundeth hu he may shrewedelichest worche;[4]
He wol take mede of that on and that other,   *bribes from one (person) or*
And late the parsoun have a wyf, and the prest another,   *permit*
    At wille:
Coveytise shal stoppen here mouth, and maken hem al stille.   *their; silent*

55   For sone so a parsoun is ded and in eorthe i-don,[5]
Thanne shal the patroun have giftes anon;
The clerkes of the cuntré wolen him faste wowe,   *court; woo*
And senden him faire giftes and presentes i-nowe,   *aplenty*
    And the bishop;
60   And there shal Symonye ben taken bi the cop.   *head*

Coveytise upon his hors he wole be sone there,
And bringe the bishop silver, and rounen in his ere   *whisper; ear*
That alle the pore that ther comen, on ydel sholen theih worche,   *in vain; they*
For he that allermost may give, he shal have the churche,   *most of all*
65   I-wis.   *For sure*
Everich man nu bi dawe may sen that thus hit is.[6]

---

[1] *Some work for the king, and gather treasure in heaps*

[2] *And the offices of generosity of Holy Church they allow to lie asleep*

[3] *There are all too many of these, if it be God's will*

[4] *Every [archdeacon] strives to work most cursedly*

[5] *For as soon as a parson is dead and placed in the earth*

[6] *Everybody nowadays may see that this is how it is*

	And whan this newe parsoun is institut in his churche,	*installed*
	He bithenketh him hu he may shrewedelichest worche; [1]	
	Ne shal the corn in his berne ben eten wid no muis,	*barn; by; mice*
70	But hit shal ben i-spended in a shrewede huis;	*cursed house*
	If he may,	
	Al shal ben i-beten out or Cristemesse day.	*before*

	And whan he hath i-gadered markes and poundes,	*gathered*
	He priketh out of toune wid haukes and wid houndes	*rides; with*
75	Into a straunge contré, and halt a wenche in cracche;	*foreign; holds; bed*
	And wel is hire that first may swich a parsoun kacche	*well for her*
	In londe.	
	And thus theih serven the chapele, and laten the churche stonde.	

	He taketh al that he may, and maketh the churche pore,	
80	And leveth thare behinde a theef and an hore,	*whore*
	A serjaunt and a deie that leden a sory lif;	*dairymaid*
	Al so faire hii gon to bedde as housebonde and wif,	*they*
	Wid sorwe.	
	Shal there no pore lif fare the bet nouther on even ne on morwe. [2]	

85	And whan he hath the silver of wolle and of lomb,	*wool; lamb*
	He put in his pautener an honne and a komb,	*snare; whetstone*
	A myrour and a koeverchef to binde wid his crok, [3]	
	And rat on the rouwe-bible and on other bok	*reads; ribible*
	No mo;	*No other (book)*
90	But unthank have the bishop that lat hit so go. [4]	

	For thouh the bishop hit wite, that hit bename kouth, [5]	
	He may wid a litel silver stoppen his mouth;	
	He medeth wid the clerkes, and halt forth the wenche,	*takes bribes; supports*
	And lat the parish for-worthe — the devel him adrenche	*go to ruin; drown*

---

[1] *He ponders how he may most schemingly work*

[2] *No poor person shall get along well there, not in the evening nor in the morning*

[3] *A mirror and a kerchief to bind his crook with*

[4] *But the bishop will be blamed that allowed things to happen this way*

[5] *For although the bishop knows about it, who could attest to it*

95	For his werk!	*pains*
	And sory may his fader ben, that evere made him clerk.	*father be*

And if the parsoun have a prest of a clene lyf,
That be a god consailler to maiden and to wif,   *good advisor*
Shal comen a daffe and putte him out for a litel lasse,   *fool; less*
100   That can noht a ferthing worth of god, unnethe singe a masse [1]
    But ille.
And thus shal al the parish for lac of lore spille.   *lack; teaching; be destroyed*

For riht me thinketh hit fareth bi a prest that is lewed, [2]
As bi a jay in a kage, that himself hath bishrewed: *cursed*
105   God Engelish he speketh, ac he wot nevere what; [3]
No more wot a lewed prest in boke what he rat   *reads*
   Bi day.
Thanne is a lewed prest no betir than a jay.

But everi man may wel i-wite, bi the swete Rode,   *know; Cross*
110   Ther beth so manye prestes, hii ne muwe noht alle be gode. *they may not*
And natheles thise gode men fallen oft in fame,   *nevertheless*
For thise wantoune prestes that pleien here nice game,   *their foolish*
   Bi nihte,
Hii gon wid swerd and bokeler as men that wode fihte. *They walk around; shield*

115   Summe bereth croune of acolite for the crumponde crok,   *crumpled*
And ben ashamed of the merke the bishop hem bitok;   *gave them*
At even he set upon a koife, and kembeth the croket, *cap; combs the locket*
Adihteth him a gay wenche of the newe jet, [4]
   Sanz doute;   *Without doubt*
120   And there hii clateren cumpelin whan the candel is oute. *"recite compline"*

And thise abbotes and priours don agein here rihtes; *act contrary to their rights*
Hii riden wid hauk and hound, and contrefeten knihtes.

---

[1] *Who doesn't know a farthing's worth of wisdom, [and] with difficulty sings a mass*

[2] *For I think it is just that a priest who is ignorant fares thus*

[3] *He speaks good English, but he doesn't know what he said*

[4] *Furnishes himself with a fun-loving wench of the latest fashion*

Simony and the Abuse of Money

    Hii sholde leve swich pride, and ben religious.

    And nu is pride maister in everich ordred hous;   *now; every*

125   I-wis,   *Indeed*

    Religioun is evele i-holde and fareth the more a-mis. [1]

    For if there come to an abey to pore men or thre,   *two poor*

    And aske of hem helpe *par seinte charité*,   *by Saint Charity*

    Unnethe wole any don his ernde other yong or old,   *Scarcely; errand whether*

130   But late him coure ther al day in hunger and in cold,   *cower*

      And sterve,   *die*

    Loke what love ther is to God, whom theih seien that hii serve!

    But there come another and bringe a litel lettre,

    In a box upon his hepe, he shal spede the betre;   *hip; prosper*

135   And if he be wid eny man that may don the abot harm,   *abbot*

    He shal be lad into the halle, and ben i-mad full warm

      Aboute the mawe.   *stomach*

    And Godes man stant ther-oute — sory is that lawe!

    Thus is God nu served thurwout religioun;

140   There is He al to sielde i-sein in eny devocioun.   *too seldom seen*

    His meyné is unwelcome, comen hii erliche or late; [2]

    The porter hath comaundement to holde hem widoute the gate, [3]

      In the fen.

    Hu mihte theih loven that Loverd, that serven thus His men?   *Lord*

145   This is the penaunce that monekes don for ure Lordes love: *monks; our*

    Hii weren sockes in here shon, and felted botes above.   *They wear; shoes*

    He hath forsake for Godes love bothe hunger and cold;

    But if he have hod and cappe fured, he nis noht i-told [4]

      In covent;

150   Ac certes wlaunknesse of wele hem hath al ablent. [5]

---

[1] *Religion is in ill repute and fares worse and worse*

[2] *His people are not welcome, whether they arrive early or late*

[3] *The gate-keeper is commanded to detain them outside the gate*

[4] *Unless he has [a] hood and furred cap, he is not esteemed*

[5] *But indeed smugness in prosperity has blinded them all*

Simony and the Abuse of Money

Religioun was first founded duresce for to drie,   *hardship; bear*
And nu is the moste del i-went to eise and glotonie. [1]
Where shal men nu finde fattere or raddere of leres?   *ruddier complected [men]*
Or betre farende folk than monekes, chanons, and freres?   *better off*
155   In uch toun   *each town*
I wot non eysiere lyf than is religioun.   *no more comfortable*

Religioun wot, red I, uch day what he shal don.   *read; each*
He ne carez noht to muche for his mete at non;   *too; noon*
For hous-hire ne for clothes he ne carez noht;
160   But whan he cometh to the mete, he maketh his mawe touht   *stomach taut*
    Off the beste;   *From the best [food]*
And anon therafter he fondeth to kacche reste.   *tries to nap*

And yit there is another ordre, Menour and Jacobin,   *Minorites; Dominicans*
And freres of the Carme, and of Seint Austin,   *Carmelites; Austins*
165   That wolde preche more for a busshel of whete   *preach; wheat*
Than for to bringe a soule from helle out of the hete   *heat*
    To rest.
And thus is coveytise loverd bothe est and west.   *lord; east*

If a pore man come to a frere for to aske shrifte,   *confession*
170   And ther come a ricchere and bringe him a gifte,
He shal into the freitur and ben i-mad ful glad,   *refectory*
And that other stant theroute, as a man that were mad   *stands outside*
    In sorwe.
Yit shal his ernde ben undon til that other morwe.   *errand; unfulfilled*

175   And if there be a riche man that evel hath undernome,   *undertaken*
Thanne wolen thise freres al day thider come;   *continually*
And if hit be a pore lyf in poverte and in care,   *anxiety*
Sorwe on that o frere that kepeth come thare [2]
    Ful loth;   *loath*
180   Alle wite ye, gode men, hu the gamen goth.

---

[1] *And now the greatest part has gone to comfort and gluttony*

[2] *Woe be to that one friar who cares to come there*

And if the riche man deie that was of eny mihte,	*die; power*
Thanne wolen the freres for the cors fihte.	*fight over the body*
Hit nis noht al for the calf that kow louweth,	
Ac hit is for the grene gras that in the medewe grouweth	*meadow*
185 So god.	*good*
Alle wite ye what I mene, that kunnen eny god. [1]	

For als ich evere brouke min hod under min hat,	*as I; hold*
The frere wole to the direge, if the cors is fat.	*funeral; body*
Ac bi the feith I owe to God, if the cors is lene,	
190 He wole wagge aboute the cloistre and kepen hise fet clene	*move; clean*
In house.	
Hu mihte theih faire forsake that hii ne ben coveytouse?	

And officials and denes that chapitles sholden holde,	*deans; chapters*
Theih sholde chastise the folk, and theih maken hem bolde.	*They*
195 Mak a present to the den ther thu thenkest to dwelle,	*dean where*
And have leve longe i-nouh to serve the fend of helle	*enough*
To queme.	*pleasure*
For have he silver, of sinne taketh he nevere yeme.	*heed*

If a man have a wif, and he ne love hire noht,	
200 Bringe hire to the constorie ther treuthe sholde be souht,	*consistory court where*
And bringge tweye false wid him and him self the thridde,	*two false people with*
And he shal ben to-parted so faire as he wole bidde	*divorced*
From his wif.	
He shal ben holpen wel i-nouh to lede a shrewede lyf. [2]	

205 And whan he is thus i-deled from his rihte spouse,	*parted; lawful*
He taketh his neiheboures wif and bringeth hire to his house;	*her*
And whiles he hath eny silver the clerkes to sende,	
He may holde hire at his wille to his lives ende	*maintain her*
Wid unskile;	*Without just cause*
210 And but that be wel i-loked, curs in here bile.	*unless; well-looked after; their*

---

[1] *You all know what I mean — you who know anything good*

[2] *He shall be helped very well to lead a wicked life*

Simony and the Abuse of Money

And yit ther is another craft that toucheth the clergie,
That ben thise false fisiciens that helpen men to die;   *physicians*
He wole wagge his urine in a vessel of glaz,   *wave; glass*
And swereth that he is sekere than evere yit he was,   *sicker*
215   And sein,
"Dame, for faute of helpe, thin housebonde is neih slain."   *lack; almost*

Thus he wole afraien al that ther is inne,   *alarm; those who*
And make many a lesing, silver for to winne.   *lie*
Ac afterward he fondeth to comforte the wif,   *But; tries*
220 And seith, "Dame, for of thin I wole holde his lyf,"   *for you; preserve*
   And liye,   *lie*
Thouh he wite no more than a gos wheither he wole live or die. *knows; goose*

Anon he wole biginne to blere the wives eighe;   *deceive the wife*
He wole aske half a pound to bien spicerie.   *buy spices*
225 The viii shillinges sholen up to the win and the ale,   *eight; pay for*
And bringe rotes and rindes bret ful a male
   Off noht; [1]
Hit shal be dere on a lek, whan hit is al i-wrouht. [2]

He wole preisen hit i-nohw, and sweren, as he were wod,   *enough; mad*
230 For the king of the lond the drink is riche and god;   *good*
And geve the gode man drinke a god quantité,
And make him worse than he was — evele mote he the,   *may he ill prosper*
   That clerk,
That so geteth the silver, and can noht don his werk!

235 He doth the wif sethe a chapoun and piece beof, [3]
Ne tit the gode man noht therof, be him nevere so leof;   *touches; glad (lief)*
The best he piketh up himself, and maketh his mawe touht,   *stomach taut*
And geveth the gode man soupe, the lene broth that nis noht   *isn't*
   For seke;   *For a sick person*
240 That so serveth eny man, Godes curs in his cheke!

---

[1] *And bring a chest crammed full with roots and rinds / Worth nothing*

[2] *It shall be an expensive leek, when all's said and done*

[3] *He causes the wife to boil a capon and a slice of beef*

201

Simony and the Abuse of Money

And thilke that han al the wele in freth and in feld,   *woodland*
Bothen eorl and baroun and kniht of o sheld,   *one shield*
Alle theih beth i-sworn Holi Churche holde to rihte.
Therfore was the ordre mad for Holi Churche to fihte,
245 Sanz faille;   *Without fail*
And nu ben theih the ferste that hit sholen assaile.

Hii brewen strut and stuntise there as sholde be pes; *strife and foolishness*
Hii sholde gon to the Holi Lond and maken there her res, *their assault*
And fihte there for the Croiz, and shewe the ordre of knihte, *knighthood*
250 And awreke Jhesu Crist wid launce and speir to fihte   *avenge*
  And sheld;
And nu ben theih liouns in halle, and hares in the feld.

Knihtes sholde weren weden in here manere,   *clothes*
After that the ordre asketh also wel as a frere. [1]
255 Nu ben theih so degysed and diverseliche i-diht,   *clothed; arrayed*
Unnethe may men knowe a gleman from a kniht,   *Scarcely; minstrel*
  Wel neih;   *Almost*
So is mieknesse driven adoun, and pride is risen on heih. *meekness; high*

Thus is the ordre of kniht turned up-so-doun,   *upside down*
260 Also wel can a kniht chide as any skolde of a toun. *town scolder*
Hii sholde ben also hende as any levedi in londe,   *polite; lady*
And for to speke alle vilanie nel nu no kniht wonde [2]
  For shame;
And thus knihtshipe is acloied and waxen al fot-lame. [3]

265 Knihtshipe is acloied and deolfulliche i-diht; *hindered; grievously disposed*
Kunne a boy nu breke a spere, he shal be mad a kniht. *If a boy knows how*
And thus ben knihtes gadered of unkinde blod, [4]
And envenimeth that ordre that shold be so god   *poisons*

[1] *As the order [of knighthood] requires as well as a friar*
[2] *And now no knight will stay to speak churlish things*
[3] *And thus knighthood is debased and has become wholly crippled*
[4] *And thus knights are collected from non-noble blood*

Simony and the Abuse of Money

	And hende;	*gracious*
270	Ac o shrewe in a court many man may shende.	*one churl; ruin*

	And nu nis no squier of pris in this middel erd,	*worth; middle earth*
	But if that he bere a babel and a long berd,	*Unless; wears; bauble*
	And swere Godes soule, and vuwe to God and hote;	*vow; promise*
	But sholde he for everi fals uth lese kirtel or kote,	*oath; tunic*
275	I leve,	*believe*
	He sholde stonde starc naked twye o day or eve.	*twice a*

	Godes soule is al day sworn, the knif stant a-strout,	*sticks out*
	And thouh the botes be torn, yit wole he maken hit stout;	*boots; strut around*
	The hod hangeth on his brest, as he wolde spewe therinne,	*vomit*
280	Ac shortliche al his contrefaiture is colour of sinne,	
	And bost,	
	To wraththe God and paien the fend hit serveth allermost.	*most of all*

	A newe taille of squierie is nu in everi toun:	*style*
	The raye is turned overthuert that sholde stonde adoun.	*raiment; crosswise*
285	Hii ben degised as turmentours that comen from clerkes plei;	
	Hii ben i-laft wid pride, and cast nurture awey	*have abandoned*
	In diche;	*In a ditch*
	Gentille men that sholde ben, ne beth hii none i-liche. [1]	

	And justises, shirreves, meires, baillifs, if I shal rede aricht,	*sheriffs; mayors*
290	Hii kunnen of the faire day make the derke niht;	*They know how*
	Hii gon out of the heie wey, ne leven hii for no sklaundre, [2]	
	And maken the mot-hall at hom in here chaumbre,	*hall of justice*
	Wid wouh;	*evil*
	For be the hond i-whited, it shal go god i-nouh.	*(see note)*

295	If the king in his werre sent after mihti men,	*war*
	To helpe him in his nede, of sum toun .ix. or .x.,	*nine; ten*
	The stiffeste sholden bileve at hom for .x. shillinges or .xii., [3]	

---

[1] *Those who should be like gentlemen are nothing like them*

[2] *They walk off the beaten track, nor do they desist for slander*

[3] *The fittest should remain at home for ten or twelve shillings*

And sende forthe a wrecche that may noht helpe himselve
   At nede.
300   Thus is the king deceyved, and pore men shent for mede.   *ruined; bribery*

And if the king in his lond maketh a taxacioun,
And everi man is i-set to a certein raunczoun,   *assigned; amount*
Hit shal be so for-pinched, to-toilled, and to-twiht,   *belabored; reproached*
That halvendel shal gon in the fendes fliht   *one half*
305   Off helle.   *Of*
Ther beth so manye parteners may no tunge telle.   *partakers*

A man of .xl. poundes-worth god is leid to .xii. pans rounde;   *goods; pence*
And also much paieth another that poverte hath brouht to grounde,
And hath an hep of girles sittende aboute the flet.   *floor*
310   Godes curs moten hii have, but that be wel set
   And sworn,
That the pore is thus i-piled, and the riche forborn!   *robbed; indulged*

Ac if the king hit wiste, I trowe he wolde be wroth,   *But; knew it*
Hou the pore beth i-piled, and hu the silver goth;   *robbed*
315   Hit is so deskatered bothe hider and thidere,   *scattered around*
That halvendel shal ben stole ar hit come togidere,   *half; stolen before*
   And acounted;   *accounted for*
An if a pore man speke a word, he shal be foule afrounted.   *wickedly attacked*

Ac were the king wel avised, and wolde worche bi skile,   *reason*
320   Litel nede sholde he have swiche pore to pile; [1]
Thurfte him noht seke tresor so fer, he mihte finde ner,   *Need; near*
At justices, at shirreves, cheiturs, and chaunceler,
   And at les; [2]
Swiche mihte finde him i-nouh, and late pore men have pes.   *let; peace*

325   For who so is in swich ofice, come he nevere so pore,
He fareth in a while as thouh he hadde silver ore;   *rudder*

---

[1] *He would have little need to rob from such poor people*

[2] *Among justices, sheriffs, escheators, and the chancellor, / and among lesser men*

Simony and the Abuse of Money

Theih bien londes and ledes, ne may hem non astonde. [1]
What sholde pore men ben i-piled, when swiche men beth in londe   *Why*
   So fele?   *many*
330   Theih pleien wid the kinges silver, and breden wod for wele.   *(see note)*

Ac shrewedeliche for sothe hii don the kinges heste;   *But cursedly; bidding*
Whan everi man hath his part, the king hath the leste,   *least*
Everi man is aboute to fille his owen purs;
And the king hath the leste part, and he hath al the curs,
335   Wid wronge.   *Unjustly*
And sende treuthe into this lond, for tricherie dureth to longe. [2]

And baillifs and bedeles under the shirreve,   *beadles*
Everich fondeth hu he may pore men most greve. [3]
The pore men beth over al somouned on assise; [4]
340   And the riche sholen sitte at hom, and ther wole silver rise
   To shon.   *To be shown*
Godes curs moten hii have, but that be wel don!   *may*

And countours in benche that stondeth at the barre,   *accountants*
Theih wolen bigile the in thin hond, but if thu be warre.   *unless; beware*
345   He wole take .xl. pans for to doun his hod,   *forty*
And speke for the a word or to, and don the litel god, [5]
   I trouwe.
And have he turned the bak, he makketh the a mouwe. [6]

Attourneis in cuntré theih geten silver for noht;   *Attorneys; doing nothing*
350   Theih maken men biginne that they nevere hadden thouht.
And whan theih comen to the ring, hoppe if hii kunne.
Al that theih muwen so gete, al thinketh hem i-wonne

---

[1] *They buy lands and possessions, none may withstand them*

[2] *And may truth be sent into this land, for treachery has endured too long*

[3] *Every [bailiff and beadle] seeks how he may most oppress poor men*

[4] *The poor men generally are summoned to the court of assizes*

[5] *And speak a word or two on your behalf, and do little good for you*

[6] *And when he turns his back on you, he makes a face at you*

205

Wid skile. [1]
Ne triste no man to hem, so false theih beth in the bile.

355 And sumtime were chapman that treweliche bouhten and solde;
And nu is thilke assise broke, and nas noht yore holde. [2]
Chaffare was woned to be meintened wid treuthe,   *Trade; wont*
And nu is al turned to treccherie, and that is muchel reuthe   *great pity*
    To wite,
360 That alle manere godnesse is thus adoun i-smite.   *struck down*

Unnethe is nu eny man that can eny craft   *knows any*
That he nis a party los in the haft;   *(see note)*
For falsnesse is so fer forth over al the londe i-sprunge,   *widespread*
That wel neih nis no treuthe in hond, ne in tunge,   *tongue*
365   Ne in herte.
And tharfore nis no wonder thouh al the world it smerte.   *injure*

Ther was a gamen in Engelond that durede yer and other: [3]
Erliche upon the Monenday uch man bishrewed other;   *Early; Monday; cursed*
So longe lastede that gamen among lered and lewed
370 That nolde theih nevere stinten, or al the world were bishrewed, [4]
    I-wis.
And therfore al that helpe sholde fareth the more amis.

So that for that shrewedom that regneth in the lond,   *cursedness*
I drede me that God us hath for-laft out of His hond,   *dismissed us*
375 Thurw wederes that he hath i-sent cold and unkinde.   *weather; unnatural*
And yit ne haveth no man of Him the more minde
    Ariht;
Unnethe is any man aferd of Godes muchele miht.   *great*

---

[1] *Everything they may acquire in this way they think they have won / With their reason*

[2] *And once there were merchants who honorably bought and sold; / And now is that custom abrogated, and has not been observed for a long time*

[3] *There was in England a game that lasted two years*

[4] *That they would never cease until all the world should be accursed*

Simony and the Abuse of Money

God hath ben wroth wid the world, and that is wel i-sene;

380   For al that whilom was murthe is turned to treie and tene.   *once; vexation; sorrow*

He sente us plenté i-nouh, suffre whiles we wolde,

Off alle manere sustenaunce grouwende upon mode   *Of; growing; earth*

   So thicke;

And evere ageines His godnesse we weren i-liche wicke.   *equally wicked*

385   Men sholde noht sumtime finde a boy for to bere a lettre,   *servant*

That wolde eten eny mete, but it were the betre.   *eat any food unless*

For beof ne for bakoun, ne for swich stor of house,   *beef; pork; provisions*

Unnethe wolde eny don a char, so were theih daungerouse   *labor; disinclined*

   For wlanke;   *pride*

390   And siththen bicom ful reulich that thanne weren so ranke.   *pitiful; arrogant*

For tho God seih that the world was so over gart,   *when; saw; proud*

He sente a derthe on eorthe, and made hit ful smarte.   *famine; painful*

A busshel of whete was at foure shillinges or more,

And so men mihte han i-had a quarter noht yore   *not long*

395   I-gon;   *Ago*

So can God make wane, ther rathere was won.[1]

And thanne gan bleiken here blé, that arst lowen so loude,[2]

And to waxen al hand-tame that rathere weren so proude.   *earlier*

A mannes herte mihte blede for to here the crie   *hear*

400   Off pore men that gradden, "Allas, for hungger I die   *Of; complain*

   Up rihte!"

This auhte make men aferd of Godes muchele miht.   *ought to*

And after that ilke wante com eft wele i-nouh,   *scarcity; abundance*

And plenté of alle gode grouwende on uch a bouh.   *growing on every bough*

405   Tho god yer was agein i-come, and god chep of corn,   *When; market for wheat*

Tho were we also muchele shrewes, as we were beforn,   *Then; scoundrels*

   Or more.

Also swithe we forgeten His wreche and His lore.   *Quickly; punishment; teaching*

---

[1] *In this way God can make scarcity where formerly there was plenty*

[2] *And then their complexion paled, which before laughed so loudly*

Tho com ther another sorwe that spradde over al the lond.   *Then; sorrow*

410   A thusent winter ther bifore com nevere non so strong.   *thousand*

To binde alle the mene men in mourning and in care   *hardened*

The orf deiede al bidene, and maden the lond al bare   *cattle died straightaway*
   So faste.

Com nevere wrecche into Engelond that made men more agaste.   *wretchedness*

415   And tho that qualm was astint of beste that bar horn,   *when; plague; ceased*

Tho sente God on eorthe another derthe of corn,

That spradde over al Engelond bothe north and south,

And made seli pore men afingred in here mouth   *simple; hungry*
   Ful sore;

420   And yit unnethe any man dredeth God the more.

And wid that laste derthe com ther another shame,   *famine*

That ouhte be god skile maken us alle tame.   *reason; obedient*

The fend kidde his maistri, and arerede a strif,   *displayed; mounted*

That everi lording was bisi to sauve his owen lyf,   *save*

425   And his good.   *property*

God do bote theron, for His blessede blod!   *provide a remedy*

Gret nede hit were to bidde that the pes were brouht,   *pray*

For the lordinges of the lond, that swich wo han i-wrouht,

That nolde spare for kin that o kosin that other;[1]

430   So the fend hem prokede uch man to mourdren other   *prodded; murder*
   Wid wille,   *Wilfully*

That al Engelond i-wis was in point to spille.   *So that; about to die*

Pride prikede hem so faste, that nolde theih nevere have pes   *they would not*

Ar theih hadden in this lond maked swich a res[2]

435   That the beste blod of the lond shamliche was brouht to grounde,   *shamefully*

If hit betre mihte a ben; allas, the harde stounde   *have been; time*
   Bitid,   *Came about*

That of so gentille blod i-born swich wreche was i-kid.   *devastation; shown*

---

[1] *Who would not for kinship spare one relative or another*

[2] *Pride urged them so vigorously that they never would have peace / Until they had created in this land such a rage*

208

Simony and the Abuse of Money

	Allas, that evere sholde hit bifalle that in so litel a throwe,	*short a time*
440	Swiche men sholde swich deth thole, and ben i-leid so lowe.	*suffer*
	Off eorles ant of barouns baldest hii were;	*earls; barons; boldest*
	And nu hit is of hem bicome riht as theih nevere ne were	
	I-born.	
	God loke to the soules, that hii ne be noht lorn!	*look after; lost*

445	Ac whiles thise grete lordinges thus han i-hurled to hepe, [1]	
	Thise prelatz of Holi Churche to longe theih han i-slepe.	*too*
	Al to late theih wakeden, and that was muchel reuthe;	*great pity*
	Theih weren ablent wid coveytise, and mihte noht se the treuthe	*blinded*
	For mist.	
450	Theih dradden more here lond to lese, than love of Jhesu Crist.	*feared; lose*

	For hadde the clergie harde holden to-gidere,	*held close together*
	And noht flecched aboute nother hider ne thidere,	*wavered*
	But loked where the treuthe was, and there have bileved,	
	Thanne were the barnage hol, that nu is al to-dreved	*baronage united ; separated*
455	So wide.	
	Ac certes Engelond is shent thurw falsnesse and thurw pride.	*ruined*

	Pride hath in his paunter kauht the heie and the lowe,	*trap; high*
	So that unnethe can eny man God Almihti knowe.	
	Pride priketh aboute, wid nithe and wid onde;	*rides; with discord; envy*
460	Pes and love and charité hien hem out of londe	*Peace; hasten*
	So faste	
	That God wole for-don the world we muwe be sore agaste.	*destroy; must; afraid*

	Alle wite we wel it is oure gilt, the wo that we beth inne; [2]	
	But no man knoweth that hit is for his owen sinne.	
465	Uch man put on other the wreche of the wouh;	*Each; blame; wickedness*
	But wolde uch man renczake himself, thanne were al wel i-nouh	*scrutinize*
	I-wrouht.	
	But nu can uch man demen other, and himselve nouht.	*judge*

---

[1] *But while these great lords thus were thrown on a heap*

[2] *We all know we are to blame for the lamentable situation that we are in*

	And thise assisours that comen to shire and to hundred,	*(see note)*
470	Damneth men for silver, and that nis no wonder.	*is no*
	For whan the riche justise wol do wrong for mede,	*peaceful justice; bribery*
	Thanne thinketh hem theih muwen the bet, for theih ham more nede[1]	
	To winne.	*prosper*
	Ac so is al this world ablent, that no man douteth sinne.	*Just; blinded; fears*

475	But bi seint Jame of Galice, that many man hath souht,	
	The pilory and the cucking-stol beth i-mad for noht,	
	Fore whenne is al a-contith and y-cast to the hepe,	*reckoned*
	Bred and ale is the derer and nevere the beter chepe	*more expensive*
	Fore that.	
480	So is trecherie a-bove, and treuthe is al tosquat.	*utterly put down*

	Hit is rewthe to speke therof, ho-so right durste deme:[2]	
	Of bedeles and of bayleffes that hath the townes to yeme,	*beadles; manage*
	That suffer such falsnesse reyne in breth and ale,	*rain; bread*
	And thow the pouer hem pleyne, ne mow they get no bale,	*though; poor; redress*
485	I wen,	*believe*
	And haulf is stole that they take of wretchethe pouer men.[3]	

	A sely workman in a toun that lyve in trewthe fre	*simple*
	And hath a wif or children, peraunter to or thre,	*by chance two*
	He sueteth many a suetes drope, and swynk he never so sore[4]	
490	Alday fore a peny or fore a peny more,	
	Be cas,	*By chance*
	At eve whan he setteth hit, half is stole alas!	*puts it down*

	Thes bakers and this brewers beth so bolde in here yifte	*their bribery*
	That fore a litel mercyment or fore a symple gifte,	*fee*
495	On may fore xij d. at a court do xl[li] schillingwerd schame,[5]	
	But how so ever hit falle, the pouer han al the grame	*happens; have; harm*

---

[1] *Then they themselves think they must fare the better, for they themselves need more*

[2] *It is a pity to speak of it, whoever rightly dares to judge*

[3] *And half of what they take from wretched poor men is stolen*

[4] *He sweats many a drop of sweat, and no matter how hard he toils*

[5] *One may for twelve pence at a court session do forty shilling's worth of wrong*

Simony and the Abuse of Money

At mele. *On such occasions (or, For supper)*
Now God amende pouermen that can wel dight and dele. *poor men; dig; delve*

That riot reyneth now in londe everiday more and more, *wanton behavior reigns*
500 The lordis beth wel a-paith therwith and lisneth to here lore, *get satisfaction*
But of the pouer mannes harm, therof is now no speche.
This bondes warien and widous wepen and crie to God for wreche
  So fast,[1]
How myghte hit be but such men mystymeth ate last. *are ruined at the end*

505 Fore al is long on lordis that suffre thus hit go.
They scholde mayntene the porayle, and they do noght therto,[2]
But take methe and sle the fole in as moche as they may. *bribes; slay*
The pore han her purgatorie; the riche kepe her day *have their suffering*
  In helle.
510 That so scorneth God and Hise, can I non other telle.[3]

How myghte hit be but God hem wreke of schame that never doth *punish them*
That clerk ne knyght, hie ne lowe, loveth right no soth. *nor truth*
Now noght this sely chepmen in that they bye or selle *simple merchants*
Or with hepe or with croc . . .
515   Of gyle.
Yit thynket hem that cometh with wrong yeldeth best the wile.[4]

But crafty Kyng of kende that ever set al thyng, *nature; ordained*
He sey how al misfarde and how they ledde the kyng. *saw; went wrong*
He sente bote of bale and awrak here deth, *remedy of destruction; avenged*
520 But thus seth men falsnesse, how hit to grounde geth *perished*
  On ende.
Fore hit may never be les, that wrong wil hom wende. *comes home to roost*

---

[1] *These husbandmen curse and widows weep and cry to God for vengeance / Very soon*

[2] *For all the problems must be attributed to lords who allow things to proceed in this way. / They should support the poor people, but they do nothing on their behalf*

[3] *Of those who so scorn God and His followers, I can say no more*

[4] *Yet those who come think that fraud yields the best results over time*

	But covetise overcombreth so al that now lyve	*overwhelms*
	That ho-so were riche ynow and hadde aght to gyve,	*whoever; anything*
525	He may han at his wille the lewthe and the clerk,	*have; ignorant man*
	And make a fals fondement and schende al the werk	*foundation; ruin*
	At anes.	*At once*
	But such baret breweres, ybrent be here bones! [1]	

	That fore alle the hard happes that God on erthe schewes,	*tough circumstances*
530	Unnethe is eny the warrer that ne wile be schrewes.	*warier; scoundrels*
	Flaterers and fals, wikketh and unwrast,	*wicked; frail*
	Of al the wreche that is come, be we noght agast	*misery*
	Ne aferd;	
	And therfore hath this schamnesse thus schak us be the berd.	*shame; beard*

535	But alther ferst grevaunce fel to the pouer wrecchen	*first; wretches*
	That lay doun be the strete — for hunger dethe they strecchen.	
	On men fel the ferst wo: such was here hap,	*their fortune*
	And seththe on the riche cam the after-clap	
	Fol sore.	*grievous*
540	And yit is to drede ther wile come more.	*it may be feared*

	But Lord, fore that blisseth bloth that ran out of Thi side,	*blessed blood*
	Graunt us rightfol lif to lede wile we here abide,	*lead while*
	So that we mow oure giltis knowe with sorwe and schrifte of mouthe,	
	And ever to serve God the bet, for that I haf yow seith nowthe	
545	Y-told, [2]	
	And come to Hym that fore us was to the Jwes sold.	*on our behalf; Jews*

Explicit Symonye and Covetise

---

[1] *But may the bones be burned of such fomenters of strife*

[2] *So that we may know our sins with sorrow and oral confession / And always to serve God better, for of that I have now / Told you*

Simony and the Abuse of Money

Above All Thing Thow Arte a Kyng

[*Money, Money!*]

(British Library MS Royal 17.B.xlvii fols. 160*v*–162*r*)

Money, money, now hay goode day!	have a
Money, where haste thow be?	been
Money, money, thow gost away	
And wylt not byde wyth me.	

Above all thing thow arte a kyng,	
And rulyst the world over all;	rule; everywhere
Who lakythe the, all joy, pardé,	worships thee; by God
Wyll sone then frome hym ffall!	soon; from

5	In every place thow makyste solas,	comfort
	Gret joye, spoorte, and uelfare;	diversion; prosperity
	When money ys gone, comfort ys none,	
	But thowght, sorowe, and care.	anxiety

	In kynges corte, where money dothe route,	court; gather
10	Yt makyth the galandes to jett,	gallants; swagger
	And for to were gorgeouse ther gere, [1]	
	Ther cappes awry to sett.	

	In the heyweyes ther joly palfreys [2]	
	Yt makyght to lepe and praunce,	causes
15	It maket justynges, pleys, dysguysynges,	jousts; masquerades
	Ladys to synge and daunce.	

---

[1] *And to wear their gorgeous clothing*

[2] *In the highways there [are] splendid palfreys (saddle-horses)*

213

Simony and the Abuse of Money

For he that alway wantyth money   *always lacks*
   Stondyth a mated chere,   *flustered countenance*
Can never wel syng, lang daunce nor springe,   *long*
20   Nor make no lusty chere. [1]

At cardes and dyce yt bereth the pryce,
   As kyng and emperoure;
At tables, tennes, and al othere games,   *backgammon, tennis*
   Money hathe ever the floure.   *is foremost*

25 Wythe squyer and knyght and every wyghte   *person*
   Money maketh men fayne;   *eager*
And causeth many in sume compeney
   Theyr felowes to dysdayne.

In marchandys who can devyse   *merchandise*
30   So good a ware, I say?
At al tymys the best ware ys   *defense*
   Ever redy money.

Money to incresse, marchandys never to cease
   Wyth many a sotell wyle;   *subtle ruse*
35 Men say the wolde for sylver and golde   *they*
   Ther owne faders begyle.   *deceive*

Women, I trowe, love money also
   To by them joly gere;   *buy; apparel*
For that helpythe and oft causethe
40   Women to loke full fayre.

In Westmyaster Hall the criers call;   *Westminster*
   The sergeauntes plede apace.   *barristers*
Attorneys appere, now here, now ther,
   Renning in every place.   *Running*

45 Whatesoever he be, and yf that he

---

[1] *"Nor provide lively entertainment, joyful welcome" (RHR)*

Whante money to plede the lawe,   *Lacks; plead*
Do whate he cane in ys mater than   *Whatever he can do in his lawsuit then*
Shale prove not worthe a strawe.

I know yt not, but well I wotte   *know*
50   I have harde often tymys tell,   *heard*
Prestes use thys guyse, ther benefyce
For moyeny to bey and sell.   *buy*

Craftysmen that be in every cyté,   *Guildsmen*
They worke and never blynne;   *cease*
55   Sum cutte, sume shave, sume knoke, sum grave,   *hammer; engrave*
Only money to wynne.

The plowman hymselfe dothe dyge and delve   *dig*
In storme, snowe, frost, and rayne,
Money to get with laboure and swete,   *sweat*
60   Yet small geynes and muche peyne.   *gains*

And sume for money lye by the wey   *wait in ambush*
Another mannes purse to gett;   *get*
But they that long use yt amonge
Ben hangyd by the neke.   *neck*

65   The beggers eke in every strete
Ly walowyng by the wey;   *Lie wallowing*
They begge, the crye, oft the cume by,   *they*
And all ys but for money.

In every coste men love yt moste,   *country*
70   In Ynglonde, Spayne, and Francs,   *England; France*
For every man lackyng yt than
Is clene owte of countenaunce.   *Is utterly humiliated*

Of what degré so ever he be,
Of werteouse conyng he have,   *useful scholarship*
75   And wante moné, yet men wyll sey,   *If [he] lacks money*
That he ys but a knave.

Simony and the Abuse of Money

Where indede, so God me spede,
   Sey all men whate they cane;   *whatever they can*
Yt ys allwayes sene nowadayes
80   That money makythe the man.

finis

In Erth It Es a Litill Thing

[*Sir Penny*]

(British Library MS Cotton Galba E.ix fols. 50*v*–51*r*)

Incipit narracio de domino denario.

In erth it es a litill thing,	*is*
And regnes als a riche king,	*reigns as*
Whare he es lent in land.	*loaned*
Sir Peni es his name calde:	*called*
5 He makes both yong and alde	*old*
Bow untill his hand.	*to*
Papes, kinges, and emperoures,	*Popes*
Bisschoppes, abbottes, and priowres,	*priors*
Person, prest, and knyght,	*Parson*
10 Dukes, erles, and ilk barowne,	*each baron*
To serve him er thai ful boune	*are; ready*
Both bi day and nyght.	
Sir Peny chaunges mans mode,	*man's mood*
And gers tham oft do doun thaire hode,	*causes them often to take off their hoods*
15 And to rise him ogayne.	*again*
Men honors him with grete reverence,	
Makes ful mekell obedience	*considerable*
Unto that litill swaine.	*little boy*
In kinges court es it no bote,	*is; remedy*
20 Ogaines Sir Peni forto mote,	*Against; argue*
So mekill es he of myght;	*great he is*
He es so witty, and so strang,	
That be it never so mekill wrang,	*much wrong*
He will mak it right.	

217

25	With Peny may men wemen till,	*seduce women (plow)*
	Be thai never so strange of will,	*strong*
	So oft may it be sene.	
	Lang with him will thai noght chide,	
	For he may ger tham trayl syde	*provide them with trailing gowns*
30	In gude skarlet and grene.	*scarlet; green*
	He may by both hevyn and hell,	*buy; heaven*
	And ilka thing that es to sell,	*each; is*
	In erth has he swilk grace;	*such*
	He may lese, and he may bind,	*loose*
35	The pouer er ay put behind,	*poor are always ignored*
	Whare he cumes in place.	
	When he bigines him to mell,	*interfere*
	He makes meke that are was fell,	*those who formerly were fierce*
	And waik that bald has bene.	*weak those who once were bold*
40	All the nedes ful sone er sped	*are accomplished*
	Bath withowten borgh and wed	*Both; security; pledge*
	Whare Peni gase bitwene.	*goes*
	The domes-men he mase so blind	*judges; makes*
	That thai may noght the right find,	
45	Ne the suth to se.	*truth see*
	Forto gif dome tham es ful lath,	*To render judgment they are so reluctant*
	Tharwith to make Sir Peni wrath,	*Thereby; angry*
	Ful dere with tham es he.	*beloved; them*
	Thare strif was, Peni makes pese;	*peace*
50	Of all angers he may relese	*relieve*
	In land whare he will lende.	*dwell*
	Of fase may he mak frendes sad,	*enemies; faithful*
	Of counsail thar tham never be rad	*advice they need never be afraid*
	That may have him to frende.	*as a friend*
55	That sire es set on high dese,	*dais*
	And served with mani riche mese,	*meals*
	At the high burde.	*table*
	The more he es to men plenté,	*abundant*

Simony and the Abuse of Money

The more yernid alway es he,   *sought after*
60   And halden dere in horde.   *And dearly held in hoard*

He makes mani be forsworne,
And sum life and saul forlorne,   *some; soul to lose*
     Him to get and wyn.
Other god will thai none have
65   Bot that litil round knave
     Thaire bales forto blin.   *Their miseries to end*

On him halely thaire hertes sett,   *wholly*
Him forto luf will thai noght let,   *love; cease*
     Nowther for gude ne ill.   *Neither; good*
70   All that he will in erth have done,
Ilka man grantes it ful sone,   *Each*
     Right at his awin will.   *own*

He may both lene and gyf,   *lend*
He may ger both sla and lif,   *cause; murder*
75   Both by frith and fell.   *woods and field*

Peni es a gude felaw;   *good fellow*
Men welcums him in dede and saw,   *i.e. word*
     Cum he never so oft.
He es noght welkumd als a gest,
80   Bot evermore served with the best,
     And made at sit ful softe.   *honored; seat*

Whoso es sted in any nede,   *Whoever is beset by any need*
With Sir Peni may thai spede,   *prosper*
     Howsoever bytide.   *Whatever happens*
85   He that Sir Peni es with all
Sal have his will in stede and stall,   *Shall; everywhere*
     When other er set byside.   *When others are set aside (rejected)*

	Sir Peny gers in riche wede	*causes; clothing*
	Ful mani go and ride on stede, [1]	
90	In this werldes wide.	*wide world*
	In ilka gamin, and ilka play,	*each pastime*
	The maystri es gifen ay	*victory is always given*
	To Peny for his pride.	
	Sir Peny over-all gettes the gré,	*victory (prize)*
95	Both in burgh and in ceté,	*town; city*
	In castell and in towre;	*tower*
	Withowten owther spere or schelde	*spear or shield*
	Es he the best in frith or felde,	*wood or field*
	And stalworthest in stowre.	*battle*
100	In ilka place the suth es sene:	*truth is seen*
	Sir Peni es over al bidene,	*everywhere completely*
	Maister most in mode.	
	And all es als he will cumand,	*is as; command*
	Oganis his stevyn dar no man stand,	*Against his voice*
105	Nowther by land ne flode.	*Neither; water*
	Sir Peny mai ful mekill availe	*help very much*
	To tham that has nede of cownsaill,	*advice*
	Als sene es in assise.	*As seen in the court of assizes*
	He lenkithes life and saves fro dede,	*lengthens; death*
110	Bot luf it noght over wele, I rede,	*don't love it too much, I advise*
	For sin of coveityse.	*avarice*
	If thou have happ tresore to win,	*have the fortune*
	Delite the noght to mekill tharin,	*too much in it*
	Ne nything thareof be;	*niggardly*
115	Bot spend it als well as thou can,	
	So that thou luf both God and man	
	In parfite charité.	*perfect*

---

[1] *Sir Penny causes [many people] to wear fine clothing / And many to go about on horseback*

God graunte us grace with hert and will
The gudes that he has gifen us till   *goods that he has given to us*
120   Well and wisely to spend;
And so our lives here forto lede
That we may have his blis to mede,   *as a reward*
        Ever withowten end. Amen

London Lickpenny

(British Library MS Harley 542 fols. 102r–104r)

	In London there I was bent,	*where; hastening*
	I saw my-selfe, where trouthe shuld be ateynte;	*achieved*
	Fast to Westminstar-ward I went	
	To a man of lawe, to make my complaynt.	
5	I sayd, "For Marys love, that holy seynt,	*Mary's*
	Have pity on the powre, that would procede.	*poor; litigate*
	I would gyve sylvar, but my purs is faynt."	*silver; light*
	For lacke of money, I may not spede.	*succeed*
	As I thrast thrughe-out the thronge	*pushed; crowd*
10	Amonge them all, my hode was gonn;	*head-covering; gone*
	Netheles I let not longe,	*did not hesitate*
	To kyngs benche tyll I come.	*Until I came to the king's bench*
	Byfore a juge I kneled anon;	
	I prayd hym for Gods sake he would take hede.	
15	Full rewfully to hym I gan make my mone;	*complaint*
	For lacke of money I may not spede.	
	Benethe hym sat clerks, a great rowt;	*company*
	Fast they writen by one assent.	*common agreement*
	There stode up one, and cryed round about,	
20	"Richard, Robert, and one of Kent!"	
	I wist not wele what he ment	
	He cried so thike there in dede;	*quickly*
	There were stronge theves shamed and shent,	*powerful thieves; ruined*
	But they that lacked money mowght not spede.	*might*
25	Unto the Comon Place I yowde thoo	*Court of Common Pleas; went then*
	Where sat one with a sylken houde.	*hood*
	I dyd hym reverence as me ought to do;	
	I tolde hym my case, as well as I coude,	
	And seyd all my goods, by nowrd and by sowde,	*north, south*
30	I am defraudyd with great falshed;	*falsehood*

222

Simony and the Abuse of Money

He would not geve me a momme of his mouthe.   *give; mum*
For lake of money, I may not spede.

Then I went me unto the Rollis   *court of Rolls*
Before the clerks of the Chauncerie.   *Chancery*
35   There were many *qui tollis*,   *(see note)*
But I herd no man speke of me.
Before them I knelyd upon my kne,   *kneeled*
Shewyd them myne evidence and they began to reade.
They seyde trewer things might there nevar be,
40   But for lacke of money I may not spede.

In Westminster Hall I found one
Went in a longe gowne of ray.   *striped cloth*
I crowched, I kneled before them anon;
For Marys love, of helpe I gan them pray.
45   As he had be wrothe, he voyded away
Bakward, his hand he gan me byd.   *he offered me*
"I wot not what thou menest," gan he say.   *know not*
"Ley downe sylvar, or here thow may not spede."

In all Westminstar Hall I could find nevar a one
50   That for me would do, thowghe I shuld dye.
Without the dores were Flemings grete woon;   *Outside; large group of Flemings*
Upon me fast they gan to cry
And sayd, "Mastar, what will ye copen or by —   *barter or buy*
Fine felt hatts, spectacles for to rede?"
55   Of this gay gere, a great cause why   *beautiful stuff*
For lake of money I might not spede.

Then to Westminster gate I went
When the sone was at highe prime.   *nine o'clock*
Cokes to me, they toke good entent,   *Cooks*
60   Called me nere, for to dyne,
And proferyd me good brede, ale, and wyne.
A fayre clothe they began to sprede,
Rybbes of befe, bothe fat and fine;
But for lacke of money I might not spede.

65	In to London I gan me hy;	*hasten*
	Of all the lond it bearethe the prise.	*is the best*
	"Hot pescods!" one gan cry,	
	"Strabery rype, and chery in the ryse!"	*Strawberry; branch*
	One bad me come nere and by some spice;	*buy*
70	Pepar and saffron they gan me bede,	*offer*
	Clove, grayns, and flowre of rise.	*branch*
	For lacke of money I might not spede.	
	Then into Chepe I gan me drawne,	*Cheapside; went*
	Where I sawe stond moche people.	
75	One bad me come nere, and by fine cloth of lawne,	*linen*
	Paris thred, coton, and umple.	*fine gauze*
	I seyde there-upon I could no skyle,	*knew nothing about it*
	I am not wont there-to in dede.	
	One bad me by an hewre, my hed to hele:	*buy a cap; cover*
80	For lake of money I might not spede.	
	Then went I forth by London Stone	
	Thrwghe-out all Canywike strete.	*Candlewick*
	Drapers to me they called anon;	
	Grete chepe of clothe, they gan me hete;	*bargains in cloth; offer*
85	Then come there one, and cried "Hot shepes fete!"	*sheeps' feet*
	"Risshes faire and grene," an othar began to grete;	*Rushes; another*
	Both melwell and makarell I gan mete,	*mulvel (cod)*
	But for lacke of money I myght not spede.	
	Then I hied me into Estchepe.	*hastened; Eastcheap*
90	One cried, "Ribes of befe, and many a pie!"	*beef*
	Pewtar potts they clatteryd on a heape.	
	Ther was harpe, pipe and sawtry.	*psaltery*
	"Ye by Cokke!" "Nay by Cokke!" some began to cry;	*(see note)*
	Some sange of Jenken and Julian, to get themselvs mede.	*reward*
95	Full fayne I wold hadd of that mynstralsie,	
	But for lacke of money I cowld not spede.	
	Into Cornhill anon I yode	*went*
	Where is moche stolne gere amonge.	*stolen goods*
	I saw wher henge myne owne hode	*hung; hood*

224

Simony and the Abuse of Money

longingly

100 That I had lost in Westminstar amonge the throng.
Then I beheld it with lokes full longe; *longingly*
I kenned it as well as I dyd my Crede. *recognized; Creed*
To be myne owne hode agayne, me thought it wrong,
But for lacke of money I might not spede.

105 Then came the taverner, and toke my by the sleve,
And seyd, "Ser, a pint of wyn would yow assay?"
"Syr," quod I, "it may not greve; *it cannot hurt*
For a peny may do no more then it may."
I dranke a pint, and therefore gan pay;
110 Sore a-hungred away I yede; *went*
For well London Lykke-peny for ones and eye, *for once and for all*
For lake of money I may not spede.

Then I hyed me to Byllingesgate, *Billingsgate*
And cried "Wagge, wagge yow hens!" *Move; hence*
115 I praye a barge man, for Gods sake,
That they would spare me myn expens.
He sayde, "Ryse up, man, and get the hens.
What wenist thow I will do on the my almes-dede?
Here skapethe no man, by-nethe ij. pens!" [1]
120 For lacke of money I myght not spede.

Then I conveyed me into Kent, *betook myself*
For of the law would I medle no more; *meddle (in)*
By-caus no man to me would take entent,
I dight me to the plowe, even as I ded before. *set myself*
125 Jhesus save London, that in Bethelem was bore,
And every trew man of law, God graunt hym souls med; [2]
And they that be othar, God theyr state restore: —
For he that lackethe money, with them he shall not spede!

Explicit London Likke-peny

---

[1] *Do you think I will perform an act of charity for you? | Here no man gets away with paying less than twopence*

[2] *And God grant reward to the souls of every true lawyer*

Notes

Beati qui esuriunt

1   *Beati qui esuriunt.* A poetic rendition of Matt. 5:6: "Blessed are they that hunger and thirst after justice: for they shall have their fill."

3   *justiciam.* So Harley MS (*i*[us]*ticia*[m]); Wr *justitiam.* See also line 5: *nequiciam/ nequitiam,* and passim.

7   *encennia.* The Royal MS reads *exhennia,* treasures.

34   *cedunt.* Above this word the MS scribe has written "*i. re*" or "i.e., *recedunt.*"

59   *cum capite cornuto.* "The head dress of the ladies of rank and fashion at this period was arranged in the form of two horns" (Wr).

73   *relatores.* Middlemen who deliver the complaint to the judges.

78   *janitores.* Door-keepers in venality satires always present special difficulties to those wishing access to courts. For similar lines, see *Crux est denarii potens in seculo* (*De cruce denarii*) especially lines 77–100; or *Qui potest capere quod loquor capiat* (*De mundi cupiditate*) lines 53–68. See also Yunck, *The Lineage of Lady Meed,* p. 80 (citing a Latin poem attacking the Court of Rome): "Si das, intrabis protinus: si non, stas, stabis eminus" (If you give, you shall quickly enter: if you don't, you remain standing; you shall remain standing, far off), and *The Simonie* lines 142–44: "The porter hath comaundement to holde hem widoute the gate, / In the fen. / Hu mihte theih loven that Loverd, that serven thus His men?"

111   *bedellis.* Bailiffs and beadles were associated with legal and bureaucratic harassment in venality satire and complaint literature. A bailiff was "an officer of justice under a sheriff, who executes writs and processes, distrains and arrests"; a beadle was "a messenger of justice; a warrant officer; an under-bailiff" (Alford, *Glossary,* s.v. *Baillif* and *Bedele*). Alford cites *PP* B.3.2: "Now is mede

... Wiþ bedelis & baillifs ybrouȝt to þe king." For a similar view of beadles, see *The Simonie* 337–41, and *Song of the Husbandman* 37–39, 51–56. The beadle became proverbial for overzealous officiousness, as the beadle in Shakespeare's *2 Henry IV* (V.iv) whom Doll Tearsheet calls, among other things, a "thin man in a censer" and a "filthy-famish'd correctioner."

114   *transmittantur.* Wr's emendation of MS *transmutantur.*

119   *averia.* "The term *averium* is commonly used to signify all kinds of moveable property; but more particularly to signify cattle and horses" (Wr).

126   *Clericos.* "The scribe has written above this word, in the MS. "i. pauperes.""

130   *ballivam.* Wr translates as "bailiwick," the jurisdiction or district of a bailiff. For similar views of bailiffs, see *The Simonie*, lines 289–94; *Song of the Husbandman*, lines, 25–28; and *God Spede the Plough*, lines 37–39.

The Simonie

1   *Whii werre.* In the Bodley MS (B) the equivalent of these opening lines occurs at lines 19–24. B opens with: "Lordyngis leve and dere, lisneþ to me a stounde / Of a new þefte that nwlich was yfounde," and continues for sixteen lines with text not found elsewhere.

9   *Treuthe.* Truth/Troth is personified in this stanza and the next. He/him in lines 10–11 and 15–18 refer to this personification. For the various meanings of this term in legal contexts, see Alford, *Glossary*, s.v. *Treuthe.*

18   *shaken his berd.* "challenge him"; or, perhaps, "cuckold him." See Whiting, *Proverbs*, § B118, and line 534 below.

24   *Si dedero.* Singing "Si dedero" (a venality satire trope) means, in effect, to pay the piper, to bribe; the sense is, "If I give, I receive; if I don't give, I receive nothing." See note to *Addresses to the Commons* line 21 (in Jakke Trewman's testimony). This trope also appears in the works of Rutebeuf. See Yunck, *The Lineage of Lady Meed*, p. 198.

38   *Seint Thomas.* Thomas à Becket, archbishop of Canterbury appointed by king Henry II, was assassinated in Canterbury cathedral in 1170. Henry II did public penance for his murder. Thomas was at first a popular saint, but by the later Middle Ages all classes came to venerate his memory and the site where he was struck down. Hence Canterbury became a major pilgrimage center and tourist attraction after Jerusalem, Rome, and St. James of Compostela.

45–47   *Summe . . . Ful stille.* The poet complains that clerks (once educated for holy orders) enter the civil bureaucracy for economic advantage, depriving the Church of their talents.

74   *wid haukes and wid houndes.* Hawking and hunting with hounds were symbols of the worldly, secular life. See line 2 of "Were beþ þey biforen vs weren" from *The Sayings of St. Bernard* (*Index* § 3310): "Houndes ladden and hauekes beren" (*EL XIII*, ed. Carleton Brown, p. 85); and Walter, of Chaucer's Clerk's Tale, who spends his time hawking and hunting (immersed in his "lust present") while neglecting his realm's welfare (IV.78–81). The author of *The Simonie* links parsons with avarice for benefices (lines 55–90) and priests with illicit sexual activity (lines 109–20).

88   *rat on the rouwe-bible.* Wordplay: he "reads on the ribible" (= rebeck, an early type of violin), with a pun on "Bible" ("and on other bok / No mo").

104–08   *As bi a jay . . . no betir than a jay.* With this might be compared Chaucer's description of the Summoner in the General Prologue of *The Canterbury Tales*:
>A fewe termes hadde he, two or thre,
>That he had lerned out of some decree —
>No wonder is, he herde it al the day;
>And eek ye knowen wel how that a jay
>Kan clepen "Watte" as wel as kan the pope. (I.639–43)

See also *UR* 1–9 (about a chough rather than a jay), and Whiting, *Proverbs*, §§ J18, J19.

115   *croune . . . crok.* "Crown of acolite for the crumpled crook" (?). The sense of the line seems to be that the "wantoune prestes" mock prelates, with perhaps an allusion to Christ's crown of thorns.

117   *kembeth the croket.* The *croket* is a rolled hair fashion introduced into the court of Henry III, which flourished into the late fourteenth century. See *PlT* line 306 and note.

118   *newe jet.* A phrase Chaucer uses for the Pardoner's dress: "Hym thoughte he rood al of the newe jet" (I.682). See *MED* s.v. *get* n.1 (a) and (b) and *Above all thing thow arte a kyng* 10 and note.

119   *Sanz doute.* A French phrase appropriate for courtly literature but highly ironic in this context.

120   *clateren cumpelin.* To "clatter [=make noise] compline" is a euphemism for their bedroom activity "whan the candel is oute." Compline is the last monastic hour of the day. In Malory, Lancelot clatters so loudly in his sleep after making love to Elayne, that Guenevere hears him in the next room and knows what has happened. The *Gawain*-poet uses the verb *clatered* to describe the noise of the ax being ground on the *gryndelston* (line 2201; cf. 731). *MED* cites this phrase as an example of *compline* sense 3: "Used humorously with reference to chatting and snoring." The other cited example is Chaucer's Reeve's Tale (I.4171).

121–22   *thise abbotes . . . contrefeten knihtes.* In the General Prologue to *The Canterbury Tales* Chaucer depicts the monk — "A manly man, to been an abbot able" (I.167) — as "An outridere, that lovede venerie [hunting]" (line 166).

123   *religious.* MS *religiouns.*

126   *a-mis.* Supplied in a different hand; so Wr and Br.

142–44   *The porter . . . His men.* On this motif of the hostile doorkeeper, see *Beati qui esuriunt* line 78 and note.

147   *He hath forsake.* Ironic, with a change of pronoun from "monekes" (line 145) and "Hii" (line 146) to "He" (line 147).

153   *Where shal . . . leres?* Compare *Preste, Ne Monke, Ne Yit Chanoun*: "I have lyved now fourty yers, / And fatter men about the neres / Yit sawe I never than are these frers" (lines 17–19). Compare also the Dominican friar in his refectory (mess hall): *PPC* lines 219–26.

183   *Hit nis . . . louweth.* "It is not only for the calf that the cow lows." That is, the cow moos for other reasons. On this phrase as proverbial, see Whiting, *Proverbs*, § C9.

193   *officials.* An *official* was "an officer subordinate to an archbishop or bishop, especially a bishop's chancellor, who presided over consistory court; a canon-law judge" (Alford, *Glossary*, s.v. *Official*).

195   *Mak a present . . . dwelle.* The dean was "a church official invested with jurisdiction over a subdivision of an archdeaconry." Alford (*Glossary*, s.v. *Dene*) cites William Holdsworth's *A History of English Law*: "It was the duty of Rural Deans to report on the manners of the clergy and laity: this rendered them necessary attendants at the episcopal visitation . . . and gave them at one time a small jurisdiction." Of such local officials, Scott L. Waugh states: "The village represented the basic level of governance. For most people, the manorial court was the primary jurisdiction and the lord's officials the paramount authority. Chaucer's reeve, for example, was feared more than the plague by those beneath him. Church officials were equally dreaded, though less conspicuous. Responsible for supervising churches, priests, and parishioners, archdeacons and rural deans were hated for their hypocritical, corrupt meddling in villagers' lives, as Chaucer's Friar's Tale reveals. One or more constables were elected by the village and were responsible for keeping order. They watched suspicious persons, organized the pursuit of wrongdoers whenever the hue and cry was raised, arrested criminals, and seized felons' chattels." *England in the Reign of Edward III* (Cambridge: Cambridge University Press, 1991), p. 154. The author of the *Apocalipsis Goliae* characterizes the dean as the "archdeacon's dog": "Decanus canis est archidiaconi" (*Die Apokalypse des Golias*, ed. Karl Strecker [Rome: Regenberg, 1928], stanza 49).

211   *And yit ther is.* In B this stanza is preceded by a stanza not found in the other MSS which reads (in Ross's transcription):

> And as I seide first, hit is a gret mischaunce,
> Þat þat synne reygnet so þorow þat synfol soffraunce.
> Þe bischop feyneþ on his side and takeð a prive mede,
> And sely denys and officialis dare noȝt seie fore drede
>   To swiche.
> Þus is Englond schent fore synne, sykerliche.

The three folios prior to the stanza are missing in B.

211–40   B follows these five stanzas on "false fisiciens" with a sixth stanza, not in A, which reads (Ross's transcription):

> He maket hym merie þe ferst, as mery as he can,
> And loke þat he fare wel his hors and his man.
> A-morwe he taket þe uryne and schaket aȝen þe sonne.
> "Dame," he seis, "drede þe noȝt. Þe maister is wonne,"   *here*
>   And li[ket].   *is delighted*
> But þus he fereð a-wey þe silver and þe wif be skikket.   *plundered*

C includes a version of the stanza.

221   *And.* So Wr and Br. MS *ad.*

228   *Hit . . . i-wrouht.* "It shall be expensive enough whan all is said and done." The phrase *dere on a lek* is reminiscent of a proverbial expression found in Chaucer: *deere ynough a leek* (*CT* VIII.795). The leek was thought to be worthless. See the note on this proverb in *The Riverside Chaucer*, ed. Benson, p. 949.

254   *also wel as a frere.* Knights should wear dress appropriate for their vocations, as do friars (or as friars should do).

264   *is.* So Wr and Br; lacking in MS but needed for the sense.

277   *Godes soule . . . sworn.* A reference to swearing on God and God's body. See the Pardoner's disquisition on swearing and oaths in the Pardoner's Tale VI.629–59.

280   *contrefaiture,* counterfeit quality. The false knight goes from a seemingly harmless imitation to outright sin such that he angers God and pays the devil most of all (line 282).

283–88   B follows this stanza with a unique stanza after which the arrangement of stanzas differs radically from A and P. The stanza reads in Ross's transcription and emendation:

> Sily man to conterfeyte, fondist in his wise,   *devotion*
> But litel fondyng is maket toward Godis service,   *devotion*

231

Where half þe bisnesse do to God þat is do to þe [fend],
To goderele al þe worle but Crist, my lef frend   *profit; world; beloved*
                        [and kynde],
Þe most deel of þe worle is blent, fore overal hit is [blynde].

285   *turmentours*. A reference to the dress of Christ's tormentors in mystery plays, which were staged by clerks.

292   *mot-hall*. "The annals of Edward's reign are filled with complaints against the King's officers . . . . In 1321, a charge was leveled against Hugh Despenser the Younger, who put his own officers into the King's household, where he was chamberlain (*Annales paulini*, in Stubbs . . . , pp. 292–97). This might be the basis for the reference in A and P to the moot-hall in the chamber" (Ross, p. 183, note 81). For various uses of the moot hall in *PP* and other works, see Alford, *Glossary*, s.v. *Mothalle*.

294   *i-whited*. "Silvered," i.e., bribed, crossed with silver.

295   *If the king*. In this section on petty justices, the poet regards the king as a victim along with the poor. The king's army suffers through bribery in the conscription process; and he loses tax monies. This was a common complaint in fourteenth-century literature. See, e.g., *Against the King's Taxes*, a macaronic poem (Anglo-Norman French and Latin) from MS Harley 2253, lines 16–20, in *Anglo-Norman Political Songs*, ed. Isabel S. T. Aspin, Anglo-Norman Texts 11 (Oxford: Basil Blackwell, 1953), p. 109. See also note to lines 313–24 below.

303   *for-pinched, to-toilled, and to-twiht*. Wr glosses these colorful terms as "pinched to pieces," "laboured away," and "twitted away" respectively. The idea, as in *Taxe Has Tenet Us Alle*, is that "The kyng therof hade smalle" (line 3).

309   *girles*. Although the word need not denote females, but only youth, here the signification seems to mean "young females."

313–24   Topos of the "king's ignorance." See *Truthe, Reste, and Pes* note to lines 45–46.

321   *Thurfte him . . . ner*. "Should he dare not seek wealth so far away, he might find it nearer to hand." This seems to be a criticism of Edward II's foreign policy.

325   *come he . . . pore*: no matter how poor he was before assuming high office.

328   *ben* inserted above the line with a karat. Wr and Br print in brackets.

330   *Theih pleien . . . wele.* "They use the king's silver for their own pleasures, and produce wood, or tallies, instead of contributing to the prosperity of the people" (Wr).

337–38 *baillifs and bedeles . . . greve.* See also *Beati qui esuriunt* line 111 and note; *Song of the Husbandman* lines 37–56 and note to line 13; and *Gode Spede the Plough* line 37. For an account of an early fourteenth-century bailiff charged with bedeviling tenants, see the case of the poor tenants of Bocking manor, who drew up a petition of grievance against John le Doo, bailiff who, by not agreeing to customary fines (amercements), "of his own conceit, increased their burdens twofold or even threefold and by such means has vexed the tenants and brought them to destruction, against all reason and the Great Charter that Holy Church ought to uphold." As quoted in Dobson, *The Peasants' Revolt of 1381*, p. 79.

345   *He wole . . . hod.* "He will take forty pence to put on his hood," i.e., to begin his official duties.

355–60 *And sumtime . . . i-smite.* Ross mentions "numerous contemporary complaints against tradesmen's offences," including "the King's ordinances which were directed against certain tradesmen, notably brewers, whose prices were too high" (p. 186, note 111).

362   *That he . . . haft.* That he is somewhat loose in the handle, i.e., unstable, unreliable. See *MED* s.v. *haft* (b). Whiting identifies the phrase as proverbial (*Proverbs*, § H10). C reads: "That he nis a party lose in the haft" (line 140); B "Þat he is more þan halfendel los in þe haft" (line 211).

363–65 *For falsnesse . . . Ne in herte.* These traditional sentiments about the failure of truth in the modern era are reminiscent of Chaucer's short poems "Truth," "Gentilesse," and especially "Lak of Stedfastnesse."

366   *And tharfore . . . smerte.* C "For sothe thei nyl sese ar God make hem to smert"; B "Þerfore is no wonþer þow al þe worle smerte."

373–78 *So that . . . muchele miht.* Although complaints against the weather were widespread in Latin and vernacular verse, this verse paragraph may allude to "the terrible storms and shortages of 1315–16" (see Ross's quotations from contemporary chroniclers on pp. 186–87, note 119).

382   *sustenaunce.* So A and B; C *frute.*

384   *i-liche wicke.* B "unwrast and wikke."

385–90   Lacking in C and B.

385–86   *Men . . . betre.* The idea in these lines (and in the verse paragraph) is that people have become too proud in times of plenty. Langland develops this idea in *Piers Plowman* passus 5 and 6 (B text). It is also a prominent feature of *Wynnere and Wastoure.* C omits this stanza.

391–96   C concludes with this stanza, whose final four lines read: "Whan bestes beth i-storve and corne waxeth dere, / And honger and pestilence in ech lond, as ʒe mow ofte here / Overal; — / But if we amende us, it will wel wers befal. Explicit" (lines 465–68).

392   *a derthe.* Perhaps a reference to the great famine of 1315. For the importance of famines in literature and history, see R. W. Frank, "The 'Hungry Gap,' Crop Failure, and Famine: The Fourteenth-Century Agricultural Crisis and *Piers Plowman,*" in *Yearbook of Langland Studies* 4 (1990), 87–104.

409   *Tho.* Although there is no large letter in A, in B the scribe left a space for a large letter in the equivalent stanza. Ross comments: "MS leaves a space here for a large capital which was never added. The scribe evidently felt that this stanza marked a divisional point in the poem, as indeed it does. The Auchinleck MS offers corresponding lines once again, beginning with this stanza" (p. 189).

415   *astint.* So Wr and Br; MS *astin.* B *a stynt* (line 283).

469   *assisours.* An assizer was "one of those who constituted the assize or inquest, whence the modern jury originated; a sworn recognitor (*OED*)" (Alford, *Glossary,* s.v. *Sisour*). Alford cites *PP* B.20.161: "Hir sire was a Sysour þat neuere swoor truþe, / Oon Tomme two-tonge, atteynt at each a queste [inquest]"; and *Jacob's Well*: "False cysourys gon vp-on qwestys, & puttyn a man fro his ryʒt thrugh a false verdyʒte, & wytnessen aʒens trewthe."

hundred. An administrative division of a county containing one hundred home-steads and having its own court.

476   A ceases with this line. Lines 465–end are supplied from B and checked against Ross's transcription.

483   *breth* (= bread). The scribe of B regularly spells final *-d* as *þ* (-th). See also *wretchethe*, wretched, line 486; *a-paith*, apaid, line 500; *methe*, meed, line 507; *lewthe*, lewd (=ignorant), line 525; *wikketh*, wicked, line 531; *blisseth bloth*, blessed blood, line 541.

494   *mercyment.* Says Skeat in his note to *Piers Plowman* B 1.159: "Blount, in his Law Dict., says — 'There is a difference between *amerciaments* and *fines*: these [i.e. the latter], as they are taken for punishments, are punishments certain, which grow expressly from some statute; but amerciaments are arbitrarily imposed by affeerors.'" Alford defines *Merciment* as "A penalty imposed 'at the mercy' of the court (as distinct from a statutory fine), an amercement." See *Glossary*, s.v. *Merciment*.

495   *at a.* B: *ata.*

    schillingwerd. B: *schilligwerd.* Ross emends to *schilli[n]werd.*

496   *han.* Ross mistranscribes as *him. Have* and *haд* are the more common forms of the verb *to have* in B, but see lines 508 and 525 where *han* is the recurrent form in B. See also lines 13, 30, 241, 394, 428, 445, 446, 496.

497   *at mele.* B: *at m.* Ross's emendation to suit the rhyme. The phrase is ambiguous and could mean "on such occasions," or "for their supper," with a pun reaching back to what "bakers" and "brewers" provide.

514   The words of this are blotted after *with*.

517–40   These lines appear as the antepenultimate and the penultimate stanzas of B. Ross in his edition transposes these stanzas to his lines 325–60. I retain the lines according to their position in B because they seem to develop the thought of the previous stanzas.

534   See note to line 18.

536   *for hunger . . . strecchen*. The meaning seems to be that they achieve death because of hunger (after first lying down in the street like beggars). See *MED* s.v. *strecchen* 5 (c).

Above All Thing Thow Arte a Kyng

Refrain, line 3. MS and Greene *goste*; RHR *gost*.

4   The word *money* in the margin appears to indicate the refrain after each quatrain for the first nine stanzas and also 11–12; stanzas 10 and 13–20 have the phrase *money &c*.

5   *place thow makyste*. MS *palce* ~~tomakt~~ *thou makyste*.

8   *But thowght*. MS *but* ~~so~~ *thowght*.

10   *galandes*. Gallants — what later ages would call "swells" — were fashionably-dressed young men. In moral lyrics they became symbols or topoi of pride and presumption. See, for example, "an acrostic on the name 'Galaunt' (built on the Seven Deadly Sins)" as printed in *A Manual of the Writings in Middle English*, 5:1469, and the three poems on *galaunts* mentioned on page 1470 (§§ 161–63). The MS seems to read *garlandes* rather than *galandes* (= RHR's and Greene's reading).

           jett. Derives from Lat. and Fr *jactare*, *jetter* but has the sense of "to carry oneself confidently or conceitedly, to talk boastfully of oneself, to boast, brag, vaunt oneself, make an ostentatious display" (*OED* s.v. *Jet* v.[1]). See also *The Simonie* 118 and note.

13   *the*. So Greene and RHR; MS *they* (anticipation of *hey weys*).

15   *dysguysynges*. "Allegorical entertainments, the forerunners of the Tudor masques" (Greene).

17   *wantyth*. MS *yt* written above the line.

18   *a mated chere*. "With the air of one checkmated or baffled" (Greene, cited by RHR).

Notes

19   *springe.* So RHR; MS *sprnge.*

22   *As kyng.* MS and RHR *at kyng;* Greene *As.*

23   *tables.* Backgammon, as in Chaucer's *Book of the Duchess,* line 51: "Then playe either at ches or tables."

25   *and knyght . . . wyghte.* MS *and & knyght . . . wyghe.* Emendations by Greene and RHR.

28   *Theyr.* MS *thery;* RHR *theyr,* Greene *Theyr.*

33   *incresse.* MS *Icresse;* Greene, RHR emend to *Incresse.*

35   *the.* So MS; Greene emends to *the[y].* RHR directs to line 67 (*the crye*), where Greene also reads *the[y].*

36   *faders.* MS ~~fath~~ *faders.*

39   *oft.* So MS and RHR; Greene *of[t].*

41   *Westmyaster.* MS *wystmyaster;* Greene emends to *Westmynster,* RHR to *westmynster.*

43   *ther.* So MS and Greene; RHR *there.*

45   *Whatesoever.* MS *Whate so euery;* RHR *Whate-so-euer;* Greene *Whatsoeuer.*

48   *Shale prove not.* So Greene and RHR; MS *shale not proue not.*

52   *moyeny.* So MS (*e* inserted above the line); RHR emends to *money.*

53   *that be in.* So MS and RHR; Greene *that in.*

55   *Sum cutte.* So RHR; MS *Su[m]* ~~knowe~~ *cutte.*

57   *dothe.* So MS and RHR; Greene *doth.*

60   *peyne.* So MS and RHR; Greene *payne.*

67   *oft the.* So MS; RHR *of them*. Greene reads *of the[y]*.

75   *moné.* So MS and RHR; Greene emends to *mone[y]*.

76   *That he ys.* So RHR; MS *that he r ys*. Greene *That i heys*.

79   *Yt ys.* MS ~~ys~~ *yt ys*.

In Erth It Es a Litill Thing

25   *till.* See *OED* s.v. *Till* v.[3] signification 1: "To draw, attract, persuade; to entice, allure, coax; to win over."

29   *For he . . . trayl syde.* "i.e. To wear low trailing gowns" (RHR). *Trayl* = "To walk with trailing garments" (RHR Glossary).

30   *grene.* The color green; but also, perhaps, "sexual passion." See MED (n.2).

33   *grace.* So RHR; MS *gce*.

34   *lese . . . bind.* Alludes to the pope's power to "bind and loose." See Matt. 16.19 and 18.18.

41   *borgh and wed. Borgh* (from OE *borg*) = surety, pledge, security-money; *to borwe* = as a pledge, as security. *Wed* (from OE *wedd*) = pledge, compact, as in Chaucer's Knight's Tale: "Lat hym be war! his nekke lith to wedde" (I.1218). The author of this lyric often writes in doublets, including some tags from the alliterative tradition. For example: "life and saul" (line 62), "get and wyn" (line 63), "lene and gyf" (line 73), "frith and felde" (line 98, compare line 75), "stede and stall" (line 86), "spere or schelde" (line 97).

44   *thai.* So RHR (*þai*); MS *he*.

52   *fase.* Scots spelling of *foes*.

67   *hertes.* RHR *hert es*, which may be the correct reading. In the manuscript the letters are crowded together, but there may be a break between *hert* and *es*.

238

81   *made . . . softe.* That is, he is seated at the place of honor.

92   *gifen.* So MS; RHR *gyfen.*

94   *gré.* The first degree, the prize, the victory, pre-eminence, top of the ladder, reward.

105   *Nowther.* So MS (*nowþer*); RHR *nouþer.*

108   *assise.* The court of Assizes determined legal matters of fact by means of assessors or jurymen (*sisours*). See Alford, *Glossary,* s.v. *Sise,* and *The Simonie* line 469 and note.

London Lickpenny

2   *trouthe.* So MS; Hammond, Holthausen *truthe.*

5   *Marys.* MS *maris.*

6   *procede.* Bring legal proceedings, litigate.

7   *I would gyve sylvar.* MS reads *I would gyve ~~money~~ sylvar.* The scribe may have anticipated *money* in line 8. *my purs is faynt.* For this language about purses and money, see Chaucer's humorous short lyric "The Complaint of Chaucer to His Purse," with its considerable word-play on "heavy" and "light."

10   *my hode was gonn,* that is, stolen. See lines 99–100. The hood in this sense is a covering for the head worn under a hat.

12   *kyngs benche.* "One of the three superior courts of common law (the other two being the Exchequer and the Court of Common Pleas)." "The King's Bench was concerned primarily with criminal law; the Court of Common Pleas, with civil actions." See Alford, *Glossary,* s.v. *Bench* and *Kinges Bench,* and Alford's citations from *Piers Plowman.* Of the courts in Westminster, Hammond quotes from Stow's *Survey of London*: "At the entry on the right hand the common place [i.e. Common Pleas], where ciuill matters are to be pleaded, especially such as touch lands or contracts; at the vpper end of the Hall, on the right hand or Southest corner, the king's bench, where pleas of the Crowne haue their

hearing; and on the left hand or Southwest corner sitteth the Lord Chancellor, accompanied with the master of the Rowles and other men . . . called maisters of the Chauncerie." She comments: "This last-named court [Chancery] handled all cases relating to revenue, and the King's Bench and Common Pleas, as Stow says, took cognizance respectively of trespasses against the King's peace and of disputes between private persons" (*English Verse*, p. 476).

20   *Richard . . . Kent.* Apparently clerks are calling names for impending court cases. The "one of Kent" might be the Kentish countryman.

25   *the Comon Place.* "Held at Westminster, the Court of Common Pleas had jurisdiction over civil actions brought by one subject against another, all real actions, and the decisions of local and manorial courts; it was inferior to the Court of King's Bench, since error lay from it to that court" (Alford, *Glossary*, s.v. *Commune Court*).

26   *a sylken houde.* Worn by sergeants at law. Alford quotes from *Piers Plowman*: "Shal no sergeant for þat seruice were a silk howue, / Ne no pelure in his panelon for pledynge at þe barre" (B.3.295; *Glossary* s.v. *Sergeaunt* II).

31   *would not . . . mouthe.* Wouldn't even say "mum"; i.e., said nothing.

34   *Chauncerie.* This court functioned as a court of appeals, "moderating the rigour of the common law, and giving relief in cases where there was no remedy in the common-law courts" (*OED*).

35   *qui tollis.* Apparently a legal formula by which clerks would summon claimants to the bar. Hammond suggests: "Thou who hast a grievance, present it."

42   *gowne of ray.* "Ray, a striped cloth, was much worn by lawyers" (Hammond).

49   *In all Westminstar Hall.* MS *In all westminstalℓᵉ hall.* The scribe seems to have anticipated the *-all* of *hall.*

51   *Flemings grete woon.* A great abundance of Flemings. For this signification of *woon*, see *OED* s.v. *Wone* sb.[3] (obsolete and poetic) II.3, 4. Stow or his copy-text rewrites this passage to: "which seing, I gat me out of the doore / where flemynge began on me for to cry" (lines 45–46 of Hammond's edition of Harley 367). The Flemings were introduced into England to help increase the wool

trade, and a number of them emigrated to England, bringing with them their expertise in cloth-making. But English laborers resented the competition from the Flemings, and many Flemings were killed during the Great Rising of 1381.

54   *felt hatts*. These words also appear in the margin of the MS.

65   *In to London.* "Our countryman crossed Long Ditch after leaving Westminster Hall by the Gate, walked by White Hall along the Strand, entered the City through Ludgate, and passed along Fleet Street to St. Paul's and the west end of Cheapside" (Hammond).

73   *Chepe.* The ward of Cheap, one of the great market areas of medieval London. In 1319 Cheap contained "mercers, pepperers, fishmongers, cheesemongers, bakers, poulterers, and cordwainers" (D. W. Robertson, *Chaucer's London* [New York: Wiley, 1968], p. 23). This Cheap in the west, near the Shambles and Newgate, should be distinguished from Eastcheap, which the narrator also visits (see lines 89–96). The word *chepe* appears in the margin of the MS.

74   *sawe.* MS *saywe.*

76   *umple.* "A fine kind of linen stuff" (*OED* s.v. *Umple*); "Fine gauze or lawn" (Hammond). Earliest *OED* citation = mid-fifteenth century. Stow or copy-text rewrites to: "here is parys thred the fynest in the land" (line 68 of Hammond's edition of Harley 367).

79   *hewre.* MED reads this word as an error for *hewve, houve, houwe* (from OE *hūfe*): "A headdress; esp. a close-fitting cap or coif." See *MED* s.v. *houve* (a). The word *herwe* appears in the left margin of the MS.

81   *London Stone.* The so-called "London Stone," or part of it, was built into the wall of St. Swithin's church. It originally might have been a Roman *milliarium* stone, or milestone, which measured distances. John V. Morris's map of fourteenth-century London on p. 14 of *Chaucer's London* designates the "London Stone" as landmark no. 29.

82   *Canywike strete*, or Candlewick Street, one of the wards of the city (near Walbrook), which contained "chandlers, weavers, and drapers" (Robertson, *Chaucer's London*, p. 41). For the location, consult the detailed fold-out "Sketch Map of London in the Time of the Peasants' Revolt, 1381," in Ruth

Bird, *The Turbulent London of Richard II* (London: Longman, 1949), following p. 156. This is based on a map by M. B. Honeybourne.

83   *Drapers* deal in cloth and other fabrics.

89   *Estchepe.* East Cheap, between Candlewick Street and Tower Street, contained "butcher's stalls, the shops of turners and basketmakers, and some cookshops" (Robertson, *Chaucer's London*, p. 59).

93   *"Ye by Cokke!" "Nay by Cokke!"* "Yes, by God!" "No, by God!" *Cokke* = euphemism for God, as in the Host's oath in Chaucer's Manciple's Prologue: "see how, for cokkes bones, / That he wol falle fro his hors atones!" (*CT* IX.9–10).

94   *Jenken and Julian.* "Evidently a song or songs by itinerant beggars" (Hammond).

97   *Cornhill.* Another great market ward of medieval London, which contained a great variety of merchants as well as more transient populations. Robertson lists the following as for sale in Cornhill: "laces, points, bows, caps, light coats, purses, hats, spurs, gaming-tables, paternosters, pen-cases, boxwood combs, pepper mills, thread, girdles, paper, and parchment" (*Chaucer's London*, p. 48). The narrator of the C text of *Piers Plowman* claims he lives in Cornhill as well as in the north country (passus 11).

100   *in Westminstar.* Hammond surmises that these words might be gloss (scribal or editorial) that has been worked into the text.

113   *Byllingesgate.* Billingsgate, one of the city gates (between Botolph's Wharf and the Wool Quay), and the fish market there, which was notorious for its bustle, noise, and abusive language.

118   *on the my almes-dede.* MS *on the ~~my~~ ^{no} almes dede.* The superscript *no* is in a different hand.

Plowman Writings

Introduction

The success of William Langland's *Piers Plowman* (three versions: 1368–74, 1377–81, and 1381–85) inspired a tradition of what might be called English "plowman writings," an important subgenre of late medieval political satire and complaint. Even before Langland certain authors, notably the anonymous poet of *Song of the Husbandman* (printed here from MS Harley 2253 of about 1330), idealized the hardworking farmer as a symbol of spiritual truth in the face of oppression and material deprivation. But Langland was the first to equate the plowman with Christ (*Petrus id est Christus*); and because Langland offered satiric attacks on the clergy in his poem, later writers, including Chaucer and John Ball of the Peasants' Revolt, used Piers the Plowman to represent true Christian virtue as opposed to the corrupt established ecclesiastical order. These plowmen not only labored, uncomplaining, for the common profit, they also came to represent faith performing good works. Through their charitable examples they tutor even the knightly classes, as when Piers instructs the world in labor and asks the knight to defend and protect the other estates (*PP* B passus 6). The best-known writings in the later plowman tradition are *Piers the Plowman's Crede* and the pseudonymous *Plowman's Tale*.[1]

The figure of the plowman has political dimensions — and poems about plowmen belong in this volume — because the plowman, in fact and in literary portrayals, was integral to the commonwealth but yet suffered poverty and hardship. The word *plough* was synonymous with the Commons, as in *What Profits a Kingdom*, line 143, "The plough, the chirche, to mayntene ryght," where *plough* and *chirche* represent two of the three estates. In the literature he provides a sharp contrast to the pampered regular clergy and to venal prelates concerned only about their temporalities.

Not all fourteenth-century English depictions of the peasant classes were positive. In his recreation of the Great Rising (*Vox Clamantis*), John Gower portrays the third estate as lazy, grasping, and proud. In this negative representation Gower is less interested in overturning the estates ideal than in recording his personal reaction to

---

[1] See *Six Ecclesiastical Satires*, ed. James Dean (Kalamazoo: Medieval Institute Publications, 1991).

the frightening events of 1381. But Langland himself, in B passus 6 and the Prologue, shows how manual laborers in good times will turn away from hard work and become slothful. They become wasters rather than winners, as in *Wynnere and Wastoure*, the alliterative poem of the early 1350s, which represents the wasters — an army of friars and merchants — as big spenders and revelers who yet help stimulate a sluggish economy. In *How the Plowman Learned His Paternoster* (STC 20034), the plowman may be expert at husbandry — indeed, his house is as fully stocked with foodstuff as a typical waster's — but he must be instructed in the Lord's Prayer by the local parson.

In fact, the plowman was not always idealized. During the years of the Great Plague in England (1348–49), labor became scarce and laborers could command increased wages for their services. In a society that had depended on serfdom and a system of tenant farmers, the rise in wages, hence higher market prices for food, combined with flight from the manor, alarmed king and parliament. As early as 1349 Edward III issued a proclamation about labor that parliament would write into law in 1351. Edward complained of "excessive wages" brought on by the death of "workmen and servants" after the plague; and he predicted "grievous incommodities" as a result of "the lack of plowmen and such laborers." He commanded that any able-bodied laborer under sixty years old not engaged in a craft "shall be required to serve in suitable service" of whosoever "shall require him." Most important, such persons shall be bound "to take only the wages, livery, meed, or salary which were accustomed to be given [five or six years previously] in the places where he oweth to serve."[2]

The first work in this section is *Song of the Husbandman*, a poem of complaint from British Library MS Harley 2253 fol. 64r (*Index* § 696, earlier fourteenth century):[3] seventy-two heavily-alliterating long lines, composed in alternating eight-line and four-line stanzas rhyming *abab* (*cdcd*), with touches of chain verse or concatenation. This lyric has often been regarded as an important witness to the so-called "alliterative revival" and as a precursor of *Winnere and Wastoure* and *Piers Plowman* and of later writings of complaint and satire. Unlike many poems of morality and complaint, this lyric, written as a first-person testimony, includes vivid, convincing descriptions of oppressions committed against peasant farmers. The poet, for example, depicts beadles — petty officials with their account books — as harassing the bondman with extortion:

---

[2] *Medieval Culture and Society*, ed. David Herlihy (New York: Harper, 1968), p. 359.

[3] This famous Harleian manuscript also supplies *Thomas of Erceldoune's Prophecy*. See above p. 11.

Introduction

Yet cometh budeles with ful muche bost:	*beadles; arrogance*
"Greythe me selver to the grene wax.	*Prepare*
Thou art writen y my writ, that thou wel wost!"	*in; well know*

Later the narrator characterizes the "maister budel" as being "bruste [bristled] ase a bore." In this poem we find a cast of unscrupulous rogues — the heyward (in charge of grain or perhaps of boundaries and fences); the bailiff (who enforced the law); the woodward (in charge of forests). The husbandman looks to the king for relief but is always disappointed; the poor rob the poor, and the wealthy prey upon rich and poor alike. The text for this edition is based on a photostat of the manuscript and is checked against the editions of Wr (in *PSE*) and RHR.

The second poem printed here, *God Spede the Plough*, exists in a unique manuscript in the British Library: MS Lansdowne 762, fols. *5r–6v* (*Index* § 363; early sixteenth century). In this refrain poem various clerical and civic officials — parson, clerk, sexton, purveyors, bailiffs, beadles, friars, summoner, priests, students, constables — demand tithes and food from the beleaguered husbandmen. To this extent the poem includes estates satire with the farmers as plaintiffs; they produce food for the common good whereas those who prey on them are managers and bureaucrats. The husbandmen are normative in that they represent the oppressed and overtaxed elements of society. The present text is based on a photostat of the manuscript checked against Skeat's edition in *Pierce the Ploughmans Crede* (EETS 30). A corner of the manuscript at the bottom right of fol. *5r* and *5v* is missing. I reproduce Skeat's speculation as to the missing portions.

The third poem in this section, "I-blessyd Be Cristes Sonde" (entitled by modern editors *God Speed the Plough*), exists in a unique manuscript: Oxford University MS Archbishop Selden B. 26 fol. *19r* (Summary Catalogue No. 3340; with music; *Index* § 3434; *Supplement* § 1405.5). This poem, which Chambers and Sidgwick date about 1450 (citing E. W. B. Nicholson's dating in *Early Bodleian Music*), celebrates husbandmen and asks God to bless the plow and to ensure plenty. The tone is quite different from the other two plowmen works in this section, which feature complaint and satire. The present text is based on an excellent electrostatic print of the manuscript and is checked against the facsimile and transcriptions in Stainer's *Early Bodleian Music* and against the editions of Chambers and RHR.

The final piece is Chaucer's portrait of the Plowman from the General Prologue to *The Canterbury Tales*: Fragment I[A].529–41. Chaucer's Plowman is one of three estates ideals — that of the commons (*laboratores*: those who work), the other two being the Knight, representative of the chivalric class (*bellatores*: those who fight) and the Plowman's brother, the Parson, representative of the clergy (*oratores*: those who pray). Like Langland's Piers the Plowman, Chaucer's Plowman is spiritualized, with few touches of individualism. As Derek Brewer has written:

> The Parson, and especially the Ploughman, are the most idealised of all the pilgrims, and the least individually realised. They are theories rather than persons. But the concrete details of the descriptions, and the moral beauty of the ideals when understood in their proper contexts, are extremely attractive and effectively presented.[4]

The Plowman works for the common profit "For Cristes sake, for every povre wight"; and he not only pays all his tithes, he is said to live "in pees and parfit charitee" and to love God "best with al his hoole herte." Although Chaucer's Plowman manifests none of the potentially revolutionary aspects of Langland's or John Ball's Piers, Chaucer does call him "a trewe swynkere," a phrase that recalls Ball's appeal to "trewe men" (those who would work for social reform). In the fifteenth century the terms "true men" and "true preachers" become code words for Lollards. The pilgrim Plowman stands as a silent rebuke to the luxurious friars and worldly monks satirized in estates literature generally and in *The Canterbury Tales* specifically.

Although the Plowman is one of Chaucer's three ideal pilgrims, he is also one of seven pilgrims for whom Chaucer wrote no tale. The reasons for his failure to include a tale for this idealized pilgrim have been a source for speculation. Perhaps he had no suitable material at hand; or perhaps the figure of the Plowman had become too highly charged politically in the aftermath of the Peasants' Revolt and Ball's invocation of Piers the Plowman. But later editors of Chaucer saw fit to insert the pseudonymous *Plowman's Tale*; and MS Christ Church Oxford 152 includes a version of Thomas Hoccleve's *Sleeves of the Virgin*, with a Prologue meant to resemble the prologues in Chaucer's *Canterbury Tales*. This has recently been printed by John M. Bowers in the Middle English Texts Series.[5]

The present text is based on the facsimile and transcription of the Hengwrt MS — National Library of Wales, Peniarth 392, abbreviated Hg — edited by Paul Ruggiers (Norman: University of Oklahoma Press, 1979), fol. 6*v* (transcription on p. 29), and is checked against the "working facsimile" of the Ellesmere MS (San Marino, Henry E. Huntington Library MS EL 27 C 9), abbreviated El (Woodbridge: D. S. Brewer, 1989), fol. 6*v*, together with the versions in *The Text of The Canterbury Tales*, ed. John M. Manly and Edith Rickert (Chicago: University of Chicago Press, 1940),

---

[4] *An Introduction to Chaucer* (London: Longman, 1984), p. 173.

[5] *The Canterbury Tales: Fifteenth-Century Continuations and Additions* (Kalamazoo: Medieval Institute Publications, 1992).

3:24–25; *The Riverside Chaucer*, ed. Larry D. Benson, 3rd ed. (Boston: Houghton Mifflin, 1987), p. 32; and *The Complete Works of Geoffrey Chaucer*, ed. F. N. Robinson, 2nd ed. (Boston: Houghton Mifflin, 1957), p. 22.

Select Bibliography

Manuscripts

British Library MS Harley 2253 fol. 64*r*. (c. 1340).

British Library MS Lansdowne 762 fols. 5*r*–6*v*. (1500–40).

Oxford University MS Archbishop Selden B.26 fol. 19*r*. (c. 1450).

Aberystwyth, National Library of Wales, Peniarth 392 (Hengwrt MS) fol. 6*v* (c. 1410).

San Marino, California, Henry E. Huntington Library MS EL 27 C 9 (Ellesmere MS) fol. 6v (c. 1415).

Previous Editions

Song of the Husbandman (Harley MS)

Brandl, A., and O. Zippel, eds. *Middle English Literature (Mittelenglische Sprach- und Literaturproben)*. 2nd ed. New York: Chelsea, 1949. [Good edition of *Song* on pp. 134–35.]

RHR, pp. 7–9.

Wright, Thomas, ed. *Political Songs of England*. London: Camden Society, 1839. [Pp. 149–52. Edition of *Song of the Husbandman* with modern English translation at the bottom of the page.]

God Spede the Plough (Lansdowne MS)

Skeat, W. W., ed. *Pierce the Ploughmans Crede*. EETS o.s. 30. London: N. Trübner, 1867. [Good edition of *God Spede the Plough*.]

I-blessyd Be Cristes Sonde (Selden MS)

Chambers, E. K., and F. Sidgwick, eds. *Early English Lyrics: Amorous, Divine, Moral and Trivial*. New York: October House, 1967.

RHR, pp. 97–98.

Stainer, John, ed. *Early Bodleian Music: Sacred and Secular Songs, Together With Other MS. Compositions in the Bodleian Library, Oxford Ranging from about A.D. 1185 to about A.D. 1505*. 3 vols. Farnborough (Hants.): Gregg, 1967. [Facsimile of the manuscript in vol. 1, plate LXIX; Stainer's transcription of the manuscript in vol. 2, pp. 132–33.]

Chaucer's Plowman

Ruggiers, Paul G., ed. *The Canterbury Tales: A Facsimile and Transcription of the Hengwrt Manuscript with Variants from the Ellesmere Manuscript*. Norman: University of Oklahoma Press, 1979. [Plowman on fol. 6v.]

Hanna, Ralph, III. *The Ellesmere Manuscript of Chaucer's Canterbury Tales: A Working Facsimile*. Woodbridge, Suffolk: D. S. Brewer, 1989. [Plowman on fol. 206v.]

Manly, John M., and Edith Rickert, eds. *The Text of The Canterbury Tales Studied on the Basis of All Known Manuscripts*. 8 vols. Chicago: University of Chicago Press, 1940. [Plowman appears in volume 3, pp. 24–25.]

Benson, Larry D., gen. ed. *The Riverside Chaucer*. 3rd ed. Boston: Houghton Mifflin, 1987. [Plowman on p. 32.]

Robinson, F. N., ed. *The Complete Works of Geoffrey Chaucer*. 2nd ed. Boston: Houghton Mifflin, 1957. [Plowman on p. 22.]

Introduction

General Studies

Hahn, Thomas, and Richard W. Kaeuper. "Text and Context: Chaucer's *Friar's Tale*." *Studies in the Age of Chaucer* 5 (1983), 67–101. [An important collaborative study of conditions surrounding the archdeacon's courts in the fourteenth century by a literary scholar concerned with historical issues and a historian interested in using literary texts as historical evidence. They demonstrate the insidious control exerted by laws and regulations on peoples' lives.]

Hudson, Anne. "Epilogue: The Legacy of *Piers Plowman*." *A Companion to Piers Plowman*. Ed. John A. Alford. Berkeley: University of California Press, 1988. Pp. 251–66. [Analyzes the late medieval and Reformation texts that derive from *PP*.]

Kinney, Thomas L. "The Temper of Fourteenth-Century English Verse of Complaint." *Annuale Mediaevale* 7 (1966), 74–89. [Places *Song of the Husbandman* in context of complaint and satire.]

Mann, Jill. *Chaucer and Medieval Estates Satire*. Cambridge: Cambridge University Press, 1973. [Authoritative study of the tradition of estates satire keyed to the pilgrims of Chaucer's General Prologue to *The Canterbury Tales*.]

Pearsall, Derek. *Old English and Middle English Poetry*. London: Routledge, 1977. [*Song of the Husbandman* on pp. 123–24.]

Scattergood, V. J. *Politics and Poetry in the Fifteenth Century*. London: Blandford; New York: Barnes and Noble, 1971. [Discusses *Song of the Husbandman* on pp. 351–52.]

Bibliographies

Adams, Robert, and Vincent DiMarco. "Annual Bibliography." *The Yearbook of Langland Studies* 1 (1987), 161–89. [Annual Bibliography contains annotations of the preceding year's publications on Langland and on issues related to Langland, beginning with 1985.]

Robbins, Rossell Hope. "XIII. Poems Dealing with Contemporary Conditions." *A Manual of the Writings in Middle English 1050–1500*. Vol. 5. Gen. ed. Albert E. Hartung. New Haven: The Connecticut Academy of Arts and Sciences, 1975. Pp.

1385–1536, 1631–1725. [Discusses "Song of the Husbandman" (§ 26) on p. 1404, bibliography p. 1651; "God Spede the Plough" (§ 111) on p. 1449; "I-blessyd Be Cristes Sonde" under § 112, p. 1449 (brief mention), bibliography p. 1677.]

Song of the Husbandman

(British Library MS Harley 2253 fol. 64r)

Ich herde men upo mold make muche mon,	*upon earth; lamentation*
Hou he beth itened of here tilyynge:	*they are weary; their plowing*
Gode yeres and corn bothe beth agon;	*Good years; have gone away*
Ne kepeth here no sawe ne no song synge. [1]	
5 Nou we mote worche, nis ther non other won,	*must work, there is no other way*
Mai ich no lengore lyve with mi lesinge;	*longer; my falsehoods*
Yet ther is a bitterore bid to the bon: [2]	
For ever the furthe peni mot to the kynge.	*fourth penny; must go*
Thus we carpeth for the kyng, and carieth ful colde,	*complain to*
10 And weneth forte kevere, and ever buth a-cast.	*hope to recover; are cast down*
Whose hath eny god, hopeth he nouht to holde,	*Whoso; doesn't expect*
Bote ever the levest we leoseth alast.	*dearest [thing]; lose at last*
Luther is to leosen ther-ase lutel ys, [3]	
And haveth monie hynen that hopieth ther-to.	*seized; [you] counted upon*
15 The hayward heteth us harm to habben of his;	*harms us by requiring use of*
The bailif bockneth us bale and weneth wel do; [4]	
The wodeward waiteth us wo, that loketh under rys;	*woodkeeper; branch*
Ne mai us ryse no rest, rycheis, ne ro.	*wealth; repose*
Thus me pileth the pore, that is of lute pris. [5]	
20 Nede in swot and in swynk swynde mot swo. [6]	
Nede he mot swynde, thah he hade swore	*He must needs waste away*
That nath nout en hod his hed forte hude. [7]	

---

[1] *They neither preserve their [old] sayings nor sing songs*

[2] *Yet is there a more bitter command into the bargain*

[3] *It is grievous to lose when [you have] little*

[4] *The bailiff summons up misery for us and thinks he does well*

[5] *Thus they rob from the poor, who are worth little (see note)*

[6] *Need must waste away in sweat and toil*

[7] *That he has no hood to hide his head in*

251

Plowman Writings

Thus wil walketh in lond, and lawe is forlore,
And al is piked of the pore, the prikyares prude. [1]

25	Thus me pileth the pore and pyketh ful clene,	*they rob*
	The ryche me raymeth withouten eny ryht;	*steal*
	Ar londes and ar leodes liggeth fol lene,	*Their; people lie; lean (poor)*
	Thorh biddyng of baylyfs such harm hem hath hiht. [2]	
	Meni of religioun me halt hem ful hene,	*Many; they bear themselves odiously*
30	Baroun and bonde, the clerc and the knyht.	
	Thus wil walketh in lond, and wondred ys wene,	*credulity is taxed*
	Falsshipe fatteth and marreth wyth myht.	*falsehood fattens*

Stont stille y the stude, and halt him ful sturne,   *quietly in; pace; sternly*
 That maketh beggares go with bordon and bagges.   *burden*
35 Thus we beth honted from hale to hurne;   *hunted; hall; corner*
 That er werede robes, nou wereth ragges.   *Those who before wore*

Yet cometh budeles with ful muche bost: *beadles; arrogance*
 "Greythe me selver to the grene wax.   *Prepare*
Thou art writen y my writ, that thou wel wost!" [3]
40 Mo then ten sithen told I my tax.   *More; times; paid*
 Thenne mot ich habbe hennen arost,   *roasted hens*
 Feyr on fyhsh day launprey and lax.   *lamprey; salmon*
 Forth to the chepyn geyneth ne chost,   *"Forth to the market gains not cost" (Wr)*
 Thah I sulle mi bil and my borstax.   *Though I should sell my halberd and my axe*

45 Ich mot legge my wed wel yef I wolle,   *must place my pledge well if*
 Other sulle mi corn on gras that is grene.   *Or sell*
Yet I shal be foul cherl, thah he han the fulle; [4]
 That ich alle yer spare, thenne I mot spene. [5]

---

[1] *And the proud riders steal everything from the poor*

[2] *Through the commands of the bailiffs such injury has befallen them*

[3] *You are written down in my book, that you know well*

[4] *"Yet I shall be a foul churl, though they have the whole" (Wr)*

[5] *That which I save up all year I must then spend*

Nede I mot spene that I spared yore, *Needs must I spend what I saved earlier*
50 Ageyn this cachereles cometh thus I mot care; [1]
Cometh the maister budle, brust ase a bore, *bristled as a boar*
Seith he wole mi bugging bringe ful bare. *my dwelling strip*
Mede I mot munten, a mark other more, *Bribery; offer; or*
Thah ich at the set dey sulle mi mare. *appointed day sell*
55 Thus the grene wax us greveth under gore, *coat (i.e., to the core)*
That me us honteth ase hound doth the hare. *They hunt us as*

He us hontethe ase hound hare doth on hulle; *hunts us as; hill*
Seththe I tek to the lond such tene me wes taht. [2]
Nabbeth ner budeles boded ar sulle, *(see note)*
60 For he may scape and we aren ever caht. *escape but; caught*

Thus I kippe and cacche cares ful colde, *seize*
Seththe I counte and cot hade to kepe. [3]
To seche selver to the kyng I mi seed solde; *To obtain*
Forthi mi lond leye lith and leorneth to slepe. *fallow*
65 Seththe he mi feire feh fatte I my folde, [4]
When I thenk o mi weole wel neh I wepe. *think of my weal I nearly*
Thus bredeth monie beggares bolde, *breed many*
And ure ruye ys roted and ruls er we repe. [5]

Ruls ys oure ruye and roted in the stre, *Spoiled; rye; straw*
70 For wickede wederes by broke and by brynke. *bank*
Thus wakeneth in the world wondred and wee *dismay and woe*
Ase god is swynden anon as so forte swynke. [6]

---

[1] *"I must thus take care against the time these catchpoles come" (Wr)*

[2] *"Since I took to the land such hurt was given me" (Wr)*

[3] *Since I possessed a (tax) account and a cottage*

[4] *"Since they fetched my fair cattle in my fold" (Wr)*

[5] *And our rye is rotten and is spoiled before we reap*

[6] *"It is as good to perish right away as to labor so" (RHR)*

God Spede the Plough

(British Library MS Lansdowne 762, fols. 5r–6v)

A processe or an exortation to tendre the chargis of the true husbondys

	As I me walked over feldis wide	*broad fields*
	When men began to ere and to sowe,	*cultivate*
	I behelde husbondys howe faste they hide,	*farmers; hastened*
	With their bestis and plowes all on a rowe.	
5	I stode and behelde the bestis well drawe	
	To ere the londe that was so tough;	*cultivate*
	Than to an husbond I sed this sawe,	*said these words*
	"I pray to God, spede wele the plough."	*may the plow prosper*
	The husbondys helde up harte and hande,	
10	And said, "That is nedefull for to praye,	
	For all the yere we labour with the lande,	*year*
	With many a comberous clot of claye,	*clot of dirt*
	To mayntayn this worlde yf that we maye,	*sustain*
	By downe and by dale and many a slough.	*swamp*
15	Therfore it is nedefull for to saye,	
	'I praye to God, spede wele the plough.'	
	"And so shulde of right the parson praye,	
	That hath the tithe shefe of the londe;	
	For our sarvauntys we moste nedis paye,	*servants*
20	Or ellys ful still the plough maye stonde.	
	Than cometh the clerk anon at hande,	
	To have a shef of corne there it growe,	*where it grew*
	And the sexten somwhate in his hande.	*sexton*
	'I praye to God, spede wele the plough.'	
25	"The kyngis purviours also they come,	*purveyors*
	To have whete and otys at the kyngis nede;	*oats*
	And over that befe and mutton,	*more than that beef*
	And butter and pulleyn, so God me spede!	*poultry*

254

And to the kyngis courte we moste it lede,
30 And our payment shal be a styk of a bough; [1]
And yet we moste speke faire for drede. *amiably; fear*
'I praye to God, spede wele the plough.'

"To paye the fiftene ayenst our ease, *(see note)*
Beside the lordys rente of our londe —
35 Thus be we shepe shorne, we may not chese, [2]
And yet it is full lytell understonde. *little understood*
Than bayllys and bedellis woll put to their hande
In enquestis to doo us sorwe inough, *inquests*
But yf we quite right wele the londe;
40 'I praye to God, spede wele the plough.'

"Than cometh prisoners and sheweth their nede,
What gret sorowe in prison theye drye. *endure*
'To buye the kyngis pardon we most take hede';
For man and beste they woll take money.
45 Than cometh the clerkes of Saint John Frary,
And rede in their bokis mennyis namyis inough. *men's names*
And all they live by husbondrye —
'I praye to God, spede wele the plough.'

"Then comme the graye Freres and make their mone, *complaint*
50 And call for money our soulis to save;
Then comme the white Freres and begyn to grone,
Whete or barley they woll fayne have;
Then commeth the Freres Augustynes and begynneth to crave
Corne or chese, for they have not inough;
55 Then commeth the blak Freres which wolde fayne have.
'I praye to God, spede wele the plough.'

"And yet, amongest other, we may not forgete *among other [things]*
The poore Observauntes that been so holy.
They muste amongis us have corne or mete; *wheat; food*
60 They teche us alwaye to fle from foly, *flee*

---

[1] *And our payment shall be with [the beating] of a stick*

[2] *Thus are we fleeced, we may not choose*

And live in vertue full devowtely,
Preching dayly sermondys inough   *sermons*
With good examples full graciously.
'I praye to God, spede wele the plough.'

65   "Than cometh the sompner to have som rente,   *summoner*
And ellis he woll teche us a newe lore,
Saying we have lefte behynde unproved som testament,
And so he woll make us lese moche more.
Then commeth the grenewex which greveth us sore,   *(see note)*
70   With ronnyng in reragis it doth us sorowe inough,   *arrears*
And after, we knowe nother why ne where-fore: *neither; nor why*
'I praye to God, spede wel the plough.'

"Then commeth prestis that goth to Rome   *priests*
For to have silver to singe at *Scala celi.*   *(see note)*
75   Than commeth clerkys of Oxford and make their mone,   *complaint*
To her scole hire they most have money.   *For their*
Then commeth the tipped-staves for the Marshalse,   *(see note)*
And saye they have prisoners mo than inough;
Then commeth the mynstrellis to make us gle —   *minstrels; entertainment*
80   'I praye to God, spede wele the plough.'

"At London also yf we woll plete,   *plead*
We shal not be spared, good chepe nor dere.   *expensive*
Our man of lawe may not be forgete,   *lawyer; forgotten*
But he moste have money every quartere;
85   And somme comme begging with the kyngis charter,
And saye, bisshoppis have graunted ther-to pardon inough;
And wymen commeth weping on the same maner.   *women*
'I praye to God, spede wele the plough.'"

And than I thanked this good husbond,
90   And prayed God the plough to spede,
And all tho that laboreth with the londe,
And them that helpeth them with worde or dede.
God give them grace such life to lede,
That in their concience maye be mery inough,
95   And heven blisse to be their mede,   *heaven's; reward*
And ever I praye, "God spede the plough."

I-blessyd Be Cristes Sonde

[God Speed the Plough]

(Oxford Univ., MS Archbishop Selden B. 26 fol. 19*r*)

	The merthe of alle this londe	
	Maketh the gode husbonde,	
	With erynge of his plowe.	*plowing*

	I-blessyd be Cristes sonde,	*dispensation*
	That hath us sent in honde	
	Merthe and joye y-nowe.	

	The plowe goth mony a gate,	*course*
5	Bothe erly and eke late,	*also*
	In wynter in the clay.	*soil*

	A-boute barly and whete,	*barley; wheat*
	That maketh men to swete,	*sweat*
	God spede the plowe al day!	*May God always bless the plow*

10	Browne, Morel, and gore	*(see note)*
	Drawen the plowe ful sore,	
	Al in the morwenynge.	*morning*

	Rewarde hem therfore	*them*
	With a shefe or more,	
15	All in the evenynge.	

	Whan men bygynne to sowe,	
	Ful wel here corne they knowe	*their wheat*
	In the mounthe of May.	

	Howe-ever Janyuer blowe,	*However January*
20	Whether hye or lowe,	
	God spede the plowe all way!	

257

Whan men bygynneth to wede   *weed out*
    The thystle fro the sede,   *seed*
        In somer whan they may,   *summer*

25 God lete hem wel to spede,   *let them prosper well*
    And longe gode lyfe to lede,   *lead*
        All that for plowe-men pray.   *who*

Chaucer's Plowman

(Hengwrt MS fol. 6v; *Canterbury Tales* I[A]529–41)

With hym ther was a Plowman, was his broother,
[530] That hadde ylad of donge ful many a foother. [1]
    A trewe swynkere and a good was he,   *worker*
    Lyvynge in pees and parfit charitee.   *peace; charity*
5   God loved he best with al his hoole herte   *whole*
    At alle tymes, thogh hym gamed or smerte,   *whether in joy or distress*
    And thanne his neighebore right as hymselve.   *just as*
    He wolde thresshe, and therto dyke and delve, [2]
    For Cristes sake, for every povre wight,   *poor person*
10 Withouten hyre, if it lay in his myght.   *payment*
    His tythes payde he ful faire and wel,   *tithes he paid*
[540] Both of his propre swynk and his catel.   *own work; possessions*
    In a tabard he rood upon a mere.   *smock; rode; mare*

---

[1] *With him (the Parson) there was a Plowman, his brother, / Who had hauled very many a cartload of dung*

[2] *He would thresh, and also make ditches and dig*

Notes

Song of the Husbandman

1   *Ich . . . mon.* Wr translates this: "I heard men on the earth make much lamentation"; but Brown and Robbins, *Index* (§ 696), place the lyric in the category of poems beginning "Each": "Ich herdemen vpo mold make muche mon," or "Each herdman on the earth makes much lamentation." The manuscript reads, however, "Ich herde men."

4   *synge.* So MS, Sampson, and RHR; Wr *syng.*

5   Wr, Brandl, and Sampson begin the "song" — with quotation marks — with this line; quotation marks conclude with the end of line 20.

6   *mi.* So MS and RHR; Wr and Sampson *my.*

7   *bid.* So MS, Wr, and RHR; Brandl emends to *bit.*

12–13   *the levest we leoseth . . . ther-ase lutel ys.* These lines, and the two stanzas, are linked according to the prosodic convention of chain verse or concatenation. Stanza linking by concatenation occurs also in lines 20–21, 24–25, 48–49, 56–57, 60–61, 68–69.

15   *The hayward.* RHR comments: "The husbandman lists the officials who extort money from him: the hayward, a local official responsible for maintaining fences separating the common from enclosed lands; the bailiff, who enforced the law; the woodward, in charge of the forest timber; and the beadle (line 37), a warrant officer working under the bailiff" (p. 250). John Alford cites the following lines from *Piers Plowman* (C.13.45–47): "If þe marchaunt make his way ouer menne corne / And þe hayward happe with hym for to mete, / Oþer his hatt or his hoed or elles his gloues / The marchaunt mote forgo or moneye of his porse." See Robbins' *Glossary,* s.v. *Haiward.* For the tyranny of such local officials, see *The Simonie,* note to line 195.

259

17   Brandl punctuates: *Þe wodeward waiteþ us, wo, þat lokeþ* . . . . This passage about the lurking woodward anticipates Chaucer's watchful pilgrim Reeve, of whom the narrator says:

> Ther nas baillif, ne hierde, nor oother hyne,
> That he ne knew his sleighte and his covyne;
> They were adrad of hym as of the deeth. (I[A]603–05)

19   *me pileth.* Ethical dative: "they rob."

22   *en.* Brandl emends to *an.*

24   *is.* Brandl emends to *haþ.*

25   See note to line 19.

26   *me.* So MS and RHR, in which case the sense is "steal from me." Brandl *me[n]*, the sense being parallel to the ethical datives of lines 19 and 25, i.e., "they (men) steal." Wr and Sampson omit.

28   *Thorh biddyng.* MS *bddyng*; Wr, Sampson, Brandl, and RHR *biddyng.* Wr translates: "through asking of bailifs such harm has befallen them."

29   *Meni.* So Wr. Brandl interprets MS as *Mem* and emends to *Men*; Sampson *Men.*

33   *Stont . . . stude.* So MS and RHR; Wr and Sampson *Stont fulle ythe stude.* Wr translates: "He stands full in the place." This should be instead: "He stands quietly in the place."

35   *hale.* Brandl *hal[l]e.*

37   *bost.* This word has at least two possible significations for this poem: "boast," "arrogance," on the one hand (*MED* **bost** senses 1 and 2), and "noise," "clamor," "outcry," on the other (sense 4[a]). For the latter signification, see *Sir Gawain and the Green Knight*, ed. Tolkien and Gordon, 2nd ed., line 1448: "Þat buskkez after þis bor with bost and wyth noyse," and *PP* C 16.89–90, ed. Pearsall: "And where be bettere to breke? lasse boest hit maketh / To breke a beggares bagge then an yren-bounden coffres." Pearsall glosses *boest* at 21.251 as "self-vaunting" (and see *MED* sense 1[c]). The *MED* traces this word to "AF

bost boasting, ostentation (prob. from Gmc.: cp. MHG *bûs* swelling, Norw. *baus* haughty." See also *MED* **boistous** adj. senses 1 and 2.

38 *grene wax*. A seal of green wax was affixed to documents delivered by the Exchequer to sheriffs (OED). See note to line 55. Like Chaucer's Pardoner, who carries "our lige lordes seel on my patente . . . that no man be so boold . . . me to destourbe of Cristes hooly werk" (VI[C]337–40), the beadle carries this greenwax document as a sign of authority as he extracts taxes from the husbandman. Line 39 reminds one of the friar in Chaucer's Summoner's Tale, who announces names on the ledger as he tries to "collect" from his congregation — "lo! Heere I write youre name" (III[D]1752).

42 *fyhsh*. So MS and RHR; Wr and Sampson *fyhshe*. Brandl emends to *fyshday*.

 and. MS and RHR &; Wr and Sampson *ant*. Also in line 44 and passim.

55 *Thus*. So the MS and RHR; Wr *Ther* (misreading the abbreviation).

 the grene wax. Documents from sheriffs sealed with green wax struck fear and grief into those who received them ("us greveth under gore"). See also *God Speed the Plough*: "Then commeth the grenewex which greveth us sore, / With ronnyng in reragis [arrears] it doth us sorowe inough" (lines 69–70).

56 *doth*. Emendation of Wr, Sampson, and RHR; MS and Brandl *deþ*.

57 *doth*. MS and Wr *doh*; Sampson *doht*; Brandl *doh[t]*; RHR emends to *doþ*. The concatenated phrase in line 56 reads, in the MS, *ase hound deþ* [for *doþ*] *þe hare*.

58 *tek*. Brandl emends to *tok*.

59 *Nabbeth . . . sulle*. RHR comments: "Difficult: tr. The beadles have never told their giver (i.e., have never said who he was). Brandl reads fulle (possible in MS.), and so Sampson, who tr. have never suffered" (p. 250). Wr translates the line: "the beadles have never asked their . . ."

70 *broke*. So MS. Wr, Sampson, and Brandl *brok*; RHR *brokes*.

72 *is*. So MS, Wr, Sampson, and Brandl; RHR *in* (an error in transcription for *is*).

God Spede the Plough

1   *As I me walked.* "This line is omitted in its right place; but is written perpendicularly on the inner margin of the leaf, with a guide-line to shew its position" (Sk).

10–88   *And said.* The husbandman's testimony takes up 79 lines of the poem. The narrator is merely a witness to the testimony.

11–12   *lande, claye.* The corner of the leaf is torn away; *lande* and *claye* are Sk's conjectures based on the rhyme words.

22   *growe.* MS *groweth.* Sk observes that *groweth* and *plough* (line 24) do not rhyme; he suggests the word might have been *grewe*, which comes closer to rhyme.

33   *the fiftene.* "Fifteenth, a tax amounting to a fifteenth of one's property" (Sk).

           ease. MS *eases.*

37   *bayllys and bedellis.* Bailiffs and beadles. See *Song of the Husbandman* note to line 15.

43   *To buye the kyngis.* I adopt Sk's conjecture about this portion of the line. The corner of the leaf is torn away. Sk comments: "The words within square brackets are conjectural, and were suggested by the fact recorded in *Piers Plowman*, that getting pardon for a bribe even from a King is not altogether a thing unknown . . . ." Words are also lacking at the beginning of lines 40, 41, and 42. I adopt Sk's likely readings of *I, Than come[th,* and *What gret.*

45   *clerkes of saint John Frary.* Clerks of the friary of St. John. "There was one such in Clerkenwell" (Sk).

49–55   *graye Freres . . . blak Freres. Graye Freres* = Franciscans (Minorites); *white Freres* = Carmelites; *Freres Augustynes* = Austins or Augustinians; *blak Freres* = Dominicans or Jacobins. Sk comments: "On fol. 9*b* of this very Lansdowne MS. we find the following. "Fratres London. Whitefreres in fletestrete, Carmelitarum. Blak freres within ludgate, predicatorum *vel* Jacob: Greye freres within newgate, Minorum. Augusteyn freres by saint Antonyes, Augustinencium. Crowched freres, Fratres sancte Crucis."

58   *poore Observauntes.* Friars observaunts. "'Observants, a branch of the Franciscan order, otherwise called *Recollects*.' Imperial Dict." (Sk).

69   *the grenewex.* "Greenwax was used for estreats [copies of court fines, for use in prosecution] delivered to the sheriffs out of the king's exchequer. These estreats were under the seal of that court, made in *green wax*. See Blount's Law Dictionary" (Sk). See also *Song of the Husbandman,* lines 38 and 55 and notes.

74   *Scala celi* or "Ladder of heaven": the name of a chapel in Rome. "It derives its name from a vision of St. Bernard's, who, while celebrating a funereal mass, saw the souls for whom he was praying going up to heaven by a ladder" (Sk). In the anticlerical context of this poem, *Scala celi* is ironic.

77   *tipped-staves.* "Tipstaves, constables. So called from their bearing a staff tipped with metal" (Sk). *Marshalse* = Marshalsea court and prison.

93   *God.* MS *Gog* here and in line 96.

I-blessyd Be Cristes Sonde

Refrain   This poem has music. "The burden and first stanza are first written for two voices; then the last line and whole first stanza are repeated for three voices" (RHR).

4   *goth.* So MS, Greene, and RHR; Stainer and Chambers *gothe* (interpreting the flourish as final *e*; also *makethe* in line 8). Chambers considerably normalizes the spelling. I do not record his normalizations in these notes.

10   *Browne, Morel and gore.* I accept Greene's reading of the first two as names for oxen. "'Browne' and 'Morel' (dark-coloured) seem to be the names of the plough-oxen. 'Gore' has presented difficulty to previous editors. Neither Stevens's 'dark-coloured' nor Robbins's suggestion of 'gray' meets the case. It is more likely that it is a dialect word for 'goad' and that the meaning is either 'Brown, Morel, and the goad' or alternatively, with 'Brown' as an adjective,

'Brown Morel and Gore,' the second ox being named for the goad" (pp. 464–65).

14   *shefe*. The clerk begs "a shef of corne" in *God Spede the Plough* line 22. A "sheaf" is an arm-load bundle, tied.

Chaucer's Plowman

2   *foother*. So Hg (rhyming with *broother*); El, Manly-Rickert, Benson, Robinson *brother / fother*. *Fother* derives from OE *foðer*, fodder (related to *food*), food for cattle but also "that in which food is carried": "a cart or cart-load." See *An Anglo-Saxon Dictionary*, ed. J. Bosworth and T. Northcote Toller (London: Oxford University Press, 1898), s.v. *Fóðer*.

3   *trewe swynkere*. The phrase could be charged, since the Lollards referred to themselves as "true preachers" or "true men," and plowmen (and workers generally) were sometimes associated with subversion of the commonwealth after the 1381 Rising. See *Addresses of the Commons*, lines 21–22 and note, and the Prologue to *The Wycliffite Bible*, lines 111–12 and note.

4   *parfit charitee*. For the tradition of *sancta rusticitas* before Langland and Chaucer, see Jill Mann, *Chaucer and Medieval Estates Satire* (Cambridge: Cambridge University Press, 1973), pp. 68–69, and the references in endnotes 65 and 66.

6   *hym*. So Hg, Manly-Rickert, Benson (*him*), Robinson (*him*); El *he*. Robinson comments: "*thogh him gamed or smerte*, in pleasure or pain; one of a number of phrases current in early English to denote 'under all circumstances,' 'in all respects'" (p. 665).

8   *dyke and delve*. Benson (*The Riverside Chaucer*, p. 820) and Mann, citing the *MED*, emphasize the formulaic nature of this phrase, which means "to work hard." Mann also quotes from *Piers Plowman*: "I dyke and I delue I do that treuthe hoteth; / Some tyme I sowe and some tyme I thresche" (B passus 5; *Chaucer and Medieval Estates Satire*, p. 70).

10   *Withouten hyre*. Working without payment, notes Helen Cooper, offers "a marked contrast to the ploughmen of Chaucer's England as represented in the

landowners' complaints about relentless demands for high wages, or to the lazy labourers of estates satire or Piers's half-acre" (*The Canterbury Tales*, Oxford Guides to Chaucer [New York: Oxford University Press, 1989], p. 53). For another mention of labor shortages after the Great Plague of 1349, see Benson, *The Riverside Chaucer*, p. 820.

13   *mere*. The poorer classes rode mares. Other horses mentioned in the General Prologue include the Monk's *palfrey* (one of his *deyntee* saddle-horses), the Wife of Bath's *amblere* (a pacing horse with a comfortable riding gait), and the Reeve's *stot*, a sturdy farm horse. In addition, the Knight's horse is characterized as "goode" and the Clerk's, as "leene . . . as is a rake."

Glossary

ac *but*

acloien *lame, hinder; obstruct;* pt **acloied**

aftir *according to*

agens, ayenst, ogaines *against; contrary to*

agensey *gainsay, deny; contradict*

agenstond *oppose; withstand*

alday *continually*

alder-, alther- *of all;* **alther ferst** *first of all;* **alderbest** *best of all*

als *as; also*

and, ande, ant *and; if*

Austyn *St. Augustine*

autour *author;* pl **autouris**

axen *ask; require*

ay *always; continually*

be *be, by*

ben *be, been, are*

bi *by*

bie, bye *buy, purchase*

biheste, *promise*

bote *remedy, cure;* **do bote** *provide remedy, redress*

brennen *burn;* part. **brennynge**

budle *beadle*

but, but yif *unless*

by *buy, purchase*

can, kan, kunnen *know*

certes, certys *certainly, indeed; in truth, in fact*

clene *pure, free from sin; completely, entirely*

clepen *call, name;* part. **clepid**

coveitise *avarice, covetousness*

demen *judge, think*

derk *dark; obscure, unclear;* **derknes** *darkness*

dom *judgment;* **Domesday** *Judgment Day*

Ebru *Hebrew*

eche, iche, uch, ych *each*

eft *again, anew*

eighe *eye*

either *either; or*

elde *old*

elles, ellis *else; otherwise*

eny, ony *any*

er, ar, or *before*

ere *cultivate, plow;* **erynge** *plowing*

eretik *heretic;* pl **eretikis**

erthe *earth*

es *is*

eten *eat*

everich *every;* **everich a** *each*

267

fadir *father*
falshed *falsehood; error*
fer *far*
figuratif, figuratyf, figuratijf *figurative; allegorical, symbolic*
fijr, fijer, fyer *fire*
fonden *strive, endeavor*
forwhi, for whi *because*
frere, freer *friar*
fro *from; away from*
ful *very; full;* **ful sore** *very hard*

gar, ger *make, do; cause, cause to be done*
gilt *sin, fault*
goostli *spiritual; spiritually*
grame *anger, rage; harm; torment*
greet *great*
gyle, gile *fraud, guile*

han *have*
hede, heed, hevid *head*
hem, ham, thame *them*
here *their; here; hear*
herte *heart;* pl **hertis**
heste *commandment;* pl **heestis, hestis**
heven, hevene *heaven*
hie, highe *high; hasten; quickly*
hii *they;* see also **thei**
hir, hire, her(e), hur *their; her*
his *its; his*
hise *his*
hit *it*
honde *hand;* pl **hondis, handis**
hu *how*
hwan *when*

ich *I; each*
i-liche *alike; equally*
i-nouh, ynou, ynow *enough*
i-piled *robbed, fleeced*
i-wis, ywis *indeed; certainly*

kan, kunne *know; be familiar with*
kunnynge *knowledge; expertise*
kynde *nature, what is natural;* **agens kynde** *unnatural, unnaturally*

lered *learned, literate*
lernen *learn; teach*
late (v) *let*
late *recently*
letten *prevent, hinder;* part. **lettide**
lesing *lie, falsehood*
lewed, lewid *ignorant, illiterate; lay*
libert *leopard*
lijf *life*
likerouse, leccherouse *lecherous; flattering; pleasant*
londe *land;* pl **londis, landes**
lore, loore *teaching; knowledge*
luytel, litelle, litil *little*

mede, methe *bribery, meed; reward*
mete *food*
mo, moo *more; other*
modir *mother*
mon *man;* poss. **mannis, mannes, mennes**
mone *complaint; complain*
morwe, morowe *morrow, morning; tomorrow*
moun, mowe *may*

muchel, mykill, mekill, miche, myche, moche *great, powerful; much*

ne *not; nor*
neithir . . . neithir *neither . . . nor*
nis, nys *is not*
no but *unless; except*
noht, nouht, nought *not; nothing*
nu *now*

o, oo *one; a single*
off *of; off*
ogaines *against*
ony *any*
oonis *once*
oonli, onely *only*
other, outher, odur *other; or* **odur . . . odur** *either . . . or*
owen *ought, should; owe*

pardé *by God, certainly, to be sure*
parfit *perfect*
peny *penny*
peraunter, peraventure *perhaps, by chance*
pes *peace*
pilen *rob, plunder;* **i-piled** *robbed*
pleyne, playne *complain, lament*
pleynte *complaint, lament*
pore, pouer, povre *poor*
povreté *poverty, indigence*
prechour *preacher; friar preacher (Dominican)*
pref, preve *proof, evidence, documentation*
prest *priest;* **prestis** *priests*

preven *prove, show; test, try;* part.
prevyd
prevytee *hidden thing; secret; allegorical figure*
puple *people*

qwhen *when*

redy *ready*
rewme, reume *kingdom, realm; domain*

sall, ssal, shal, schul *shall;* **salbe** *shall be*
saught, *assault; onslaught*
schewes *shows, reveals, permits*
schrift *confession*
seie *say;* 3 sg **seith;** pl **seyn;** pt **seide**
sely *innocent, simple, good; hapless*
sentense, sentence *meaning; true meaning*
shent *ruined, destroyed*
singnefien *signify, mean*
sith, siththen, seththe *since; afterward; then*
skile *reason;* **by skile** *reasonably*
soth, sooth, suth *truth*
sorwe, sorowe *sorrow*
speche *speech*
spede *succeed; prosper; hasten*
speken *speak*
stinten, stenten *stop, cease, desist*
suffre, suffer *allow, permit; suffer, endure*
suid *followed, adhered to;* **suynge** *following, holding to*
summe *some*

Glossary

swich, suche, swylk *such*

swinken, swynken *work, toil, labor*

synne *sin*

thanne *than; then*

tharfen, thurfen *need, require*

thei, theih *they*

theih *though*

therto *of it, about it, concerning it*

thilke *that, that same, that very (one)*

thenken, thynken *think*

ther(e), thair *their; there; where*

thise, this *these*

tho, thoo *those*

thorw, thurgh, thorugh, thruh *through; by means of*

thow, thah *though, although*

thridde *third*

togidere *together*

travaile *work, labor, toil*

trewe *true*

trouthe, trothe *truth, troth*

uch *each*

undirstonding *interpretation; understanding*

unnethe *scarcely, with difficulty*

verry, very *true*

waried *cursed*; part. wariyng

wenen *believe, think, suppose;* pt wende

werk *work*

werre *war*

whanne, *when*

wheither, whether, wher *whether; (tell me) whether*

wher *whether*

whilom *once; once upon a time*

wid *with*

witen, weten *know; understand*

witen, wyten *blame, censure*

wo, woo *woe*

wouh *evil, wickedness; wrong, bad*

wol *will; wish;* pt. wolde

wood, wode *mad*

worschipe, worchip *honor; reputation, renown; worship*

y *I; in*

yeden *went*

yif, yef *if*

yit, yut *yet*

ypocrisie *hypocrisy*

ypocrite *hypocrite*

yvel *evil*

Notes

Notes

Notes

Notes

Notes

Notes